AMERICA'S SPLENDID LITTLE WARS

AMERICA'S SPLENDID LITTLE WARS

A SHORT HISTORY OF
U.S. MILITARY ENGAGEMENTS:
1975–2000

Peter Huchthausen

VIKING

VIKING

Published by the Penguin Group

Penguin Group (USA) Inc., 375 Hudson Street, New York, New York 10014, U.S.A.

Penguin Books Ltd, 80 Strand, London WC2R 0RL, England

Penguin Books Australia Ltd, 250 Camberwell Road, Camberwell, Victoria 3124, Australia

Penguin Books Canada Ltd, 10 Alcorn Avenue, Toronto, Ontario, Canada M4V 3B2

Penguin Books India (P) Ltd, 11 Community Centre, Panchsheel Park, New Delhi–110 017, India

Penguin Books (N.Z.) Ltd, Cnr Rosedale and Airborne Roads, Albany, Auckland, New Zealand

Penguin Books (South Africa) (Pty) Ltd, 24 Sturdee Avenue, Rosebank, Johannesburg 2196, South Africa

Penguin Books Ltd, Registered Offices: 80 Strand, London WC2R 0RL, England

First published in 2003 by Viking Penguin, a member of Penguin Group (USA) Inc.

10 9 8 7 6 5 4 3 2 1

LIBRARY OF CONGRESS CATALOGING-IN-PUBLICATION DATA

Huchthausen, Peter A., 1939–
    America's splendid little wars : a short history of U.S. military engagements: 1975–2000 / Peter A. Huchthausen.
        p. cm.
    Includes bibliographical references and index.
    ISBN 0-670-03232-8
    1. United States—History, Military—20th century. 2. Intervention (International law)—History—20th century. 3. Presidents—United States—History—20th century.
    4. United States—Military Policy. I. Title.
    E840.4 .H83 2003
    973.92–dc21   2002038025

This book is printed on acid-free paper.

Printed in the United States of America
All maps by Mark Stein Studios

To my grandchildren, Ewan, Bailey Anne, Blake, and Nicholas;
if ever called on to fight for your country, do so well,
but always with compassion for the beleaguered.

Acknowledgments

I deeply appreciate the assistance and counsel of Jim and Dorothy Clunan, both dedicated foreign service officers and longtime friends. Their rich experience in diplomatic posts in Moscow, Kuwait, Belgrade, Ankara, London, and Naples made their contributions from the political-military field indispensable, and their patient editing was invaluable. Special thanks to Ambassador Paul D. Taylor, who provided his capable views of Latin America in the chapter on Panama. I am also grateful for the insights and forbearance of Joyce Bibber, professor emeritus of history at the University of Southern Maine in Gorham. Special thanks to Diane Barnes, former professor of history at Tuskegee University and the University of Maine, for her unique ideas, and Jack Barnes, veteran educator, author, literary critic, world traveler, and farmer, for his advice and encouragement. I also thank Jan Snouck-Hurgronje, who conceived the idea for this book and persevered in getting the project under way.

    I am indebted to my U.S. Naval Academy classmate Admiral Sir Leighton "Snuffy" Smith, one of the few U.S. naval officers in history to be granted knighthood by a British monarch, who offered deep insight into the military events in the Balkans, and whose leadership of U.S. and NATO forces during the intervention in Bosnia proved so vital. Thanks also to Brigadier General David Grange, Vice Admiral Joe Metcalf III, and the late Captain John Michael Rodgers for their invaluable contributions from their personal experiences in the *Mayaguez* and Iran rescue missions, Grenada, and the Gulf War.

The views of U.S. Army Lieutenant Colonels Peter Mueller and Ben Weiss on their participation in the Gulf War gave me a unique perspective from the trenches. I am also deeply thankful for the guidance and inspiration of Ernest H. Knight, veteran, historian, and oracle of Raymond, Maine, and for the fresh suggestions of Kathy, who cared for and fed me while I undertook this project.

Contents

Maps

Introduction

Since the evacuation of Saigon in April 1975, the United States government has committed its forces to combat in more than a dozen military operations. In some cases, the United States briefly invaded a country to protect or evacuate American and foreign noncombatants caught in volatile security situations. In other instances, U.S. forces intervened at the request of friendly nations and joined with allies to liberate occupied lands, to stop mass killing, and to thwart blatant violations of human rights. Until now, there has been no book that encompassed the full American military experience since 1975 in one volume or explored this period in relation to past conflicts and its larger impact on modern world history. There are books that address the individual conflicts and some that study American warfare of the 1990s in general, but this book focuses on each U.S. military engagement of the last twenty-five years of the twentieth century.

In the first thirty years following the end of World War II, struggles in Greece, Korea, Berlin, Vietnam, and the Caribbean foiled American aspirations for peace in a seemingly never-ending global contest with Communism. In the decades after the U.S. withdrawal from Vietnam, as the Communist sphere withered away, America, now the sole world military power, was plagued by other nasty conflicts. By the turn of the new millennium, it was clear that the Pax Americana had been as troubled as the Pax Britannica of the Victorian age and the Pax Romana of ancient times.

The following chapters explore the underlying motivation for military intervention, which, in many cases, was peripheral to vital U.S. national interests. Each engagement, from the 1975 operation to recover the hijacked merchant ship SS *Mayaguez* and her crew in the Gulf of Siam through the Iran hostage crisis and conflicts in Grenada, the Middle East, Panama, the Persian Gulf, Somalia, the Balkans, and finally Kosovo, the last American military operation of the twentieth century, is examined in a purely historical context. Sometimes American forces were successful; on occasion they merely interrupted the ugly work of dictators. In a few cases, the U.S. government initiated action on humanitarian grounds only after the world media deluged the public with wrenching coverage of suffering—often in countries of little obvious relevance to U.S. national interests. One largely unknown military action in 1991 was an exceptional, bloodless success. Called Operation Eastern Exit, this extraordinary evacuation of 281 American and foreign personnel from Mogadishu, Somalia, was a joint navy and marine operation that involved extreme-range helicopter flights and air-to-air refuelings. Other engagements, like Operation Desert Storm in 1991, were full-scale wars, albeit brief, that Americans fought with a broad coalition of allies, using both conventional and special operations forces. The United States employed limited conventional and semi–special operations forces during the 1991 and 1993 conflicts in Somalia. In 1987, convoying operations in the course of the Iran-Iraq War were conducted primarily by naval forces. In the 1990s, America and NATO intervened in Bosnia and Kosovo to stop the blatant slaughter of innocent civilians by Balkan dictators and their marauding ethnic clans. Tactical air operations dominated the fighting in these more recent conflicts and presented their own set of unique operational challenges and strategic solutions. Each military engagement in this history demonstrates the progression of a blend of battlefield hardware, improved communications, and command-and-control technologies. This melding has led to both great success, as in Kuwait, and heavy loss of life for little purpose, as in Somalia.

Across the breadth of the United States, in places large and small, subtle exhibits remind us of the men and women who participated in one or more of the jarring post-Vietnam confrontations. Small glass cases display military awards, and aging photographs of sons and daughters in uniform dot the dusty corners of diners, shops, and homes, reminding families of their offspring's service.

In an 1898 letter to Lieutenant Colonel Theodore Roosevelt following the fall of Santiago, Cuba, U.S. Ambassador John Milton Hay used the phrase "splendid little war" to refer to the bloody victories of the Spanish-American War. The U.S. military encounters from 1975 to 1999 were neither splendid nor small. Instead, the personal adventures of the blood-caked veterans described in these pages more accurately reflect the words of the duke of Wellington in 1815: "[A] great country can have no such thing as a little war." Because most of these veterans do not speak in public about their battle experiences, it is necessary to record the details of these events so that neither the participants nor their descendants forget what they achieved.

PART ONE

Gerald R. Ford:
Rebounding Against Piracy

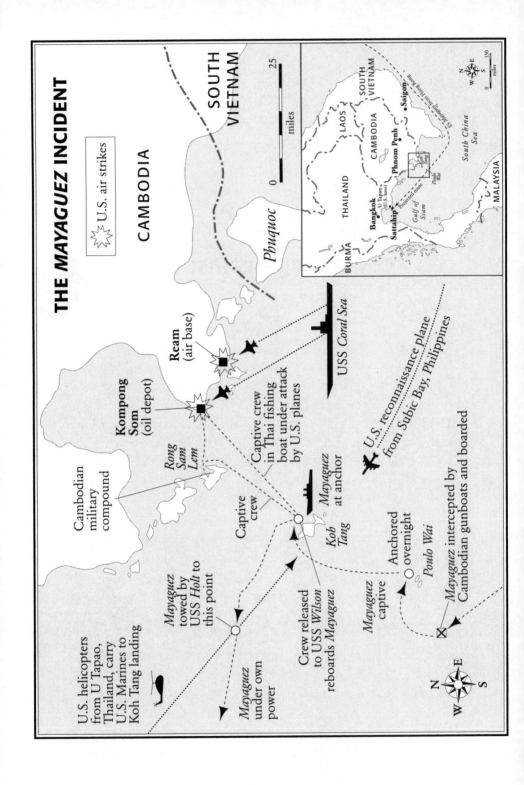

THE *MAYAGUEZ* INCIDENT

SOUTH VIETNAM

CAMBODIA

Phuquoc

U.S. air strikes

Ream (air base)

Kompong Som (oil depot)

USS *Coral Sea*

Captive crew in Thai fishing boat under attack by U.S. planes

Rong Sam Lem

Cambodian military compound

U.S. reconnaissance plane from Subic Bay, Philippines

Captive crew

Mayaguez at anchor

Koh Tang

Mayaguez towed by USS *Holt* to this point

Crew released to USS *Wilson* reboards *Mayaguez*

Anchored overnight

Ponlo Wai

Mayaguez under own power

Mayaguez captive

Mayaguez intercepted by Cambodian gunboats and boarded

U.S. helicopters from U Tapao, Thailand, carry U.S. Marines to Koh Tang landing

N E S W

0 miles 25

Inset map
SOUTH VIETNAM

LAOS

BURMA

THAILAND

CAMBODIA

Phnom Penh

Saigon

Bangkok

U Tapao (U.S. base)

Sattahip

Gulf of Siam

Projected route

SS Mayaguez from Hong Kong

South China Sea

Poulo Wai

Koh Tang

MALAYSIA

N E S W

0 miles 150

CHAPTER 1

Recovering SS *Mayaguez* and the Fight on Koh Tang

The Gulf of Siam, May 12–15, 1975

After Prince Norodom Sihanouk of Cambodia was overthrown as head of state on March 18, 1970, North Vietnamese soldiers rampaged throughout the country. Another war had erupted as a side show to the Vietnam conflict, one in which Sihanouk's followers, allied with Hanoi, and the Cambodian Communists, called the Khmer Rouge, fought the forces of U.S.-backed Lon Nol, who was the former defense minister and one of Sihanouk's aides. By May 1975 Lon Nol had been defeated, and the country was on the brink of a long period of bloody internal upheaval. What followed was the last armed incident of post-Vietnam disengagement and a test of American resolve to use force to protect its interests abroad. Under the War Powers Act of 1973, new limitations were placed on the U.S. president requiring him to consult with the Congress before committing Americans to combat. The seizing of the *Mayaguez* by Khmer Rouge forces, though never proved to have been a deliberate act sanctioned by the Cambodian government, was clearly the first trial of America's fresh global thinking. This incident would not only take on a magnitude of importance far out of proportion with the value of the ship or the number of men involved but also cast its shadow over America's future military encounters.

On May 12, 1975, SS *Mayaguez*, an ungainly vessel with steel containers piled two high and six abreast, owned by Sea-Land Service and flying the American flag, steamed peacefully across the shimmering waters of the Gulf of Siam, some fifty miles off the Cambodian coast. It was May 12, 1975, just two weeks after American armed forces had closed the long and painful chapter of the struggle in Southeast Asia by evacuating the last Americans from Cambodia and Vietnam. As sailors watched through the pilothouse window on that Monday afternoon, a tiny smudge on the horizon transformed slowly into the distinct outline of a small craft speeding directly toward the ship. The boat kept closing in from Poulo Wai, a small group of islands lying fifteen miles to port of the *Mayaguez* as she steered northward, bound for Sattahip, Thailand, from Hong Kong. When what the crew thought was a fast-moving fishing boat morphed into a stub-nosed gray gunboat flying a red flag, the deck watch immediately called the master of the *Mayaguez*, Captain Charles T. Miller.

Ironically, what Captain Miller saw was an American-built Swift boat manned by Khmer Rouge soldiers wearing the familiar black pajamas all too recognizable to Americans. The fifty-foot, nineteen-ton coastal and river patrol boat had been used extensively in Vietnam by the U.S. Navy and Coast Guard. As it neared the 450-foot-long *Mayaguez*, the small craft ripped off a burst of .50-caliber machine-gun fire across the container ship's bow, followed shortly by a rocket-propelled grenade. This was the third attack on international shipping in the Gulf of Siam by armed Cambodian forces in the past two weeks: A South Korean ship had been fired on and chased, and a Panamanian ship had been seized and released after twenty-four hours.

Within minutes, as Captain Miller watched from his bridge, the patrol craft swung parallel to the *Mayaguez* and sent a second rocket streaking across the freighter's bow. Miller stopped his engines. By 2:20 P.M. a boarding party of seven barefoot men carrying Chinese AK-47 assault rifles and a rocket launcher had taken over the ship. The leader of the group was a slender man in his mid-thirties who carried a machine gun and a portable radio. He spoke no English. After inspecting the bridge, he beckoned Captain Miller into the pilothouse. Pointing to a local chart, the Khmer drew an anchor at a point behind the inner atoll of the Poulo Wai Islands. Captain Miller tried to stall, claiming the depth was inadequate, but finally steamed his ship ahead at one-third speed to the indicated spot.

Curious about the ship's sudden change of course and speed, Third Mate Dave English appeared on the bridge. After briefly assessing the situation, he withdrew without being noticed and made his way quickly to the radio shack. Once inside English ordered the radio operator to send an emergency signal. Although frightened that the two might be discovered by the Cambodian soldiers, the operator made several attempts on the International Distress Frequency band telegraph key but received no responses. Finally English used the single sideband high-frequency radio voice distress net to call in the Mayday, give their position, describe the situation, and ask that the message be passed to U.S. authorities. After some initial confusion the message was answered by someone who spoke English. He repeated back their position—9 degrees 48 minutes north latitude, 102 degrees 53 minutes east longitude, about seven miles southeast of the Poulo Wai Islands—and said that he would forward their distress signal. The Mayday had been received by the Delta Exploration Company in Djakarta, Indonesia, which passed it to the U.S. embassy in Djakarta, which then relayed the message to Washington.

After Captain Miller anchored the *Mayaguez* a mile north of Koh Tang as ordered, twenty-four hours passed during which the crisis took root in Washington, D.C. The U.S. Pacific Fleet Commander, who read the distress message at the same time as Washington, immediately ordered a U.S. Navy P-3 Orion, a long-range patrol aircraft, to fly to the area. It took off from Cubi Point in the Philippines and arrived over the *Mayaguez* the same night at 10:30 local time. The P-3 dropped flares and identified the ship in a contact report to the Naval Air Station Cubi operations center. During the next four days the ship was kept under constant surveillance by navy aircraft.

The wheels of diplomatic machinery began to turn almost immediately after the first distress message had been received in Washington. At 7:40 A.M., slightly more than six hours after the *Mayaguez* had transmitted her distress message, Lieutenant General Brent Scowcroft, deputy assistant for National Security Affairs, informed President Gerald Ford of the incident. Ford convened a National Security Council (NSC) meeting at noon. Among those present was Secretary of State Henry Kissinger.

After the session, the White House released a statement calling the incident an act of piracy, and stating that the United States would hold the Cambodian government accountable. The statement further hinted that the United States might retaliate with armed force if the crew and ship were not soon released. President Ford instructed Henry Kissinger to appeal to the People's Republic of China in Peking through George Bush, the senior U.S. liaison chief. Bush was to ask the Chinese to persuade the Cambodian government to release the ship and crewmen immediately. Deputy Secretary of State Robert Ingersoll summoned Huang Chen, the chief of the Chinese Liaison Office in Washington, to the State Department, gave him the same message, and asked him to relay it forthwith to Phnom Penh.

On May 13, several flights of U.S. Air Force F-4 Phantom fighter-bombers took off from bases in Thailand and appeared over the *Mayaguez*. The aircraft circled overhead and strafed in front of and around the containership in a futile effort to prevent the Cambodians from removing the crew and complicating matters by moving the ship. In desperation, the Cambodians on board returned fire with small arms. Following the strafing, four of the armed Cambodian guards, by now somewhat shaken, hustled the *Mayaguez* crew off the ship in two groups onto two small fishing boats and took them toward Koh Tang Island. Instead of landing on the island, however, they moored the boats in a nest with two other boats full of armed Cambodians, just off the island's northern shore. After spending a sleepless night at the mooring, the American crewmen watched as F-4s again buzzed the *Mayaguez* in a further attempt to persuade the Cambodians not to move the ship or crewmen from the area. In the meantime, U.S. Navy surveillance aircraft reported that the captured crewmen had been taken to the island of Koh Tang.

In rapid response to the navy report, and assuming that the crew were being taken ashore, President Ford ordered a marine assault on the island and air strikes to be launched against targets on mainland Cambodia.

In reality, the two fishing boats carrying the crew of the *Mayaguez* were still moored off the island. Early the next morning one boat was observed heading for the Cambodian mainland port of Kompong Som. When the navy P-3 aircraft approached the single fishing craft at low level as it chugged the fifty miles northeast to the mainland, the airmen spotted Caucasians on board, and they reported that these men may be some of the American hostages. Because the second fishing boat had not left for the mainland, the impression continued that some of the crewmen had been taken ashore on Koh Tang. Unfortunately, this assumption proved incorrect—the entire crew had left Koh Tang.

More U.S. jets buzzed the small boat with the *Mayaguez* crewmen and their Cambodian guards as it continued toward the mainland. The airplanes fired into the water around its hull, trying to make it reverse course, fearing that the Americans would be dispersed on the mainland, further complicating a rescue. Aircraft rockets slightly wounded several of the *Mayaguez* crewmen, while their terrified captors hid belowdecks. Despite the attack, the fishing boat arrived in Kompong Som, and Captain Miller and all thirty-nine crewmen were put ashore on Rong Sam Lem, an island inside the harbor. They were kept there for some hours, their fate apparently in the hands of a local Khmer Rouge commander.

Meanwhile, some twelve hundred miles to the north, U.S. Navy Commander John Michael Rodgers, commanding officer of the guided missile destroyer USS *Henry B. Wilson,* was piloting his ship out of Kaohsiung, Taiwan, where he and his crew had spent three days relaxing. The visit to Kaohsiung had followed the emotional days spent evacuating the last Americans and thousands of loyal South Vietnamese from the beleaguered capital, Saigon, two weeks earlier. It had been a draining experience for the men of the *Wilson,* and Rodgers had let his crew choose their favorite liberty port.

USS *Wilson,* Rodgers's fourth command at sea, had gained a reputation as one of the most efficient ships in the Seventh Fleet. During the Saigon evacuation, he had been ordered around to the mouth of the Rung Sat River near Vung Tau at Cape Saint Jacques. His mission was to find and escort a convoy of tugs towing large steel barges filled with fleeing Vietnamese. Off Vung Tau, Rodgers saw two sets of radar contacts going south in the narrow canals from Saigon into the Rung Sat. The contacts were two American-manned tugs operated by contract engineers. As the tows passed close to the shore at Vung Tau they came under heavy fire from the bank, presumably from Communist forces. While some Vietnamese aboard the crowded barges returned fire with small arms, Rodgers saw the danger, approached the coastline, and began to suppress the shore fire with his five-inch guns. "That worked for a while," said Rodgers, a no-nonsense New Englander, "until I observed the tugs had slipped their tows and begun to race away to safety, leaving the barges, crowded with thousands of hapless Vietnamese, stranded and still under fire from the shoreline. I grew very angry." Without awaiting orders, Rodgers quickly demonstrated his character. He steamed alongside the lead tug and trained his forward five-inch gun on it, then radioed the skipper via the International Distress Frequency. A harried first mate answered. "Tell your master," said Rodgers, "to reconnect your tow immediately, or I will blow you out of the water." After a short pause, another voice from the tug came over the radio: "Right away, Captain."

As the *Wilson* passed the sea buoy heading out of Kaohsiung, Rodgers retired to his sea cabin. He switched on the radio to the BBC and heard the news announcer give details of an act of piracy: An American merchant ship had been boarded and detained by the Khmer Rouge off the island of Koh Tang in the Gulf of Siam. Rodgers returned immediately to the bridge navigation plot and quickly laid out a rough track to Koh Tang. Without waiting for orders, Rodgers sent a brief message to his immediate tactical commander and to the commander of the Seventh Fleet: "Unless otherwise directed, am proceeding at 33 knots to Koh Tang island to render assistance. Estimated time of arrival forty-eight hours, request tanker enroute." (The phrase "unless otherwise directed" is used traditionally in the navy by a junior to pry a timely response for his action from his senior commanders.) The *Wilson* commenced a two-day full-power run toward the scene of the action, while Rodgers and his men anticipated a fight. They would arrive off Koh Tang at 7:00 A.M. on May 15, just after a second U.S. Navy ship, the frigate USS *Harold E. Holt,* arrived from Subic Bay.

As the *Wilson* steamed south, navy officials diverted the aircraft carrier USS *Coral Sea* from Indonesian waters where she was heading for Australia to participate in a commemoration of the Battle of Coral Sea. As the carrier raced north toward Cambodia she was ordered by President Ford to launch air attacks against a naval base and fuel dumps on mainland Cambodia. While these strikes were under way, on May 15, navy and air force fighters engaged and sank at least half a dozen Khymer patrol boats along the coast.

While the air strikes were in progress, a contingent of marines and air force personnel led by Lieutenant Colonel Randall W. Austin, commander of the Second Battalion of the Ninth Marine Regiment, prepared to land on Koh Tang to seize, occupy, and defend the island. Their specific tasks were to search for the crew of the *Mayaguez* and to deny the use of the island as a base of fire that could interfere with the recapture of the containership. The president ordered the attack before receiving the navy report that part of the crew may have been taken toward the Cambodian mainland.

The assault on the island—which would last seventy-eight hours—was being pulled together quickly, and the specific intelligence to help prepare the marines was scanty. Lacking concrete detailed information on the strength and disposition of Cambodian forces on the island, the Intelligence Center Pacific (IPAC), located in Hawaii, had estimated that possibly one hundred to two hundred Khmer Rouge infantry, called Khmer Kraham, with small arms supported by heavy weapons, might be present on the north end of the island. The estimate was nearly correct numerically but was unfortunately vague regarding their specific location, their disposition, and the status of entrenchment on the island. There was no mention of the existence of permanent, bunkered emplacements of heavy weapons or antiaircraft positions on the island. This was to prove costly to the 179-man marine force that landed in the first wave.

During the brief hours before the planned assault, the marine commander of the landing force and one staff officer made a single hurried reconnaissance flight over the island. They noted it was approximately five miles long and covered with jungle canopy; a cleared path ran through the jungle across its narrow northern neck. Although the marines successfully completed their reconnaissance flight, aerial photographs of the island were not provided in time for a thorough study of the defenses. Some photographs were brought out to the airfield and shown to Captain James Davis, the G Company commander who was to lead the blocking platoon of his company, as he stood on the dark runway just moments before boarding his helicopter. When viewed by flashlight, these images confirmed that there were fixed bunkers and open heavy-caliber gun pits on the northern part of the island, but their locations were not exact. It proved too late to modify the planned assault.

The Second Battalion of the Ninth Marine Regiment was scheduled to land by Seventh Air Force HH-53 and CH-53 helicopters in two waves, four and a half hours apart. They flew from U Tapao, Thailand, 195 nautical miles from Koh Tang. The plan called for the first wave, one reinforced platoon of G Company with Captain Davis, to land on the west coast of the island and the remainder of the company, led by battalion commander Lieutenant Colonel Austin, to land simultaneously on the east side. The two groups would then converge toward the center of the island, clearing a corridor across, sweeping the northern tip, then taking a hill in the south that was the highest point of the island. As the assault on the island began, another company of marines from the First Battalion of the Ninth Marine Regiment would board and retake the *Mayaguez,* which remained at anchor off the northeast tip of the island, from the decks of USS *Harold E. Holt.* A second wave of marines would follow four and a half hours later—the time required to shuttle more marines from Thailand and reinforce the marines on both sides of the island.

At 4:00 A.M. on Thursday, May 15, the 227-man assault team, flying in eleven helicopters, swooped south from Thailand. Three would divert to retake the containership, and the remaining eight would attack the island. Forty-eight marines and twelve navy men rappelled down ropes onto the deck of the *Holt* from three air force HH-53 helicopters. The frigate then moored alongside the *Mayaguez*, and the marines crossed to retake the containership without a fight.

As 179 marines from Captain Davis's company began the attack on the island supported by air force fighter-bombers, they immediately ran into heavy resistance. During the storming of the east side of the island, where three platoons and the battalion command group were to land, two helicopters were immediately hit by heavy-caliber ground fire from bunkered positions. One helicopter burst into flames and went down in the water, killing seven marines, two navy corpsmen, and the air force copilot; three more men died in the surf while the remaining thirteen swam out to sea and were rescued by the USS *Henry B. Wilson* four hours later. One of the marine swimmers used his survival radio to direct air force fighter-bombers to targets on the island while treading water in the offshore seas. A second helicopter managed to land on the east side of the island despite having its tail destroyed. The twenty marines and four air force men it carried disembarked, formed a perimeter in the trees along the beach, and held out under intense fire for the remainder of the day.

More helicopters from the first wave tried repeatedly to land their marines on the eastern side of the island but came under heavy automatic weapons fire. That landing area turned out to be the most heavily defended, with gun pits and bunkers located directly on the beach. By 6:10 A.M. there were only thirty marines ashore of the planned ninety from the first wave, and after repeated attempts to reinforce those on the eastern shore, the additional helicopters were driven off by intense fire. Two of the eastern first-wave helicopters diverted to the west shore and landed the battalion commander, Lieutenant Colonel Austin, and twenty-nine men at a random point there. At first this group was pinned down on a small beach one kilometer to the south of the blocking platoon's planned position on the west side of the island. They attempted to fight their way north, where other marines were expected to land.

The helicopter assault on the island's west beach by the single blocking platoon led by Captain Davis began at 6:30 A.M. when four helicopters approached from the northwest and tried to land but encountered intense heavy fire from machine guns and rocket-propelled grenades. The first helicopter from this group was shot down after its marines disembarked and landed in the water; the four crewmen were killed. The second, with Captain Davis aboard, was severely damaged, aborted its landing, and returned to Thailand. The third helicopter successfully landed the remainder of the blocking platoon. The fourth was driven off and withdrew, awaiting clearance to try again to land its marines. Austin's group, which had diverted to the west side, then fought its way north against stiff opposition and joined the main group in the west, expanding their number to eighty-two men.

Three helicopters had gone down, two on the eastern side and one in the water on the west side, while two others limped back to base badly damaged, all the marines, including the company commander, still aboard. All but one of the eight helicopters bringing in the first wave of marines to the island were destroyed or damaged. That meant only five helicopters were available to bring in the 127 marines for the second wave. The marines on the east side of the island had been pinned down immediately and separated into two groups. After the fiercely opposed landing, the marines fought a fourteen-hour pitched battle against more than one hundred well-disciplined Khmer Rouge infantry.

At 7:00 A.M. USS *Henry B. Wilson* sailed into radio range of the air force officer acting as the on-scene commander located on board the Airborne Battlefield Command, Control, and Communications EC-130 Hercules aircraft flying over the island. Captain Rodgers reported that he had arrived to render assistance. He was amazed when the airborne commander told him to orbit at ten thousand feet and await instructions. After gently explaining that he would have to confine his altitude to sea level because of the restraints of gravity, Rodgers steered close to the eastern side of Koh Tang and at 7:20 observed heavy firing ashore. The *Wilson* crew sighted the downed heli-copters and detected round spheres, which, Rodgers said, "appeared to be coconuts in the water off the island." Suddenly realizing that the coconuts were instead the helmets of helicopter flight crewmen, Rodgers sent the ship's motor whaleboat and his captain's gig, well armed with machine guns and small arms, to haul the surviving heli-copter crews from the waters near the beach. They attracted intense fire from the Khmer Rouge forces.

Air force fighter-bombers from bases in Thailand attempted to support the marines during their fight on the island, but their air-control team on the ground had been separated in the landings and several team members were killed. As a consequence, overall air sup-port was makeshift and spotty, although Rodgers's small boat crews provided some accurate guidance to the pilots. Several A-7 bombers also directed other aircraft in supporting strikes.

For reasons unknown to this day, but probably because of the ini-tial air strikes on the mainland, the Khmer Rouge suddenly released the *Mayaguez* crew in the midst of the fighting, sending them out from Kompong Som in a commandeered Thai fishing boat. Captain Rodgers received a report from an orbiting P-3 aircraft that a small gun-boat was approaching from Kompong Som. Given permission to close, engage, and destroy the gunboat, Rodgers turned the *Wilson* toward the approaching boat and bore down on it at twenty-five knots, preparing his forward five-inch gun mount to take the boat under fire. Fortu-nately, a gunner's mate perched aloft saw the craft through the power-ful optics of the gunfire director and noticed it was a fishing boat. He then reported that he saw Caucasian faces aboard. Rodgers held his fire, and by 10:00 A.M. the entire crew was safely in his hands.

After Captain Miller and his men were safely on board the *Wilson*, Miller told Rodgers that he had promised the Cambodians who re-leased them that, upon reaching U.S. forces, he would ask that further air attacks against the mainland and Koh Tang be called off. Rodgers immediately reported the request in a message to his superiors, as he and the merchant skipper looked aloft to see the sky alive with aircraft from the USS *Coral Sea* heading directly for Kompong Som. It was too late to call back the next strikes. Miller shrugged: "I tried."

With the *Mayaguez* crewmen safely aboard the *Wilson,* President Ford ordered the Marines on Koh Tang, who had been fighting for more than twelve hours, to disengage and withdraw from the island. Rapid communications with Washington almost spelled tragedy for the beleaguered marines when five more helicopters flying south from Thailand, bringing the badly needed reinforcements, complied with the president's order to withdraw and turned back. These helicopters reversed course a second time at the furious insistence of Lieutenant Colonel Austin, who was by now leading the combined force of the two groups on the island. The fighting on Koh Tang had become so intense that the relief troops were unquestionably needed to protect the withdrawal of their comrades.

Four of the five helicopters carrying the second wave landed one hundred more marines. The fifth helicopter tried to pick up the twenty-four men trapped on the eastern beach, but it was heavily damaged and returned to Thailand. At that point there were 225 U.S. troops on the island. For eight more hours after the order was given to disengage, the marines continued to fight against more than a full battalion of Khmer infantry supported by a heavy-weapons company. As the ground fighting continued, sailors in the *Wilson*'s whaleboat continued to support the marines with .50-caliber machine-gun fire. Air force fighter-bombers flew over the island before dark to assist the marines, but their pilots were unable to see them through the jungle. Meanwhile, the frigate *Harold E. Holt* was towing the *Mayaguez* clear of the action.

Just after dark, at 6:10 P.M., air force pilots made another attempt to rescue the marines. Three helicopters landed on the east side of the island in the face of heavy ground fire. A small covering infantry force landed to protect the helicopters, while the stranded marines scrambled aboard. Helicopter crews stood in the cargo bay firing their GAU-5 mini-guns with one hand and pulling marines aboard with the other.

The final effort on the ground was the withdrawal of the larger group from the west beach. Thirty marines were still heavily engaged on the southern flank of the west beach with Lieutenant Colonel Austin in command. Twenty-seven fought their way onto the last helicopter, which had set down on the narrow beach with its tailgate down facing the island. Air crewman Technical Sergeant Wayne Fisk charged out of the last CH-53 into a hail of automatic weapons fire to take one last look for any remaining men. He found two young marines still firing into the tree line. Fisk sent them to the helicopter and continued to search for more of the missing. Fisk and a second marine barely made it back to the helicopter's rear door while being pursued by Khmer Rouge soldiers. As the helicopter lifted off, the ramp suddenly released, in a terrible moment, causing the last men to begin tumbling out the back. They were saved from falling from the helicopter by the other marines, including Captain Davis, who formed a human chain to hoist the dangling men from the rear door.

After the chaotic but largely successful withdrawal, there was a frantic head count of marines. As those pulled out earlier had been taken to various ships and air bases, the count was prolonged and confused. Eventually the battalion commander determined that three marines were unaccounted for, probably left behind in the hasty departure. The three missing were part of a machine-gun team from E Company that had landed in the second wave. They were last seen by another marine who recalled passing them ammunition during the hasty retreat before the last helicopter departed. Twenty-five years later, Cambodian veterans of the action told western researchers that all three marines left behind had been killed. Over the years, American journalist-researchers who revisited the scene found evidence on the island that the three remaining marines had resisted until the last, although their remains have still not been positively identified.[1]

Cambodian forces engaged during the fight included approximately twelve patrol boats and at least one Cambodian battalion of Khmer Kraham infantry. Losses in the action included a Khmer base and oil-storage facility destroyed, eight or ten patrol boats sunk, and about one hundred Khmer infantry killed or wounded. U.S. casualties were eighteen killed and fifty wounded.

The reaction in Washington to the hijacking of *Mayaguez* reinforces the view that senior statesmen like Secretary of State Kissinger, tempered by the many years of cold war, had a tendency to relate lesser regional events to the larger global superpower competition. In this case, Kissinger and the National Security Council aides hastened to make the point that the United States could still act forcibly despite the fall of Saigon two weeks earlier. They were determined not to suffer another USS *Pueblo* incident.[2] Using this reasoning, Kissinger persuaded President Ford to order immediate air strikes against Kompong Som and to assault Koh Tang Island without waiting for diplomatic measures to secure the release of the *Mayaguez* crew. We now know from information from the Cambodians that the crew was in the process of being released as the air strikes and island assault were under way, unbeknownst to the authorities in Washington.

After an analysis of Khmer communications intercepted by air force intelligence, it became apparent that the seizure of the *Mayaguez* might have been the deed of a local commander and not an official government act. President Ford subsequently canceled additional B-52 strikes he had previously ordered to launch from Guam to hit Cambodian targets on the mainland. It was nevertheless too late to call back the navy air strikes from the *Coral Sea*, which continued even after the *Mayaguez* crew was safely aboard the *Wilson*.

After the fight was over and the *Mayaguez* crew recovered, some criticized the United States for reacting hastily with excessive force. However, this incident was not a complex political crisis that called for a measured response. Since no response was ever received from the Cambodian government through diplomatic channels, the seizure was considered a brazen deed that validated a rapid and forceful response. While twentieth-century piracy certainly did not cease with the recapture and rescue of the *Mayaguez* crew, no more American-flagged ships have been seized by pirates since.

Militarily, the *Mayaguez* rescue and the fight on Koh Tang were important events, and successfully demonstrated that the United States could take swift and decisive action. It is clear that the rapid application of land- and carrier-based air power caused the Cambodians to change whatever plans they had in store for the captured

American ship and crew. However, the precise relationship between the Cambodian government and those who conducted the seizure is still uncertain. The successful outcome of the *Mayaguez* rescue mission, despite its high cost in casualties—more killed and wounded than the number of crew originally captured—was the beginning of a slow process to reassert U.S. military prestige after it had reached its nadir in Vietnam. Not all of the U.S. rescue attempts that followed would be as successful.

PART TWO

James E. Carter, Jr.:
Choosing Military Action

CHAPTER 2

America and Special Warfare

April 1980

During the long cold war the United States sought to contain the spread of Communism in Southeast Asia by committing massive U.S. resources throughout the region. In 1965 the strategy in Vietnam shifted to introducing sizable ground combat units, and soon scores of American draftees were fighting and dying in a war on the Asian mainland. Eight years later, American ground forces had left and conscription ceased. American military leaders were discouraged by the failure to win the ground war despite their great advantages in firepower and mobility. The Vietnam experience had shaken their faith in the "American way of war"—reliance on mass industrialized violence and highly mechanized mobility.

Since colonial times Americans had viewed a professional army with some distaste and mistrust. However, after Vietnam, Americans began to search for a way to restore the armed forces' role as a credible instrument of U.S. policy. An all-volunteer force was formed. Politicians and career military officers agreed to banish the draft for two reasons: (1) the numbers were no longer required and (2) it was widely believed that the conscription formula had been implemented unfairly. There was also a renewed emphasis on special operations.

Years of frustration brought about by U.S. involvement in Southeast Asia also started a trend to elevate technology above the traditional focus on the individual fighting man. It became unacceptable for the United States to suffer large numbers of casualties. American science and technology developed superweapons systems and envisioned "Star Wars" battlefields where the enemy and target images are projected in detailed video presentations thousands of miles from the front. A popular aversion to seeing loved ones returned in body bags changed the philosophy of making war, and the new science and technology seemed to make the revisions possible. The basis for deciding whether or not to use military force shifted from the traditional criterion of "How long will it take to achieve the objective?" to "How many casualties will it cost?" The American military command and control system grew more sophisticated and spawned a generation of high-tech warriors who believed the number of men on the ground to be less important than new and complex electronic battlefield equipment. New aircraft with all-weather capabilities, night-vision devices, long-range video observation technology, and smart and highly accurate precision-guided weapons began to turn many defense leaders away from a theory reliant on large standing armies. Many military thinkers agreed that special operations forces, a favorite idea of President John Kennedy from the early 1960s, could take over complex fighting missions and accomplish daring surgical operations with impunity. This thinking became more popular in the post-Vietnam, post-*Mayaguez* period as Americans sought to modernize yet reduce the manpower of the armed forces. Many political leaders believed it would be better to rely increasingly on specialty fighting forces supported by the new standoff air and naval weapons.

Guerrilla warfare was not new to Americans but included a full array of renowned behind-the-lines fighting legends such as the Revolutionary War guerrilla leader Francis Marion and Civil War–era raiders like James Ewell Brown "Jeb" Stuart. During World War II American forces used special warfare tactics with limited success both in German-occupied France and in Burma and the Philippines against the Japanese. U.S. Navy Underwater Demolition Teams successfully infiltrated and destroyed enemy defenses before Allied landings in the Pacific and European theaters. Combined operations under Lord Louis Mountbatten gained a great deal of fame for British special forces as well after some very daring and costly operations along the German-occupied coasts of Norway and France. The Royal Marine Special Boat Squadrons known as the "cockleshell heroes" became a hallmark of courage after their small explosive-laden kayaks were used to stage daring and spectacular raids against German shipping in France and the Japanese in Singapore. The British Special Air Service commando forces, direct offspring of the remarkable Long Range Desert Group squadrons that fought so successfully behind German lines in North Africa, were among the most celebrated founders of the modern-day special operations forces.

After the war, the U.S. government organized a new type of special forces in occupied Germany to train armed teams made up of displaced Russians and other fiercely anti-Communist refugees from eastern Europe. The U.S. Navy tapped the valuable experience of its Underwater Demolition Teams, upgraded their training with the help of the British Royal Marine Special Boat Squadron, and in 1961 formed naval commando units called Sea, Air, Land, or SEAL, teams. The SEALs became the first postwar American special warfare forces to deploy on combat missions when they conducted beach reconnaissance and commando raids in Cuba to prepare for the invasion anticipated during the October 1962 Cuban missile crisis.

During the long war in Vietnam special operations forces from all services fought in the jungles, highlands, and rivers of Indochina. From the very beginning U.S. Army Special Forces had acted as advisers, training and leading Vietnamese counterpart organizations, and the navy did likewise with its SEALs. As the war progressed, American special operations forces fought with varying degrees of success, interdicting the North Vietnamese supply lines of the Ho Chi Minh Trail and across the Cambodian border. However, the early American commitment to special operations under President John F. Kennedy and Secretary of Defense Robert S. McNamara in Southeast Asia in the 1960s was seriously discredited, because the Americans failed to integrate the political into the military as the British and French colonial services had done. U.S. Special Forces combat operations in Vietnam were frequently conducted without simultaneous pacification and civic action efforts and often conflicted with the attempts of other agencies to gain the support of South Vietnamese locals. The sometimes unsavory reputation of these Special Forces reached a head toward the end of America's time in Vietnam, when the commander of the Green Berets and some of his officers were arrested and charged with using the enemy's own methods of coercion, torture, and execution of prisoners. They were later acquitted of wrongdoing. Bad press naturally followed, but the U.S. Army, Navy, and Air Force special operations forces had proven effective on a small scale. America was slow to learn that wars cannot be fought and won under strict rules imposed on one side only. To counter terrorists with little heed for principles, one needs to turn their tactics against them rather than rely on traditional codes of good sportsmanship. This strategy was proved by the successful, but necessarily secretive, operations of the SEALs in Vietnam and the British Special Air Service in Malaysia and Northern Ireland.

The regular army harbored a serious mistrust of these special forces, however. Like the battleship navy of the early years of World War II that held out against aircraft-carrier warfare, the regular army represented a conservative block that competed with progressive advocates. Interservice rivalry resulted in a post-Vietnam reduction in size and funding of the famed Green Berets and the fading of their popularity. For a regular army or noncommissioned officer, a too-close tie to the elite special troops was not healthy for a career. Nevertheless, the rise of worldwide terrorism, as well as the spectacular successes of special antiterrorist squads in the Israeli raid against hijackers in Entebbe, Uganda, and the German attack against terrorists in Mogadishu in the late 1970s, made a similar American capability worth reconsidering. The services finally accepted the need for special operations, though not without resistance.

In 1977 President Carter authorized the army to form a special antiterrorist task force. The army gave this job to the veteran Green Beret Colonel Charles Beckwith and earmarked $4 million to establish a highly trained, superbly equipped, and secret antiterrorist unit able to operate anywhere in the world. He was given two years. He modeled

Delta Force on the British Special Air Service commandos, and also used British selection procedures and training.

In 1979 the United States was faced with a frustrating situation in Iran. On November 4, Iranian students, in an action claimed to be independent of the revolutionary government of Ayatollah Khomeini, violated the Vienna Convention regarding the conduct and inviolability of diplomats, overran the U.S. embassy in Tehran, and took fifty-five Americans hostage. Occurring just two years after the formation of Delta Force, this incident became the focus of its first major operation.

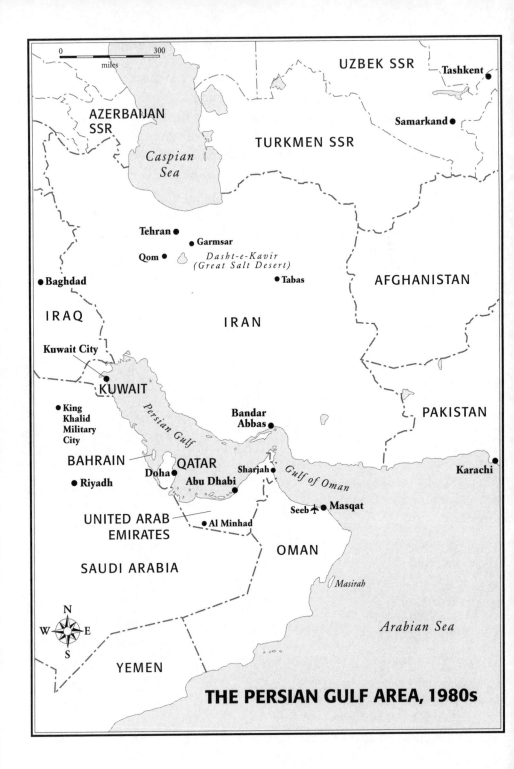

THE PERSIAN GULF AREA, 1980s

CHAPTER 3

The Hostage Rescue Attempt

April 24, 1980

> *You cannot take a few people from one unit, throw them in with*
> *some from another, give them someone else's equipment, and hope*
> *to come up with a top-notch fighting outfit.*

> —Colonel Charles Beckwith,
> U.S. Army rescue force commander

It is helpful to look to the history of the Middle East, Persian Gulf, and horn of Africa for the background of some of the future applications of U.S. military force. The Iran hostage rescue operation, the Persian Gulf escort naval engagements in 1987, the Gulf War in 1991, and even the 1993 intervention in Somalia bear some relationship to the clash of British and Russian forces in the region during the nineteenth century.

Beginning with Peter the Great in 1723, Russian interest in the Persian Gulf region was based on the goal of access to warm-water ports. With his dreams of maritime expansion, the czar declared war on Persia and sought unsuccessfully to expand from the southern shore of the Caspian Sea into the gulf to open sea lanes to India. This threat from Russia consumed the British for centuries and resulted in the prolonged presence of significant British forces in the area. Although the British rarely confronted the Russians on the field of battle, the

Russian threat triggered several smaller British wars in the region, most notably in Afghanistan, an inhospitable land noted for long and tortuous defeats of invaders. In the mid-1800s, the great powers of Britain and Russia were feeling their way toward each other in central Asia, like two blindfolded giants, each confused by ignorance of the other's intentions. The study of Britain and Russia in Asia is of a war that never happened.

America's first serious involvement in Iran came during World War II. British and Soviet forces entered the country in 1941 to secure an overland route for lend-lease supplies flowing to the Soviet Union and to preempt German occupation of the vast Persian oil fields. The British and Soviets jointly unseated Reza Shah Pahlavi, the uncooperative Iranian monarch then in power, and installed his twenty-one-year-old son Mohammad Reza Pahlavi on the Peacock Throne. During the Tehran Conference in 1943, Churchill, Stalin, and Roosevelt pledged formal support for Iran's territorial integrity and independence. Six months after the war ended, British and American forces withdrew from southern Iran, while Soviet forces remained in northern Iran and tried to establish a client state. Their efforts to seed Communism in Iran failed, however, when their antireligious rhetoric undermined their efforts in a society deeply devoted to the Islamic faith. Strong pressure from the United States through the United Nations helped bring about a withdrawal of Soviet forces from northern Iran in 1946.

Thereafter, the Soviets changed their tactics to subverting the young shah's rule, and their influence in Iran persisted during the postwar period through the Iranian Communist Tudeh Party. This subversive Soviet threat became a key concern and overriding factor in the American determination to retain the shah during the years of the cold war. When a Soviet-backed coup threatened the shah in 1953, President Dwight D. Eisenhower authorized an operation, code-named Ajax, to oust Mohammad Mossadegh, a popular and therefore threatening opposition leader who had gained the support of the Tudeh Party. The plan, originally concocted by the British, was directed by Kermit Roosevelt of the Central Intelligence Agency.[1] The operation succeeded, and Britain and America successfully maintained their influence in the Persian Gulf. In return for their support, the shah granted American and British oil companies each 40 percent of the Iranian oil consortium.

With the Allies' man in power for two decades, Iran achieved unprecedented economic prosperity. The shah stressed the Soviet threat to his kingdom and asked for a long list of modern military equipment. Although his appeals were ignored by President Eisenhower, the shah found an enthusiastic supporter in Vice President Richard Nixon, who seemed enraptured by the shah's growing anti-Communist convictions. While this Nixon-shah association was not productive at the time, it reemerged twenty years later as one cornerstone of the American policy of Persian Gulf security. During the late 1950s and early 1960s the shah began to face serious opposition from revolutionaries led by the Shiite clergy. Resistance developed into open rallies, and then riots came to a head in 1963. The shah suppressed the clashes by brutal military force; in June 1963 hundreds of protesters in the Muslim holy city of Qom were killed.

The unrest was instigated by the cleric Ayatollah Khomeini, but at the time he was not taken seriously by American observers. Jailed and exiled to France after the 1963 riots, Khomeini continued to fuel Iranian dissent with a steady stream of sermons smuggled into Iran on audiocassette tapes.[2] By 1978 Khomeini's persistence had paid off, as he grew to personify Iranian dissent. It is astonishing that the vast intelligence mechanism made up of the U.S. Central Intelligence and Defense Intelligence Agencies, Britain's MI-6, and Iran's own heavy-handed intelligence service, SAVAK, failed to uncover signs that a religious revolution was at hand, led by the same Iranian clergy who had fomented the unrest in 1963. From 1963 to 1978 the risk of an internal uprising against the shah went largely unheeded as the United States focused on the external threat of the Soviet Union. In 1973 the United States initiated a major military buildup within Iran. The Western allies were distracted by the unprecedented economic gains the country made and were bemused by the shah's investment in their military assistance program. The religious turmoil throughout the land was simply overlooked.

In the post-Vietnam years it was disturbing to many in both the West and Iran to see vast quantities of modern weapons, ships, aircraft, tanks, ground equipment, and antitank and air-defense missiles pour into Iran as part of a vast and accelerating security assistance program. It was totally out of proportion to any threat the country faced or to the Iranians' ability to absorb and successfully operate these armaments. The Nixon Doctrine in the Persian Gulf region took the form of a "two-pillar" policy in which America strove to build regional security by providing military material support but not troops to the two friendly regimes, Iran and Saudi Arabia. The complex social and religious upheaval churning in the shadows was ignored. At the core of the unrest lay the hatred of the imitation of Western culture by the shah's regime, denounced by Khomeini as "Westoxication."[3]

While President Carter was elected in 1976 on the principal issues of human rights and reducing American arms sales abroad, torture and political persecution had become routine in Iran under the shah, and his personal manipulation of the economy merely provoked the growing opposition. The Iranian revolution began in 1978, two months after the death of the Ayatollah Khomeini's son, allegedly at the hands of SAVAK.[4] The Iranian police opened fire on a religious demonstration in Qom, killing a number of students, an act that set off a series of violent demonstrations that subsequently started the revolution in earnest. The shah's regime began to come apart at the seams and the shah was forced to flee for his life in January 1979. The rest of the world, including an incredulous American government, was left in shock. After seeking shelter in two reluctant Arab states, Egypt and Morocco, the shah landed in America. Then, while the Carter administration cogitated and sought solutions, events in Tehran boiled over. In February Khomeini returned from exile in France. The rapid deterioration and collapse of the shah's government had caught the United States by surprise. The Ayatollah Khomeini's newly emerging regime vehemently opposed American presence in the area in any form. The new Iran also sought to spread the Islamic revolution throughout the Persian Gulf region by encouraging the overthrow of Arab states.

Then, on November 4, 1979, after the fall of the interim govern-

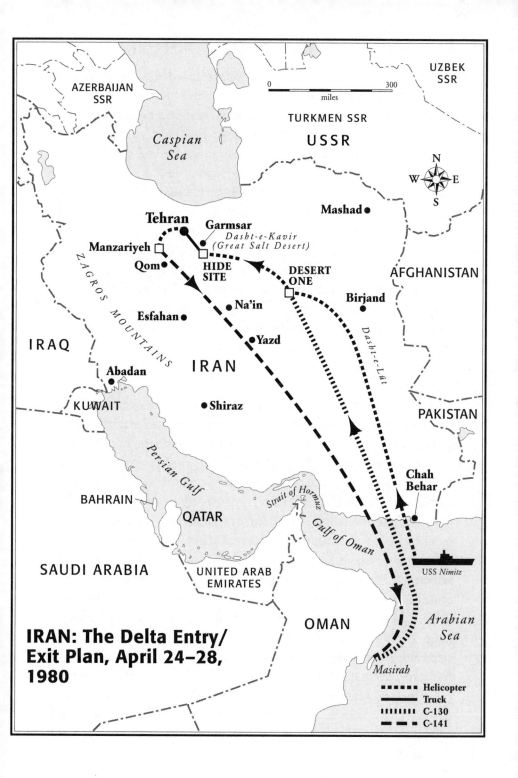

IRAN: The Delta Entry/
Exit Plan, April 24–28,
1980

ment, a handful of Iranian revolutionary guard students scaled the walls and seized the American embassy compound in Tehran. Certainly they had the blessing of Khomeini, who had been in the country only nine months. The former shah had been admitted to the United States earlier. It was not the first time the embassy had been attacked, and it is therefore puzzling why such an action took the embassy by surprise. Nine months earlier, on February 14, revolutionaries had attacked and captured the ambassador and some of his staff. On that occasion members of Khomeini's staff, recently returned in triumph with their leader, had intervened on the ambassador's behalf, and within twenty-four hours all the American captives had been released. They further made provisions for token protection by offering the embassy a band of young revolutionary guards to act as security. When the ultimate provocation came in November, it triggered a long standoff between Iran and the United States that did not end until 444 days later, when a shattered President Carter left the White House.

The Ayatollah's takeover in Iran and the seizure of the U.S. embassy in 1979, coupled with the Soviet invasion of Afghanistan in December of the same year, prompted the president to declare his Carter Doctrine in his State of the Union Address on January 23, 1980. It stated: "An attempt by an outside power to gain control of the Persian Gulf region will be regarded as an assault on the vital interests of the United States of America, and such an assault will be repelled by any means necessary, including military force." This policy provided the direct rationale for developing the U.S. Rapid Deployment Force, a large conventional unit designed to respond quickly at extreme distances from home. Events of that year also drew more American naval forces into the area, where they would remain at reduced levels for the next twenty years. Given the lack of reliable U.S. military bases on Saudi Arabia's soil, and that country's reluctance to make binding defense arrangements with Western powers, America was limited to developing only minimal logistic facilities there and elsewhere in the region. These provided the capability to handle potential surges of American forces on a temporary basis should the need arise.

President Carter frequently but reluctantly considered military action against Iran to gain release of the American hostages. A long and anguishing period during which negotiations and limited economic sanctions failed produced no results, but a rescue seemed a long shot. The military choices addressed by his national security advisers included imposing a blockade, mining Iranian ports, unleashing selected air strikes against Iranian oil refineries, and a carefully crafted, complex rescue mission to be conducted by Delta Force, the newly formed army special operations antiterrorist unit.

After the first occupation of the embassy compound in February, Delta Force had requested permission to send a team to Tehran to conduct a detailed survey of the embassy and its surroundings in anticipation of some sort of future operation. The Army Chief of Staff, General Edward C. Meyer, denied permission for Delta to survey the area, an unfortunate decision that proved in the end to greatly complicate planning when the army was ordered to formulate a hostage-rescue plan later that year. Then Delta Force requested a covert reconnaissance flight into Iran to locate staging areas for a possible rescue attempt. This request was first sought from the president on February 28. President Carter denied the request on the basis that the mission might fail and jeopardize diplomatic negotiations.[5] On March 7 National Security Adviser Zbigniew Brzezinski and Secretary of State Cyrus Vance resubmitted a proposal for the reconnaissance mission and were again turned down by the president because he felt that such a mission, if discovered, might further provoke the Iranians.[6]

After four months of frustrating talks with Iran, President Carter called a meeting of the National Security Council to review a military solution. During this gathering, which was held at Camp David on Saturday, March 22, 1980, the president finally approved a reconnaissance mission and the commitment of special operations personnel to attempt to rescue the hostages by force. The meeting began at 10:45 A.M. and continued until 3:30 P.M. The shah was then visiting Panama to investigate the possibility of settling there. He was also considering an invitation by President Anwar Sadat to end his flight in Egypt. President Carter had just spoken to Sadat and persuaded him that Egypt was a more prudent place of refuge than the United States. Sadat believed he could weather the political consequences, and the shah flew to Egypt the next day, just as air force General David Jones, the chairman of the Joint Chiefs of Staff, briefed the president on the details of a planned rescue mission.

The lack of intelligence that had frustrated any possibility of an immediate rescue mission had finally been overcome, and the U.S. military was receiving reports from allied foreign observers in Iran. Additionally, some agents from the Defense Intelligence Agency's Intelligence Support Activity had been sent into Iran. Any rescue plan would be particularly difficult to formulate, because it would take place in a landlocked capital in a country surrounded by states openly hostile to the United States: the Soviet Union, Iraq, and Soviet-occupied Afghanistan. Although the locations of the hostages were generally known, it was not likely that they could be mustered together quickly and moved easily during a rescue. Thus, it was necessary that a rescue plan include enough time for the rescue forces to search a large number of buildings in the embassy compound before gathering the hostages and rescue forces together and whisking them out of the city and the country. General Jones was certain that if the rescue forces could get into the compound without alerting the revolutionary guards, the operation stood a high chance of success. Getting into the compound and evacuating the Americans seemed less difficult than getting the rescue forces to the embassy and surprising the guards.

The army devised a rescue plan that consisted of separate phases, each of which could be terminated and the forces withdrawn, if necessary, without making the situation between the two countries worse. The first phase of the plan required positioning forces covertly at various tactically advantageous locations throughout the Middle East. Certainly one of the most challenging aspects of the entire operation was to keep secret a large movement of specialist units from the observant eyes of the free press and the Soviets. The potentially high visibility of the particular ground, air, and naval forces that might be expected to take part in an engagement of this kind made the operational security of the effort a key aspect of the plan.

The main purpose of the March 22 Camp David meeting was to set a timetable in motion so that once the president decided to go, a rehearsed force would be ready with minimal delay. A staging base called Desert One was selected in the remote Great Salt Desert, near the town of Tabas, two hundred miles southeast of Tehran. The plan was to fly in a force at night in a combination of fixed-wing aircraft and long-range helicopters coming from different directions. The force would converge at Desert One, where the helicopters would refuel from huge bladders delivered by the fixed-wing aircraft, load the assault force, and take off again for a spot called the hide site near Garmsar, eighty miles southeast of Tehran. They would then land and conceal the helicopters, rest, and wait in darkness for their assault on the embassy compound.

The plan required long-range helicopters to fly an incredibly long distance with maximum fuel load and minimal cargo. The mission, code-named Eagle Claw, included more than one hundred participants. Two Iranian generals who had fled Iran during the revolution were to help the rescuers get in and out of the embassy. Altogether, the team consisted of ninety Delta rangers, twelve drivers for the convoy of hostages and rescuers, and a twelve-man road-watch team, including interpreters, that would secure Desert One against chance intruders. An additional thirteen-man Special Forces assault team would enter the Iranian foreign ministry and free three hostages who were held separately. Delta's ninety-man assault team was divided into three groups: Red, White, and Blue. After the road-watch teams were withdrawn from Desert One, 120 men would continue to the hide site.

The rescuers expected the assault on the embassy compound to be the most certain part of the operation, and it had been rehearsed repeatedly. Getting the hostages and rescue teams out of Tehran was also well rehearsed and was not considered to be the most difficult part of the operation. The long flights in and out of Iran, however, were made complex and difficult by the necessity for concealment. The rescue force had to take off from an aircraft carrier in the Gulf of Oman. Because the helicopters had to be hidden below the flight deck in the carrier's hangar bay, which required them to have folding tails, the choice of aircraft was limited to navy helicopters. The mission of the helicopters was so closely held, and the importance and vitality of the effort so well concealed, that when the navy mine warfare squadron commanders were ordered to provide some of their helicopters for an undefined joint operation, they naturally offered up their aircraft with the worst maintenance records. The plan settled on using navy RH-53D Sea Stallion helicopters, since they had the range and folding tail assembly that allowed them to be concealed in the aircraft carrier hangar bay.

At first the navy wanted the helicopters to be flown by navy pilots, but it had no pilots experienced in the type of low-level night flying required by the special rescue force. Nevertheless, navy pilots came with the helicopters and began training with Delta Force, but it soon became obvious that they were unsuited to the type of flying required by the mission. The Joint Chiefs of Staff then selected Marine Corps pilots to fly the helicopters even though they, too, had little special operations flight training. For reasons of secrecy the participants had not once trained together. Incredibly, the entire force never met until the operation began. Why Delta Force was not assigned pilots with the required training is still a mystery. With the mixed bag of services involved in the operation, experts claim that the mission commander, Colonel Charles Beckwith, never really had overall command of the effort.

The mission began on April 24, 1980. The helicopters lifted off on time from the carrier *Nimitz* but promptly flew into two big clouds of suspended dust and sand that caused them to veer off course and to delay their arrival by more than an hour at Desert One. The first six of the eight helicopters arrived at Desert One from sixty to ninety minutes late, and the other two never arrived. One of the missing landed with mechanical failure and was abandoned. The crew boarded the eighth, which was not damaged, and returned to the carrier *Nimitz*. At Desert One a third helicopter was declared unusable owing to a hydraulic failure. Faced with having only five out of the minimum six helicopters that he needed for the mission, Colonel Beckwith made the difficult decision to abort. Then, to make matters worse, while preparing to evacuate the staging area, one RH-53D helicopter collided with one of the six fixed-wing HC-130 Hercules in the mission and both aircraft burst into flames, killing eight men (five air force men and three marines) and seriously wounding several more.

The rescue plan itself was complex, haphazard, and characterized by the Vietnam-era practices of employing civilian management techniques that avoided centralized command and impeded individual initiative. Even more deplorable was the finger-pointing that followed. Senior administration figures second-guessed the determination and even the courage of the mission participants, particularly the helicopter pilots. In postaction accounts several senior White House officials claimed that two of the three helicopters that aborted the mission because of mechanical failure could have continued on. Specifically, they referred to the cockpit instrument warning lights, the BIM (Blade Inspection Method) in the two helicopters that aborted. These lights had indicated possible early stages of internal structural failure in the rotors and that the blades were losing the pressure of the inert nitrogen gas inside.[7] Some critics claimed these indications did not necessarily make the helicopter inoperable.[8] Such criticism is unwarranted, and those who participated in the mission were the most qualified to judge those matters.

When President Carter told the American people that a rescue attempt to free the hostages had been unsuccessful, the event became a symbol of military failure that was hard to overcome. After the disaster at Desert One, the secretary of defense appointed a special investigative panel chaired by Admiral James L. Holloway III, a former chief of Naval Operations, to seek recommendations and elucidate lessons learned. Made public in August 1980, the report of the rescue mission prepared by Admiral Holloway and five other officers from all the participating services was a comprehensive, independent evaluation of all aspects of the mission.[9]

The choice of using navy helicopters flown by Marine Corps pilots was a point of considerable censure in the Holloway report, and was singled out as one of the primary reasons for the failure of the mission. Another glaring issue that marred the operation was the absence of the helicopters' unit maintenance personnel aboard the USS *Nimitz*. By default, necessary maintenance for the unusual helicopters had to be performed by the men of the *Nimitz* helicopter squadron, who were trained on their own Sea Kings and not the RH-53D Sea Stallion, a totally different kind of helicopter. Spare-parts shortages and poor maintenance plagued the rescue mission, which was characteristic of the poor defense management of the 1970s. These errors, compounded by secrecy and haste, made the long and difficult flight to Desert One nearly impossible to achieve successfully. It is unlikely that the precise cause of the mechanical failures will ever be determined. Flying at extremely low altitude over five hundred miles of desert beneath Iranian radar coverage, a total of six hundred miles from the carrier, was a superhuman and heroic feat in and of itself.

Whether a rescue mission with properly trained personnel and well-maintained equipment could have succeeded remains an open question. Gary Sick, who served on President Carter's National Security Council staff, said that the rescue was a military failure, not a failure of political judgment or command.[10] Retired Brigadier General David Grange, who served as a Ranger company commander and part of the rescue force, saw it differently: "Due to the audacity, surprise, and training of the ground forces, we would have been successful. During the American embassy assault . . . and extraction out of Iran, the force would have had some casualties, and some of the hostages would have been hurt, but I am convinced the mission would have been a success."[11] Former hostage Moorhead Kennedy disagreed. "The Iranians had warned us as early as February," Kennedy said, "that they hoped Mr. Carter would do nothing foolish like a helicopter rescue attempt, for they were ready for it, and some if not all of us would be killed. . . . Don't you think if everyone in Washington knew that Mr. Carter was running out of options, the students might have arrived at the same conclusion and taken precautions accordingly?"[12]

Another critical point in studying the mission in hindsight is the fact that despite the massive security assistance present in Iran, the U.S. government lacked any effective remaining intelligence sources on the ground and had been forced to begin intelligence collection operations nearly from scratch.[13] The Holloway Commission's findings ultimately resulted in the creation of the Special Operations Advisory Panel that was to pave the way in the future for forming a separate Joint Special Operations Command.

The failure of the rescue mission in Iran was the lowest point of American military esteem in the post-Vietnam era. It happened in the midst of a period of international instability, a domestic economic crisis caused by the oil shortage, and the deteriorating conditions of American military life in late 1970s. During this time all services were struggling to remain operationally ready. The austere defense budgets of the 1970s had forced the navy to decrease its number of ships by half in ten years, and many were unable to go to sea for lack of adequate manning. Air force aircraft were frequently cannibalized for spare parts to keep a bare minimum number flying, and 7 percent were grounded because of a spare parts supply shortage. The junior grades of the armed forces were paid less than 85 percent of the federal minimum wage, and many servicemen had no choice but to put their families on food stamp programs. Less than half of the military were high school graduates. Morale was at an all-time low, which was reflected in the retention rates of all services. Navy pilot retention, for example, was barely 28 percent, which seriously diluted the fleet's air capabilities.

The failure of the Iran rescue mission had a severe and lasting effect on American military leadership. Never again would U.S. forces be committed without possessing an overwhelming advantage in numbers and firepower. The operation had been planned and rehearsed over a period of more than six months, and its failure could not be dismissed as simply due to mechanical problems. Not having an adequate number of helicopters to back up those that failed proved to be an error that would affect many future military operations. Caspar Weinberger, President Reagan's secretary of defense, stated that during the preparations for the next American military engagement, the intervention in Grenada three years later, he had ordered General John Vessey, the chairman of the Joint Chiefs of Staff, to double the assets he thought necessary to do the job because of the results of the failed hostage-rescue mission. Costly and futile as the Iran rescue attempt was, the end result was a necessary boost to the acceptance of the special operations troops as not only legitimate but also necessary, given the changing nature of human conflict.

There has always been a general feeling in the United States that its diplomats abroad should be protected. Throughout history Britain has shared the same belief concerning its subjects. In 1850 British Foreign Secretary Lord Henry Palmerston declared in a debate in the House of Commons: "As the Roman in days of old held himself free from indignity, when he could say *civis Romanus sum,* so also a British subject in whatever land he may be, shall feel confident that the watchful eye and strong arm of England will protect him against injustice and wrong." In 1864, when Emperor Theodore of Abyssinia imprisoned Queen Victoria's consul to the Abyssinian court and tortured him because of a diplomatic faux pas, the British reacted with a force that triggered the Abyssinian War. The Crown sent forth an expedition consisting of thirteen thousand British and Indian soldiers in a campaign lasting more than three years. In April 1868 they attacked the Abyssinian fortress of Magdala, killed seven hundred Abyssinians, and rescued the consul and a group of forty-eight other European prisoners held by Emperor Theodore.[14]

Just two years after the hostage rescue attempt in Iran, Italian Red Brigade terrorists kidnapped U.S. Army Brigadier General James Dozier. The Pentagon, State Department, and Central Intelligence Agency spent an inordinate amount of time struggling over who would take action to find and free Dozier, but the Italians succeeded in rescuing him. Congressional leaders were outraged and discouraged by interservice bickering, and in 1987 Congress passed a law ordering the Defense Department to form a new Joint Special Operations Command. Senior military leaders fought the issue, feeling that Congress was meddling in their affairs, but in the end the joint command was formed and did extremely well, beginning with the storming of Panama in 1989. However, more failures and embarrassing operations were undertaken before that milestone was reached.

PART THREE

Ronald W. Reagan: Lashing Out

BEIRUT

French MNF

WEST BEIRUT

EAST BEIRUT

Italian MNF

Sabra

Shatila

GREEN LINE

British MNF

U.S. MNF

Airport

0   2200
yards

N W E S

Tripoli

Zegharta

Batrun

Baharn

Jubayl

Juniye

Beirut

Zahle

SHUF MOUNTAINS

BEKAA VALLEY

Mediterranean Sea

Suq al Gharb

Awali River

LEBANON

Saida

SYRIA

Damascus

Tyre

Tibnin

Bent Jubayl

En Naqura

ISRAEL

LEBANON, 1983

0   25
miles

CHAPTER 4

Intervention in Lebanon

June 1982–February 1984

In 1982 the United States sent marines into Lebanon as part of a United Nations–sponsored multinational force including British, French, and Italian army units. Their mission was to supervise the simultaneous withdrawal of the U.S.-backed Israeli and Soviet-backed Syrian military forces poised for battle inside Lebanon. The buildup followed the Israeli invasion in 1982 and threatened to transform Lebanon into a full-scale battleground. Over time, however, the mission of the international force failed to adjust to the dynamics among the belligerents, and the chances for successful peacekeeping gradually evaporated.

Roughly the size of the state of Connecticut, Lebanon was created out of the wreckage of the Ottoman Empire's Greater Syria after World War I, when the victorious Allies drew up artificial boundaries. It has a rich history and a mixed ethnic population with a myriad of religious beliefs. Following World War II, Lebanon emerged as a relatively stable state governed by a parliamentary system in which the Christians enjoyed a majority. In subsequent years, the Muslims became the majority group, but the Christians retained control of the government through manipulation of various power blocs during rigged elections. For more than ten years Lebanon continued to

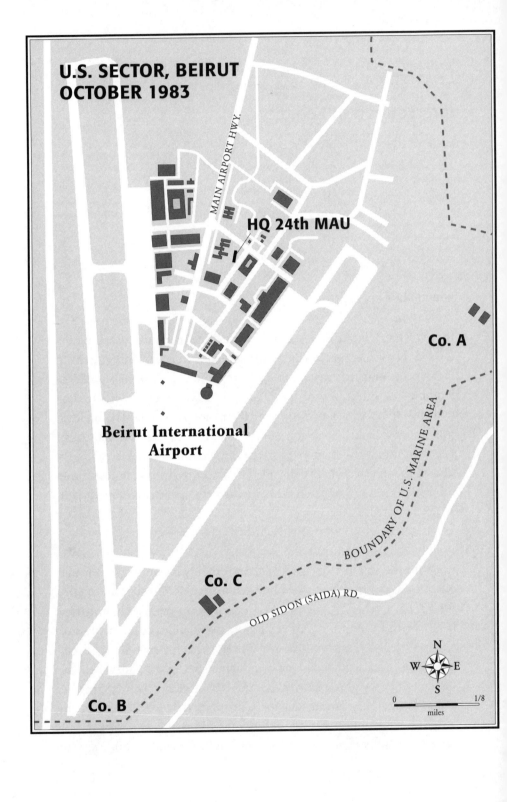

U.S. SECTOR, BEIRUT
OCTOBER 1983

MAIN AIRPORT HWY.

HQ 24th MAU

Co. A

BOUNDARY OF U.S. MARINE AREA

Beirut International
Airport

Co. C

OLD SIDON (SAIDA) RD.

Co. B

N
W E
S

0   1/8
miles

maintain a basically stable, if weak, government with the capital, Beirut, acting as both a cultural hub and one of the main commercial trade centers of the Middle East.

The saga of U.S. intervention in Lebanon began in 1958, when President Dwight D. Eisenhower sent in a military force to forestall what was perceived to be an attempt by acolytes of United Arab Republic leader Gamal Abdel Nasser, backed by the Soviet Union, to overthrow the government of Lebanese president Camille Chamoun. The American intervention, involving seventeen thousand army troops and marines, appeared to shore up the government's stability, and after a few months the troops were successfully withdrawn. However, over the next ten years the situation in Lebanon steadily deteriorated as the country became more and more embroiled in internecine strife.

Renewed unrest began in 1970 with King Hussein's expulsion of the Palestine Liberation Organization (PLO) from Jordan. Led by Yasir Arafat and with nowhere else to go, the Palestinian fighters settled in southern Lebanon and began to operate out of those areas, using terror tactics to gather worldwide support for their cause. Several thousand dedicated PLO fighters settled in Lebanon and began forays against Israel from the vicinity of Beirut, which had a long history of peaceful coexistence among its Muslim, Jewish, and Christian residents. With the influx of the PLO, however, Lebanon began to suffer serious sectarian violence. By early 1975 civil war erupted between the Christians and the Muslims and their Palestinian allies. Over time Lebanon's relatively weak central government gave way under the pressure of inter-Arab disputes and the outbreak of long-dormant internal conflict, and by the early 1980s southern Lebanon had become the primary locus of Arab-Israeli horrors. Additionally, by 1981 the Shiite Muslims, who were among the largest and most destitute sectarian communities in the world and occupied the bottom of the Lebanese political structure, formed a new alliance with the Palestinians in order to improve their economic and political status. With a belief system centered on Ali, the son-in-law of Muhammad, the Shiite branch of Islam had long been characterized by a sense of persecution. During the 1980s, it grew into one of the most fanatical political groups in the Middle East and harbored a more virulent hatred for the West than other branches of Islam. Shiites felt that an accurate census in Lebanon would prove they might indeed have a plurality, but their efforts were consistently curbed by the more numerous and more moderate Sunni Muslims and the Maronite Christians, the Phalangists. Further grievances sprang from what they perceived as the disproportionate Christian wealth and power. The governing Maronite Christian sect, headed by the Gemayel clan in the 1980s, held the Palestinians primarily responsible for the loss of order.

While neighboring Syria had generally supported Palestinian efforts against Israel, its politically astute President Hafez al Assad ensured that no single faction became too powerful in Lebanon. To prevent the PLO from gaining superiority in Lebanon in 1976, Syria even intervened sporadically on behalf of the Phalangists—a curious alliance, but typical of President Assad's political methods. After that, to protect its interests, Syria kept tens of thousands troops equipped and trained by the Soviet Union in Lebanon. Syria viewed Lebanon as a convenient place from which to stage attacks against Israel, while Israel saw Lebanon as a potential buffer to protect it from Syrian or Palestinian attacks.

Matters came to a head in April 1981, when Phalangist leaders devised a scheme to draw the Israelis into a clash with the large Syrian forces around the town of Zahle, the third largest city in Lebanon, with a population of two hundred thousand (mostly Greek Orthodox). Zahle was the capital of the Bekaa Valley, the long narrow valley lined by mountains that separates central Lebanon from Syria. The Phalange leader Bashir Gemayel informed the Israelis that the city was a major Phalange stronghold about to be surrounded and overrun by Syrian commandos. Then, to confirm this claim, a Phalangist unit attacked Syrian soldiers guarding a bridge on the Beirut–Damascus highway and destroyed two tanks. President Assad reacted immediately and rushed Syrian reinforcements to Zahle by road and helicopter. The Syrians troops behaved with considerable brutality, burning crops and shelling the city. The ground fighting precipitated an air battle in which Israel downed a Syrian military helicopter, and Syria immediately installed Soviet-made SAM-6 antiaircraft missiles in the Bekaa Valley.[1] This militarization of the strategic valley quickly led to a series of Israeli air strikes against Syrian and PLO positions in Lebanon and, in response, to an increase in Palestinian artillery and rocket attacks against northern Israel launched from Lebanon.

Seeking to de-escalate the spiraling conflict, U.S. Ambassador Philip Habib hammered out a cease-fire. The agreement was complex, and the Israelis immediately began enforcing their own interpretation: First, any Palestinian attack against Jews anywhere in the world constituted a violation of the delicate regional cease-fire. Second, Israeli forces were free to advance into any area peacefully, meaning as long as they were not actively shooting. If they were fired upon, that action would constitute a violation of the cease-fire by the opposing side.[2]

While the PLO in Lebanon was focusing its hostility against Israel, most Israelis viewed the situation as a perfect opportunity to finish off the PLO in one fell swoop. Furthermore, some Israelis, such as Defense Minister Ariel Sharon, viewed the entire Arab-Israeli conflict at the time as merely a sideshow of the Soviet–U.S. cold war. Sharon believed that destroying the PLO might bring an abrupt end to worldwide terrorism and be a regional tactical defeat for the Soviet Union. Secretary of State Alexander Haig held views similar to Sharon's.

The Israelis claimed justification for a full-scale invasion of Lebanon when a "Palestinian" gunman wounded the Israeli ambassador in London, even though four days later the would-be assassin was found to be from a completely different faction—the anti-Arafat Iraqi Abu Nidal group. The head of the hit squad was the cousin of Abu Nidal. In any event, on June 6, 1982, Israel invaded Lebanon in a fierce effort to destroy the PLO completely, and end years of intermittent warfare in which the victims had been mostly civilians.

The Israelis successfully advanced deep into the Bekaa Valley against Syrian forces while the PLO fought to hold on in Beirut and indeed to survive, as Israeli forces cut off and surrounded the city. Grave concern for innocent civilians who might be caught in violent urban fighting if Israel advanced into Beirut formed the basis of a Lebanese request for a multinational force to be brought in to separate the belligerents. France, Italy, the United States, and Britain were asked to contribute to the force. Secretary of State Haig backed American participation, arguing that the main obstacle to peace was the presence of three foreign armies in Lebanon—the Syrian "peace-keeping" force, the military arm of the PLO, and the Israeli army—all of which were stronger than the Lebanese army.[3] The idea of participating in such an international force was at first opposed by Secretary of Defense Caspar Weinberger and Chairman of the Joint Chiefs of Staff General John Vessey.

Desperate to keep the peace in Lebanon and to prevent escalation to a full-scale war, the United Nations Security Council passed Resolution 508 in July 1982 calling for the withdrawal of Israel from Lebanon. The United States agreed to participate in a multinational Force (MNF), the purpose of which was to supervise the withdrawal of both Israeli and Syrian forces, whose presence in Lebanon had been roundly condemned by the United Nations.

On August 25, 1982, elements of the Thirty-second Marine Amphibious Unit, commanded by Colonel James M. Mead, landed in the port of Beirut. A Marine Amphibious Unit is a self-contained force of roughly twelve hundred troops with its own artillery, heavy weapons, helicopters, and fixed-wing aircraft. After going ashore, the marines assisted in the evacuation of 6,436 Palestinians and Syrians. PLO leader Arafat was escorted to safety and eventually to Tunis by French and American forces. By September 3 the mission seemed complete and the marines withdrew without having fired a shot, reboarding their ships on September 10. It appeared that intervention had worked and the mission was seen as a model of successful peacekeeping.

Four days after the marines withdrew, the leader of the Israeli-backed Christian Phalangist movement, President-elect Bashir Gemayel, was assassinated, presumably by PLO supporters. The following day Israeli forces overran the Muslim sector of West Beirut. During the next two days, angry Phalangists, under the protection of the Israeli forces in West Beirut, massacred hundreds of Palestinian civilians, including women and children, in the refugee camps of Shatila and Sabra south of Beirut. There were strong indications that the senior Israeli commander, Ariel Sharon, ignored these actions and turned a blind eye to the slaughter. Directly following the horrible massacre, Amin Gemayel, the new Lebanese president and brother of the slain Bashir, requested that the MNF once again intervene to protect the Muslims of West Beirut and guarantee the withdrawal of Israeli and Syrian forces from the city. The government of Lebanon, as well as most Christian and Muslim factions, supported the reintroduction of the MNF.

On September 29, despite the opposition of the Joint Chiefs of Staff, President Reagan ordered Colonel Mead's Thirty-second Marine Amphibious Unit back into Beirut, this time with the mission of providing a "presence in Beirut, that would in turn help establish the stability necessary for the Lebanese government to regain control of their capital."[4] The mission of the marines as written in the JCS Alert Order of September 23, 1982, was defined as follows: "To establish an environment which will permit the Lebanese armed forces to carry out their responsibilities in the Beirut area."[5] The French, Italians, and British again agreed to participate. President Ronald Reagan had assured Congress that the marines were in Lebanon not to engage in combat, but to pacify Lebanon. However, the mission was less than a model of clarity for the marines, who were not sure whether they were supposed to act as peacekeepers or to maintain order between feuding factions backed by the Soviet Union on one side and Israel on the other.

Two days after going ashore, the marines began to receive sporadic fire from both the Syrians and the Lebanese Muslims. The MNF totaled three thousand troops, including a British force of 155 observers. The French portion of the MNF was stationed in Beirut, and the Italians were stationed near the heavily populated refugee camps in the south. The U.S. Marine contingent, which had grown to a force of twelve hundred, was assigned to an area south of the Italians at the Beirut International Airport. There was no single commander of the force; each contingent had its own leadership that was authorized to coordinate with the other contingents. Three U.S.

Marine rifle companies came ashore initially and displaced Israeli forces from the airport. The marines had the Mediterranean on one flank and the Old Sidon Road in the east on the other. As an experienced combat commander, Colonel Mead immediately sought to place his marines on the high ground across the road, but he was overruled by his commanders. The United States did not wish to appear to be supporting Israeli forces that were still using the Sidon Road for the logistic support of their forces positioned elsewhere. This forced the marines into a tactical situation that would prove to be seriously flawed.

The marines' terrain was difficult to defend. They were deployed around the airport. Traffic was heavy there, with more than thirty flights and twenty-four hundred passengers moving through on an average day. The marines established their headquarters in a two-story concrete building that had previously been the airport firefighting training school. The full marine battalion used a partially bombed-out four-story reinforced concrete building, located to the southwest of the headquarters, as a barracks. It had been the Lebanese Aviation Administration Bureau. On October 30, the Twenty-fourth Marine Amphibious Unit, commanded by Colonel Thomas M. Stokes, Jr., came ashore and relieved the Thirty-second. The new unit consisted of 1,806 Marines and 81 navy personnel, including corpsmen, chaplains, and construction personnel called Seabees. As the new marine contingent came ashore, a car bomb exploded on the beach nearby, an ominous warning to the new peacekeepers. In an attempt to emphasize a renewed determination to improve the situation, the marines began to patrol actively by jeep and on foot. They also began to train the Lebanese Armed Forces Rapid Reaction Force in small-unit tactics, the use of arms, and command and control procedures. This outward support of the Lebanese military was a further attempt to show that the mission was there not to support Israel, as the Muslim factions believed, but to make concrete progress shoring up the defensive capability of the government of Lebanon.

By the end of 1982, when it became clear to all the factions that neither Israel nor Syria intended to withdraw anytime soon, they began to attack one another as well as the MNF. The American training and equipping of the Lebanese army were neither sufficient nor effective in helping to quell the fighting on all sides. Nor was the Lebanese army able to deal with the thirty thousand Syrians and as many Israelis still present in Lebanon.

The marines' first serious confrontation with a major conventional force occurred on February 2, 1983, when the Israeli army dispatched three Centurion tanks at high speed down the Sidon Road after one of its supply columns had been ambushed. It perceived that the attackers had emerged from the territory under U.S. control and intended to flush out the culprits. The three tanks were stopped abruptly in the middle of the road by Captain Charles B. Johnson, an outraged marine company commander. Johnson bravely stood in the road and faced off the tanks until they complied with his order to stop, which they did only after he climbed onto the lead tank and threatened the Israeli commander at gunpoint. This act was initially acclaimed by the local Muslim community as indicating that the American forces were sincerely neutral in their mission, but the sentiment was short-lived. On February 14 the Thirty-second Marine Amphibious Unit relieved the Twenty-fourth in Beirut, beginning Colonel James Mead's third tour in Lebanon. Difficulties between the marines and Israeli forces continued until Ambassador Philip Habib applied pressure, and the Israeli army installed a direct radio link for coordination between the U.S. and Israeli on-scene commanders.

As the MNF was increasingly perceived by Muslims to be the official ally of the Christian-dominated Lebanese government, hostility grew. On March 15 an Italian patrol was ambushed by Muslim forces who killed one soldier and wounded nine. The next day five U.S. Marines were wounded when a Muslim tossed a hand grenade at a patrol north of the airport. Thereafter, the Marines curtailed foot patrols and increased vehicular patrols with loaded weapons. Two days later, after coming under sniper fire, the marines returned fire for the first time against the unidentified assailants. Then, on April 18, a man drove a pickup truck loaded with explosives past a Lebanese guard into the lobby of the American embassy in West Beirut. It exploded, killing sixty-three people, including seventeen Americans. Evidence proved that suicidal and determined Iranian revolutionary guards were active in the area and were assisting the Palestinian Shiites with considerable financial support. It seemed that the rapid acceleration of violence among the local factions had drawn other similarly motivated activists.

After the bombing attack at the embassy, the marines' mission expanded. The U.S. European Command, under whose authority the marines operated, changed the rules of engagement to permit the marines to initiate fire if they perceived an imminent threat. They doubled guards on all posts and for the first time employed armored amphibious tractors on main routes around their positions. On May 5, Colonel Mead's helicopter was hit by small-arms fire from unidentified shooters, but there were no casualties.

Israel and Lebanon signed a U.S.-sponsored withdrawal agreement on May 17, but Syria and the Muslim factions opposed it as inequitable, and tensions rose still higher. At the end of May, the Twenty-fourth Marine Amphibious Unit replaced the marines ashore, and Colonel Timothy J. Geraghty relieved Colonel Mead as the U.S. MNF commander. During this deployment, Lebanese army personnel began to accompany the marine patrols. On July 22 twelve Soviet-built rockets and mortar rounds landed in Beirut airport, wounding two marines and an American sailor, killing one civilian, and wounding thirteen others. The rounds were determined to have been fired by a Syrian-backed left-wing Muslim Druze military faction. Apparently all of the disparate Muslim factions had begun to work together in an altogether natural process of focusing on a common "enemy" force—the intruder from far away—without consideration of that force's purpose.

The U.S. Marines found themselves in an increasingly untenable tactical position while vainly trying to support the local Lebanese army. The Soviet-equipped and -supported Syrian army backed the local Muslims, an increasingly united front consisting of the Druze and Shiite militias, who were still locked in combat against the Christian-led Lebanese army and Phalangists backed by the Israelis. In the middle stood the marines, appearing to each side to be supporting its antagonists.

On August 8, after Druze artillery and mortar fire erupted again, the marines employed their counterbattery radar to knock out the source of shooting for the first time. On August 28, without prior warning to the MNF, Israeli army units began to withdraw. Simultaneously, hostile fire concentrated on the U.S. area, and the marines began routinely to return fire against snipers. The next day, when two of their men were killed and three wounded by a heavy mortar round that hit their position, the marines began to fire their heavy 155mm howitzers and to use U.S. Navy gunfire support. The cruiser USS *Belknap* and destroyer USS *Bowen* provided the first naval gunfire by shooting illumination rounds to cover the marines at night. The marines also began to employ their Cobra helicopter gunships for the first time. One Cobra destroyed a Druze armored personnel carrier that had fired on the marines' position. A second Cobra was hit and made an emergency landing on USS *Iwo Jima,* which was offshore in the Mediterranean. From that day on, the marines were deeply engaged in daily sporadic warfare and continued to take casualties with no achievable objective in sight. Their mission had been to support the government of Lebanon and to prevent the situation from deteriorating, but it had inevitably expanded in response to the reality of the intense hostility. Although the initial deployment of the MNF had been accomplished with good intentions, it soon became clear that it required full firepower just for self-defense, employing the complete array of modern American weaponry, including naval gunfire support and limited air power. This response is consistent with "the American way of war."[6] A man taught and trained as a marine is expected to take the traditional steps of returning fire in kind when fired upon, and to use all means at hand to win. However, this was not consistent with the role of peacekeeper and would not accomplish the mission but rather create a new situation of self-perpetuating combat.

The U.S. government was now faced with three options: withdraw the U.S. force, which was what the theater commander, U.S. Army General Bernard Rogers, wished to do; reinforce and reposition the marines to compensate tactically for the Israeli withdrawal; or stay with the status quo and make no changes. The question went directly to Secretary of Defense Caspar Weinberger, who decided to leave the marines in their indefensible position. In Weinberger's view, the mission of the marines had not changed, but the situation surely had since the withdrawal of the Israeli forces—they were now engaged in repeated firefights with experienced Syrian troops and Iranian revolutionary fighters situated directly outside their positions.

General Rogers authorized Vice Admiral Edward H. Martin, the commander of the Sixth Fleet, to provide the marines with aerial reconnaissance and naval gunfire support from ships located off the coast in a position called Bagel Station. The Sixth Fleet commander also moved the helicopter carrier USS *Tarawa* closer to shore with another Marine Amphibious Unit embarked as reinforcements. The marines ashore suspended patrols and hunkered down in defensive positions while maintaining two vulnerable outposts beyond their perimeter for early warning. By August 31 combat had increased to the point that the marine foot patrols into Beirut were totally suspended and two aircraft carriers, USS *Eisenhower* and the French *Foch*, moved in to provide air support to the besieged MNF.

By September 4 Israeli forces had withdrawn beyond the Awali River in southern Lebanon. However, the Lebanese army did not fill the gap left by the departing Israelis, thus leaving a vacuum into which the irregular forces of the multiple factions could and did infiltrate with impunity. Despite the Israeli departure, Syria continued to refuse to withdraw its forces. Ironically, the United States, after condemning Israel for invading Lebanon in the first place, was now appealing for Israeli forces to remain and help keep order in the seriously deteriorating tactical situation. The Israelis refused to pause in their withdrawal.

Early on September 6 twenty-one heavy rockets hit the marines' position, killing two men and wounding two more. The Lebanese government forces were pushed eastward, leaving the Druze militia dominating the high ground overlooking Beirut and the airport. This put the marines in an even less tenable position, which in normal combat would have called for an immediate assault against those entrenched above them. Diplomatic and political restrictions governing the MNF overrode the designs of combat, echoing the American experience in Vietnam.

From September 7 on, the marines were calling in routine naval gunfire support from the destroyers USS *Bowen* and USS *John Rodgers*. The Thirty-first Marine Amphibious Unit arrived from the U.S. Pacific Fleet on September 12 to act as reinforcements for the entrenched Marines. On September 19 navy ships fired more than 350 five-inch rounds in support of the Lebanese forces holding their ridgetop positions at Suq al Gharb, nine miles southeast of the center of Beirut. This represented a significant escalation by American forces. On September 20 navy carrier aircraft began to support the marines, who were forced to withdraw their two vulnerable outer warning outposts and consolidate their perimeter.

The order to support Lebanese forces with naval gunfire was given to Colonel Geraghty directly by Assistant National Security Adviser Robert C. McFarlane, who had replaced Ambassador Habib as special envoy and the principal Middle East negotiator. McFarlane had been pressing for authorization to send the marines into the mountains to support the Lebanese army. The marine commander ashore, Colonel Geraghty, opposed calling in heavy naval gunfire support for the Lebanese army, knowing such an action would result in additional fire and pressure against his own marines, who were still restricted from going on the offensive and were stagnating in their indefensible positions. In the view of the Syrians, the Druze, and their Shiite allies, the American force's stance as neutral peacekeepers was further diminished with the increase in direct gunfire support by the navy. Then, to exacerbate the situation, on September 25 the battleship USS *New Jersey* began firing its sixteen-inch guns.

A fragile cease-fire went into effect on September 26, and the Beirut airport closed for six days. During the cease-fire the Americans increased their support to the Lebanese army by providing them with armored personnel carriers, howitzers, and tanks. At the same time, the PLO began to fight its way into the abandoned refugee camps of Sabra and Shatila, and the Iranian leftist group called Islamic Amal erected bunkers in front of the marine positions. So the peacekeeping marines, already fighting a full-fledged war against first-rate Syrian soldiers, now had a new adversary in Iranian revolutionary guardsmen dug in directly outside their perimeter.

Despite the cease-fire, the marines were engaged in a vicious sniper war. Firefights became nearly continuous, and six marines were killed and forty wounded. For a fleeting period it seemed that the violence might have reached a peak, but in reaction to the marines' successes with their night-vision devices and superb fire discipline during sniper exchanges, a small extremist Shiite splinter group with direct ties to Iran arrived unannounced on the scene. These new fanatics were closely linked to the Islamic Jihad, or Holy War, and grew determined to exact revenge. This was the group linked to many past car bombings and kidnappings in Beirut and Israel. It was probably at this juncture that the idea of massive retaliation against the marines was formulated, and since these radicals did not possess heavy weapons of their own, they would resort to bombs to do the job.[7]

On October 12 the U.S. Congress voted to allow President Reagan to keep the marines in Lebanon for an additional eighteen months as an extension of the authorization to send troops, Public Law 98-119. On October 19 four marines were wounded when a remote-controlled bomb, hidden in a blue Mercedes, exploded next to their resupply convoy. At home the U.S. government tried to downplay the fighting, and often reported that the artillery and mortar fire landing among the marines were just accidents intended for the combating Lebanese militia forces, but the marines were in fact the targets.

On Sunday morning, October 23, 1983, while more than three

hundred marines and naval personnel slept, a yellow Mercedes five-ton open-bed truck drove down the road west of the headquarters and entered the parking lot in the south front of the building. The driver suddenly accelerated and, gaining momentum by driving in circles in the lot several times, drove at high speed through the barbed wire and concrete barricade between two guard posts. Before the guard could open fire, the truck, loaded with more than twelve thousand pounds of TNT, hit the building and exploded. Almost everyone inside was killed: 241 Americans including 220 marines, 18 navy medical corpsmen, and 3 soldiers—the largest number of marines killed in a single day since the invasion of Iwo Jima. The explosion destroyed the building and blasted a forty-by-thirty-foot hole eight feet deep beneath the concrete floor.

Immediately following the bombing there was a strong call in the United States for retaliation. Secretary of Defense Weinberger stated publicly in November that Iranians had carried out the attack with the "sponsorship, knowledge, and authority of the Syrian government."[8] The initial reaction was to plan to strike back by bombing the Iranian training camp in the Baalbek region of the Bekaa Valley. However, there was grave concern for the security of the marines still ashore with their battered battalion who were busily reestablishing their defenses. Despite strong recommendations by Secretary of the Navy John F. Lehman, Jr., to retaliate against someone for the bombing, Weinberger and General John Vessey, the chairman of the Joint Chiefs of Staff, opposed immediate strikes, and the United States hesitated.

In November the Twenty-second Marine Amphibious Unit arrived to relieve those embattled marines of the Twenty-fourth who remained in Lebanon. Under the revised security procedures, only rifle companies remained ashore while all headquarters and supporting units stayed aboard amphibious ships off the coast. Lebanese troops replaced one marine rifle company north of the airport, and the remaining marine units dispersed their forces into freshly prepared hard bunkers and command posts.

The French, who had also suffered casualties from terrorists, struck back by bombing the Iranians in Baalbek on November 16. But still the Americans delayed. The Israelis conducted a large air strike against Syrian targets east of Beirut on December 3. Later the same day, the U.S. Navy conducted a photo reconnaissance flight with two F-14s flying from the carrier USS *John F. Kennedy*. While flying low over the Beirut area, the F-14s were fired at by Soviet-made SA-7 shoulder-launched surface-to-air-missiles but not hit.

The firing of these antiaircraft missiles finally triggered approval from Washington to mount major air strikes against Syrian gun and radar positions in Lebanon. On December 4 the Sixth Fleet attacked Syrian targets with a major carrier air strike and in the process lost two airplanes to surface-to-air missiles. An A-6 Intruder bomber and an A-7 Corsair II were hit and downed. One airman died; another was captured and released a month later. Poor planning, haste, and bad tactics caused these losses.

The marines ashore came under heavy rocket attack immediately and lost eight men. From this point until the final withdrawal ordered by President Reagan in February 1984, the U.S. and other MNF contingents came under relentless attack from weapons of all types, including surface-to-surface missiles, antitank rockets, small arms, and even tanks. The original mission of deterrence and peacekeeping had given way completely.

In February 1984 vicious fighting erupted between Lebanese government troops and the various Muslim factions. The Lebanese army lost control of the situation when the hard-line Amal faction succeeded in forcing all Muslims to leave the Lebanese army and the Amal and Druze went on the offensive. These Muslim militias and the Lebanese army became locked in combat, and the militias eventually overran Christian-controlled West Beirut. The Lebanese army collapsed, and the Amal factions who did not wish to fight the marines pulled back, while the marines filled the positions vacated by some of the surrendering Lebanese army. The mission to support the territorial integrity of Lebanon had failed, and there was no other choice than to depart. British forces withdrew on February 7, followed by the Italians and French. The remaining U.S. Marines, except for eighty who were guarding the U.S. embassy in East Beirut, were flown out by helicopter on March 31 and returned to their ships off the coast. The Druze militia occupied the marines' former positions, and the U.S. force remained on board ship off the coast until April 10.

U.S. troops had been on the ground in Lebanon for 533 days, during which 266 Americans of all services were killed and 151 were wounded. On September 20, 1984, the annex of the U.S. embassy in Beirut was struck by yet another suicide truck attack, which killed twenty-three people and wounded eight marines. Three Muslim "martyrs" in Lebanon had proved how effective suicide bombings could be as a tool to achieve their objectives—in this case, the withdrawal of the MNF.

The purpose of the intervention in Lebanon had been to keep the warring factions apart in Beirut, but the end results were sectarian violence that continued well into 1993 and claimed more than sixty-three thousand lives. Thirty thousand Syrian troops continued to occupy the country in 2001, and the newly formed radical revolutionary group Hezbollah controlled southern Lebanon. America's eighteen-month involvement in Lebanon had failed despite the great cost.

In November 1983 Secretary of Defense Weinberger established a commission headed by retired Admiral Robert L.J. Long, a former commander in chief Pacific, to investigate what went wrong in Lebanon. The Long Commission found that the rules of engagement did not cover attacks on the Beirut embassy and the marine barracks. Blame for not supervising the marines' security was placed on the chain of command. In the commission's report issued in December, Syria and Iran were held at least indirectly responsible for the attack. A House Armed Services subcommittee conducted its own investigation and found not only that the security had been "inadequate" but also that the Marine Amphibious Unit commander had "made serious errors of judgment in failing to provide better protection for his troops. . . ."[9]

Why didn't the marines take adequate security measures? Their presence in Beirut had certainly been highly visible within the U.S. chain of command. The marine command in Lebanon had endured a stream of recurring visits by senior Defense Department officials, the chairman of the Joint Chiefs of Staff, the European Supreme Commander, the chief of Naval Operations, the commander of the Sixth Fleet, and the commandant of the Marine Corps as well as the commander of the Amphibious Task Force. A total of twenty-four generals and admirals had visited the marines during the entire period of their operation before the bomb destroyed their barracks. These visits served no purpose other than to distract the small command from its focus on the issues at hand—no precise or significant guidance was offered toward interpreting the marines' rules of engagement or, more seriously, the changing nature of their mission. The Long Commission found this fact disturbing, especially since no corrective actions were taken to change or improve the marines' security or their mode of operations.

Noninterference was viewed as a good thing by many in the chain of command who remembered the long and frustrating years of war in Southeast Asia beleaguered by political micromanagement and obstruction at all levels. The marines had been billeted in the same area for more than a year, and their limited defensive measures and lack of adequate control points were justified by some as being in keeping with their diplomatic mission. At the congressional hearings into the deaths of the marines, Ambassador Philip Habib was asked if increased defensive measures would have affected the political goals of the marine intervention. "It would have impaired the diplomatic mission," he replied.[10] Said Admiral Robert Long, "Our marines didn't belong in Beirut under those conditions."[11]

On the very day the explosion ripped through the marine barracks in October 1983, President Reagan signed the approval for U.S. forces to intervene on the Caribbean island of Grenada to protect American citizens whose lives might have been threatened by two Marxist political factions locked in a vicious power struggle. The final days of the American involvement in Lebanon were overshadowed by the intercession of combined United States and Caribbean forces in Grenada. The long and painful American involvement in Lebanon, although executed with valor and determination by forces made up mostly of marines, seemed to have been in vain. Worse yet, the same mistakes would be repeated in a civil war in Somalia in 1993. Little was learned from the intervention in Lebanon.

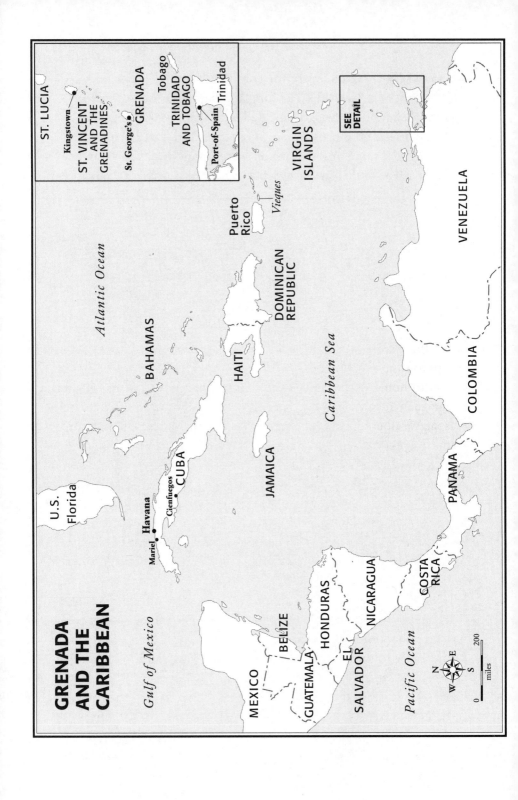

CHAPTER 5

Intervention in Grenada

October 24–26, 1983

Since the 1970s, Fidel Castro had dispatched thousands of Cuban troops to support revolutions in Angola, Mozambique, and Ethiopia. Closer to home, Cuba was actively supporting the Sandinistas in the Nicaraguan revolution of 1979. According to Secretary of Defense Caspar Weinberger, after an April 1983 visit to the United States by Prime Minister Maurice Bishop of the small Caribbean island of Grenada, which is located near the coast of Venezuela, U.S. leaders became concerned that the Soviet Union and its ally Cuba were pouring large amounts of money and arms into the island nation. Sensing a looming threat to the safety of more than one thousand Americans studying on the island, the Reagan administration began to contemplate taking action. Within six months over fifteen thousand U.S. servicemen and women would be involved.

This alarm over Grenada arose only three years after the hostage debacle in Iran. That memory was seared into the minds of many senior members of the Reagan administration, and Weinberger had been closely following reports about the Grenadian situation for several years. Grenada had received more than $33 million in aid from Cuba and stockpiled enough Soviet arms to equip an army of ten thousand. A six-hundred-man construction force from Cuba was building an airfield considerably larger than what might normally be used for tourist purposes, one suitable to handle Soviet long-range

TU-95 Bear bombers and reconnaissance aircraft. These planes frequently made training flights from the northern base of Olenogorsk in the Soviet Union southward along the East Coast of the United States, landing in Havana. The threat that these flights might be extended to Grenada was worrisome because of its proximity to the busy shipping lanes between Venezuela's rich oil fields through the Caribbean and into U.S. ports in the Gulf of Mexico. The thought of Grenada's deep-water port at St. George's being used by Soviet and Cuban naval forces was even more alarming. The U.S. Navy's advocates were deeply concerned about the Soviet Union's attempts to support its nuclear submarines in ports in Cuba and disturbed that it had even stationed nuclear submarine support ships in the ports of Mariel, twenty-five miles west of Havana, and Cienfuegos, on Cuba's southern shore.

The United States made no secret of its concern about the military buildup in the Caribbean, and in March 1983 launched a large-scale military exercise called Ocean Venture 1983 on the nearby training island of Vieques, off the coast of Puerto Rico, to focus on the events on Grenada. President Reagan told the press in the summer of 1983 that the growing military presence of the Soviet Union in the area posed a definite threat to U.S. shipping carrying oil supplies through the area. It was becoming more evident that Grenada could become a bastion of Communist armed strength and another platform for exporting revolution into Latin America. Then on October 19 a series of bizarre events in Grenada brought the situation to a climax.

Grenada, a small nation of one hundred thousand people and about 133 square miles, is situated near Barbados and Trinidad and anchors the crescent-shaped island chain that begins east of Puerto Rico. The island was discovered by Christopher Columbus in 1498 and initially settled by the French. After it changed hands several times, the British took permanent possession in 1783. Grenada receives heavy tropical rains that inundate its rich volcanic soil, producing ample supplies of fruit and vegetables—grapefruit, guava, tomatoes, and yams. The island has a thriving fishing industry and a potentially tremendous tourist trade. The inhabitants are mostly literate and work small farms that export cacao, nutmeg, and other rich spices to make a modest living. Grenada is a member of two regional security organizations, the Caribbean Community (CARICOM) and the Organization of Eastern Caribbean States (OECS), which was headed in 1983 by Eugenia Charles, prime minister of Dominica, one of Grenada's neighbors to the east.[1]

A key feature of the economy on Grenada is the St. George's University School of Medicine, established in 1977 by American investors with headquarters in Brooklyn, New York. Eight hundred to one thousand students are enrolled. It is a popular choice for Americans who cannot attend a U.S. medical school for financial or other reasons. The medical students spent approximately $2.5 million in 1983, a valuable asset to the economy of Grenada and a major basis for U.S. concern about the human rights environment on the island.

Britain set Grenada on the road to commonwealth status in 1967, but the days preceding independence were marked by unrest, strikes, and rioting in which several people died. The island finally achieved independence on February 7, 1974, with an unpredictable prime minister, Sir Eric Gairy, at the helm. Gairy was an eccentric character who soon grew bored with parliamentary democracy and gradually formed his government into a powerful dictatorship and surrounded himself with gangs of thugs to maintain his position. His Mongoose Gang, named after the animal introduced to rid the island of its notorious rats, was made up mostly of laborers. In 1976, a coalition of opposition parties was formed that made up about 48 percent of the electorate. The situation gradually deteriorated, as the country fell further into economic stagnation and a violent struggle between political strongmen. After twelve years Gairy had managed to squander the wealth of the island until it was nearly bankrupt.

Twenty-six-year-old Maurice Bishop returned home in 1970 after gaining his education in London and became active in politics. Bishop began to organize opposition to Gairy on a platform against corruption. In 1972 Bishop formed the Movement for Assemblies of the People, which merged a year later with another opposition group called the Joint Endeavor for Welfare, Education, and Liberation

(JEWEL), the coalition becoming the New Jewel Movement (NJM) with Bishop as its leader.

Bishop learned that the necessary ingredient in wielding power in Grenada was controlling the workers, and he gained his political experience in the streets during the period of widespread brutality by the Gairy regime. His father was shot and killed during the strikes that led to independence in 1974. Bishop and many of his followers had been severely beaten by Gairy's goons. In a bloodless coup on March 13, 1979, Maurice Bishop took over as prime minister of Grenada. There was little doubt that most people supported Bishop during the transition; the Grenadians were more than pleased to be rid of Gairy. But on the same day that Bishop took over, he announced he would seek an arms and economic assistance pact with his friend Fidel Castro. President Carter's administration, surprised by the move, expressed disappointment and cautioned Bishop without effect against his new relationship with Cuba. The U.S. government was slow to recognize that Maurice Bishop and his closest followers, Defense Minister General Hudson Austin and Deputy Prime Minister Bernard Coard and his wife, Phyllis, were devoted Marxist-Leninists.

Had Bishop called elections shortly after his ascension to power he no doubt would have won and legitimized his People's Revolutionary Government (PRG), but his promised elections were postponed and then canceled. He installed a Cuban-style dictatorship and suspended the constitution. In July 1979 his followers suppressed political opposition, broke up a political protest for democracy, and closed the opposition newspaper *Torchlight*. The editor of another paper, The *Grenadian View*, was arrested, and Bishop's People's Law No. 18 banned all opposition press the following year. Sadly, political arrests and torture continued as usual under the new prime minister, and many of the new political dissidents disappeared into Fort Rupert, the prison on the hill outside St. George's, where they were subjected to brutality.

Bishop brought in Cuban experts to train his followers in the use of propaganda. Soon political posters adorned with pictures of Castro and Bishop began sprouting up across the island, urging the workers to strive for a total revolution. Bishop developed a Department of Politics in his People's Revolutionary Army (PRA) and constructed a political commissar system parallel to that of the Soviet Union. He built an extensive military infrastructure, a Communist-style police force, and a personal security apparatus designed by East Germans and complete with Cuban bodyguards.

In April 1979 shipments of arms and military advisers began to arrive in Grenada from Cuba, and by late 1981 Grenada and Cuba had signed a protocol of military cooperation.[2] In the southwest corner of the island Bishop established a Cuban military mission boasting twenty-seven military specialists. Bishop also wasted little time establishing close links with the Soviet Union, and Grenada's representative voted in January 1980 against the United Nations resolution condemning the Soviet invasion of Afghanistan. That year additional Cuban military advisers and construction workers arrived in Grenada and began constructing a new airport with a ten-thousand-foot runway. In 1980, while visiting Havana, General Hudson Austin, Grenada's defense minister, signed a military aid agreement with the Soviet Union, and another was arranged in July 1982. Bishop entered additional trade agreements with the Soviet Union, Czechoslovakia, Bulgaria, and East Germany. The same year an agreement with Cuba included the first armored vehicles—eight Soviet-made BTR-60 armored personnel carriers, two BRDM-2 armored cars—and other significant military equipment.

In the midst of sending large shipments of military supplies to Grenada, the Soviet Union built an embassy near the island's Quarantine Point, and in 1982 it dispatched its first ambassador, Major General Gennady Sazhenev of Soviet military intelligence (GRU). Bishop signed three more formal military agreements with the Soviet Union by the end of that year through which, according to U.S. intelligence estimates, the Grenadian People's Revolutionary Armed Forces (PRAF) could have fielded four infantry divisions equipped with more than sixty armored personnel carriers and one hundred Soviet ZSU 23mm antiaircraft guns, plus a dozen military aircraft and a half dozen naval patrol craft, by 1986. Their militia could field at least fourteen battalions. Grenada was dependent solely on Soviet support for all the equipment, including spare parts, ammunition, and finances. In 1983 Prime Minister Tom Adams of nearby Barbados called Grenada "one of the perhaps dozen most militarized states in the world in terms of population under arms."[3]

Bishop fell further into the grip of Cuba and the Soviet Union while his small country's economy continually faltered as it embraced the goals of socialism. After a time Bishop realized that he was not going to succeed economically while in the pocket of the Soviets and Cubans, so he made a few overtures for improved relations with the United States. He was so badly in need of hard currency by 1983 that he was forced to approach the American medical school in St. George's, hat in hand, to plead for early payment of their taxes.

In early April 1983 Bishop's advisers urged him to mend relations with the United States, which had recently excluded Grenada from its Caribbean Basin Initiative and had blocked loans and assistance to the island from the International Monetary Fund. When invited to Washington, Bishop met with National Security Adviser William Clark. Clark and other representatives suggested that Bishop develop a more democratic stance and cautioned that by foiling his political opponents and speaking against the United States he risked isolation. Following his visit to Washington, and in response to his ostracism by the West, Bishop suddenly announced plans for a new constitution and free elections.

Grenada's tenuous relations with the West, and the precarious situation on the island, were further complicated by the emerging power struggle between Bishop and Deputy Prime Minister Coard, an ardent Marxist who was working to undermine Bishop's support with the NJM Central Committee. Popular discontent with the deteriorating situation on the island fueled the fire: Grenadians were disenchanted with the failure of state farming efforts, the collapse of cash crops on the world market, and the fishing industry. Coard, working to build his popular support, accused Bishop of inadequately socializing the economy.[4]

At the same time Bishop was in the midst of signing another secret military pact, this time with North Korea—whose interests in the Caribbean were less than clear. The Soviets, who were displeased by

Bishop's wavering and apparent rapprochement with the United States, preferred the more reliable Coard. Fidel Castro, on the other hand, considered Bishop a close friend.

As the personal rivalry between Bishop and Coard intensified, Coard began pressing Bishop for a power-sharing plan in the Party Central Committee. In 1983, during a much-publicized meeting with Soviet Foreign Minister Andrei Gromyko, Bishop pledged to support the Soviet policy of keeping the Caribbean "cauldron boiling."[5] In September Prime Minister Bishop flew to Eastern Europe, where he toured Prague and Budapest, and returned via Havana after a visit with Castro. It had looked increasingly as if he would give in to Coard's demand for a dual leadership role, but while in Havana, apparently after receiving encouragement from Castro, Bishop seemed once again to harden his position against Coard—which he made known in a telephone conversation with his supporters.

When Bishop returned to Grenada on October 8, the scanty reception he received at the airport tipped him off that something was amiss; to make matters worse, he could not find many of the other Central Committee members at all. He quickly tried to consolidate his power within the NJM during hastily called meetings in which he pledged to review the matter of joint leadership with Coard. But Bishop was fighting a losing battle; on October 12 he was placed under house arrest by a faction led by Coard and General Hudson Austin.

A week later a crowd numbering about three thousand gathered at Bishop's home to protest his arrest and, after a period of chanting and shouting, forced the guards to free Bishop. In the melee that followed, Bishop and several other members of his cabinet were whisked away by followers in a motorcade. While driving they expected to encounter an even larger crowd of Bishop supporters at Market Square; however, the motorcade turned away from Market Square, where the jubilant crowd waited, and spirited Bishop to Fort Rupert, the main military headquarters of the People's Revolutionary Government, high on a hill overlooking the harbor.

Shortly after noon, the angry crowd, estimated at four thousand, converged on the fort, demanding that Bishop emerge. Coard and

Austin had ordered a convoy of three Soviet BTR-60 armored personnel carriers, each with eight to ten infantrymen inside, to go from Fort Frederick to Fort Rupert. The convoy drove up the two-mile winding road from the west side of the island with orders to attack the crowd at the fort and capture Bishop and his cabinet, who were inside. When the convoy appeared at the top of the hill, the crowd, believing they were arriving to help Bishop, parted before the vehicles. The infantry dismounted. One soldier launched a rocket-propelled grenade at a car in front of the fort, and as it disintegrated in flames, the soldiers strafed the crowd with heavy 12.7mm machine guns mounted on the armored personnel carriers. The column of troops then moved into the fort, firing their weapons as they walked. Onlookers leaped from the high walls of the fort to evade the bullets. Thirty to forty civilians were killed and many more were seriously wounded. During a firefight between the Bishop supporters, who were armed, and the PRAF detachment at least four soldiers were killed. Once inside the fort, soldiers captured Bishop and his followers after a brief scuffle. They were ordered out of the fort and into a yard used as a drill field and basketball court, where they were held for about forty-five minutes until the troop commander returned to the hill with the order from Coard and the Central Committee to execute Bishop and the others. Shortly after 2:00 P.M. machine gunners opened fire at short range, killing Bishop and seven of his cabinet members and supporters.

The next day, Coard and the Political Department of the Central Committee proclaimed, in Soviet style, their victory over the "counterrevolutionaries and betrayers of the masses opposed to Socialism." The announcement said that Bishop and his followers had been shot to death by PRAF troops loyal to the Central Committee. After issuing a twenty-four-hour curfew and a warning that anyone seen in public would be shot on sight, General Austin, commander of the Grenadian armed forces, severed all communications with the outside world.

Grenada's neighbors were not ignoring the situation. Two days later, the Cuban government denounced the murder and called for the situation to return to normal. On October 13 U.S. Ambassador to Barbados Milan Bish had reported that the situation in Grenada was deteriorating and that there had been riots with armored personnel carriers firing into crowds. On October 14, the day Bishop was expelled from the party, the Joint Chiefs of Staff alerted the U.S. Atlantic Command to begin planning to evacuate American citizens. At the time of Bishop's murder on October 19, the possibility of some kind of military option was already under active consideration by the planners of the area's regional security organizations and the Barbados Defense Force. The chairman of the OECS, the outspoken anti-Communist Eugenia Charles, called for a meeting. Immediately following the massacre, the prime minister of Barbados, Tom Adams, proposed an intervention. He suggested that the OECS request assistance from Barbados and Jamaica, asking Barbados to invite the United Kingdom and the United States to participate.

Based on the October 19 events in Grenada and the actions of the OECS, President Reagan immediately authorized diverting the Twenty-second Marine Amphibious Unit, which was about 350 miles out of Norfolk and headed to the Mediterranean, to join the USS *Independence* carrier battle group and Amphibious Squadron Four. A combined twenty-one-ship force headed to the Caribbean. The diversion had a immediate deterrent effect on Castro, who forthwith informed the United States that he would not interfere by deploying his armed forces to Grenada. Although Castro had condemned the Coard action and Bishop's execution, he did send senior Colonel Pedro Comas Tortoló, former head of the Cuban military mission in Grenada and then chief of staff of the Army of the Center of Cuba, to organize the defense of Grenada. Soon Cuban workers and advisers began to install runway barriers on the Point Salinas airfield in Grenada to block all aircraft from landing.

On October 20, the day following the killings in Grenada, the U.S. government began to look more seriously into the safety and well-being of the American medical students and other citizens present on the island. Admiral Wesley McDonald, the commander in chief Atlantic, submitted contingency plans for six different ways to evacuate U.S. citizens from the island, ranging from a show of force to evacuating them from a hostile environment should the need arise. Unfortunately, some of the planning was based on a mistaken assumption that all American medical students in Grenada resided at the campus just to the east of the Point Salinas airfield, an error that would later cause a great deal of embarrassment. The Joint Chiefs of Staff then issued the order for Operation Urgent Fury. The original plan approved on October 21 had been overlaid by numerous additions for expanding the forces involved to include more units from the other services and special operations forces.

There could be no plea for assistance from Grenada itself, since there was no legitimate government after Coard and Austin established martial law on October 19. The Revolutionary Military Command established by Bernard Coard went unrecognized; therefore, the sole constitutional authority left on the island was British Commonwealth Governor-General Sir Paul Scoon, who represented the queen but was under house arrest. His opinion regarding intervention would have weighed heavily in London and Washington. Prime Minister of Barbados Tom Adams met with U.S. Ambassador Milan Bish and succeeded in convincing him that the only way to return democracy to Grenada was to remove the PRA by force. Adams and Eugenia Charles thought there was little chance that Cuba or the Soviet Union would intervene, and the OECS agreed to invoke article 8 of its 1981 Treaty of Association. The text of the OECS request for assistance read in part: "The Authority proposes therefore to take action for collective defense and preservation of peace and security against external aggression by requesting assistance from friendly countries to provide transport, logistic support, and additional military personnel to assist the efforts of the OECS to stabilize this most grave situation within the eastern Caribbean."[6] Worried by the violence and fearing that Grenada had become a threat to the peace of the region, four of the seven members of the Caribbean security alliance appealed for British and American help. The British declined.

Eugenia Charles transmitted the eight-point official written request for assistance to the U.S. government on Sunday, October 23, 1983, the day of the bombing of the marine barracks in Beirut. While still shocked by the heavy losses of marines in Lebanon, President Reagan ordered U.S. armed forces to invade and secure Grenada. His stated objectives were to protect American lives, deny the island to Communist control, and encourage true democracy.

Once the president had ordered the invasion, it fell to Secretary of Defense Caspar Weinberger and Chairman of the Joint Chiefs of Staff General John Vessey to carry it out. Vice Admiral Joseph Metcalf III was assigned to command the joint task force that would assault Grenada. The intervention had two specific operational missions: (1) to free British Governor-General Sir Paul Scoon and (2) to secure the welfare and safety of the roughly one thousand American medical students. The American troops would no doubt be in the spotlight of the international press after the bombing in Beirut and the previous failed rescue in Iran. The United States badly needed a military success. Weinberger later praised the action, writing, "[President Reagan] began the long and difficult task of restoring America's hopes, her greatness and strength."[7]

The result of President Reagan's order was the rapid assembly of a force of fifteen thousand U.S. troops, plus a contingent of three hundred soldiers and police from six neighboring Caribbean states. They faced approximately one thousand Grenadian soldiers, another one thousand local Grenadian militia, and about six hundred Cubans. The Cubans in the construction force working in the southwest corner of the island at the Point Salinas airfield were expected to resist a landing by American forces. There were additionally forty Cuban advisers assigned to the Grenadian army, eighty-seven Cuban soldiers, eighteen diplomats from a number of countries with military ties to Grenada, and, of course, Cuban Colonel Comas Tortoló, who had just been sent by Castro to supervise the defense.

On Sunday October 23 Vice Admiral Metcalf, the commander of the U.S. Second Fleet, which was responsible for the defense of the western Atlantic, was attending a clambake. He was called in to Atlantic Fleet Headquarters to meet with Admiral McDonald, who told him he would be the joint task force commander for the invasion of

Grenada. Admiral Metcalf convened a meeting at 7:00 A.M. the next day on board his Second Fleet flagship, the amphibious command ship USS *Mount Whitney,* which was berthed at Norfolk.

The operation order for the intervention was separated into sections for each service: army, navy, marines, and air force. Because navy and marine secure radio signals were not compatible with army and air force radios, Admiral Metcalf feared there would be communications difficulties. As a short-term solution, he chose to put two army–air force secure satellite radios with specially rigged antennae on the *Whitney,* which enabled his staff to communicate with all participating units.[8]

Admiral Metcalf's Second Fleet staff was augmented with additional army personnel, including Major General Norman Schwarzkopf, who was then the commanding general of the Twenty-fourth Mechanized Infantry Division at Fort Stewart in Georgia. To Admiral Metcalf the forces at hand–the Twenty-second Marine Amphibious Unit, which was commanded by Colonel James P. Faulkner, supported by the *Independence* carrier battle group with an embarked air wing–were completely self-sufficient.[9] A Marine Amphibious Unit consists of a self-sustaining force of two thousand marines with tanks and armored personnel carriers, assault and attack helicopters, field artillery, self-propelled artillery, and the necessary support equipment and ammunition. However, the equipment of the Twenty-second had been loaded onto other ships for the peacekeeping mission in the Mediterranean. The unit had been reduced in size to the Second Battalion of the Eighth Marine Battalion Landing Team, which was commanded by Lieutenant Colonel Roy Smith, Marine Medium Helicopter Squadron 261, and a command and logistics group. The Second Battalion had 43 officers and 779 enlisted men, which was 10 percent less than usual. The rifle platoons had been reduced from forty-five to thirty-six men each and were organized into eleven-man squads. The battalion's total firepower had been increased by additional grenade launchers, Dragon antitank missiles, and heavy .50-caliber machine guns. The marines were loaded on board the amphibious assault ship USS *Guam,* the amphibious transport dock USS *Trenton,* and the landing platform dock USS *Fort Snelling,* the latter two of which were capable of launching landing craft and amphibious vehicles from a well deck. The group also included the

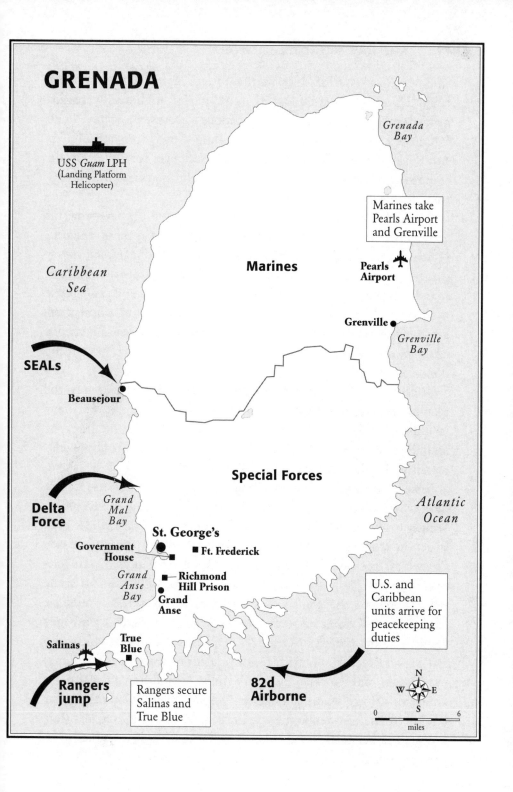

GRENADA

USS *Guam* LPH
(Landing Platform
Helicopter)

*Caribbean
Sea*

*Grenada
Bay*

Marines take
Pearls Airport
and Grenville

Marines

**Pearls
Airport**

Grenville

*Grenville
Bay*

SEALs

Beausejour

Special Forces

*Atlantic
Ocean*

Delta
Force

*Grand
Mal
Bay*

St. George's

**Government
House**

■ **Ft. Frederick**

*Grand
Anse
Bay*

■ **Richmond
Hill Prison**

**Grand
Anse**

U.S. and
Caribbean
units arrive for
peacekeeping
duties

Salinas

**True
Blue**

**Rangers
jump**

Rangers secure
Salinas and
True Blue

**82d
Airborne**

N
W   E
S

0   6
miles

landing ship tanks USS *Manitowac* and USS *Barnstable County,* which could deliver vehicles of all types onto dry land. Additionally, participants from each service's special operations forces were organized into a Joint Special Operations Task Force under the command of U.S. Army Major General Richard Scholtes. Although controlled by the competing services, these units together sought to achieve the successful outcome that had eluded them in the past.

The political intelligence regarding the situation in Grenada was extremely good, based on information supplied by experienced officers and members of the OECS staff and the Caribbean security organization, but intelligence regarding the infrastructure on the small island was woefully lacking. There were very few maps, and those available were outdated. Because there were no ongoing priority targets on the small island, there were few overhead reconnaissance photographs. Intelligence from agents in Grenada was practically nonexistent.

With the addition of the Joint Special Operations Task Force, the plan to take control of Grenada was finally hammered out. The navy would cordon off the island with ships and aircraft. Marines from the amphibious unit would fly by helicopter to the island's only operating airfield (called Pearls Airport), in the northeast end of the island, and take the town of Grenville and its garrison on the east side at dawn. Simultaneously U.S. Army Rangers from the Seventy-fifth Ranger Regiment would fly in and seize both the airfield under construction at Point Salinas and the medical school campus nearby (known as True Blue). Once Point Salinas was secured, two battalions of the Eighty-second Airborne Division were to land in aircraft at the field to relieve the Rangers. Special operations forces would be landed at St. George's on the west side of the island. There they would take the Governor-General's residence, the main island radio station, and the two Grenadian army garrisons—Fort Rupert, located in the town, and Fort Frederick in the hills. An additional Delta Force antiterrorist force would land at the Richmond Hill Prison above the city to release any remaining political prisoners. The Rangers were prepared either to fly in and land on the airfield, if possible, or to parachute in to take their objectives.

On October 23, two nights before the landings, a team of navy SEALs was poised to land covertly at Point Salinas and conduct a reconnaissance of the area. Its mission was to determine what the Rangers would encounter and set up beacons for them. A thirty-seven-man Delta Force Team was to land in the dark and clear the airfield ahead of the Rangers. The Rangers and special operations commandos had intended to jump into Salinas at 1:00 A.M. in darkness from twelve hundred feet but were overruled by the Atlantic Command. They prepared instead to land in the early hours of dawn by jumping from six hundred feet in a combat jump, relying on the early reconnaissance by the SEALs; however, the SEALs' mission was aborted.

A team of twelve SEALs and four air force combat controllers was to parachute from six hundred feet into the sea, each man carrying equipment weighing more than a hundred pounds. The sixteen men were divided into two teams that would be picked up by two Boston Whalers launched from a destroyer, the USS *Clifton Sprague,* positioned at the drop zone. Then they were supposed to land, reconnoiter, and place beacons on the Point Salinas airfield. They parachuted and landed in medium seas with winds greater than twenty knots. Four SEALs drowned when they became entangled in their parachute shrouds; their heavy equipment pulled them down into the water. After a difficult recovery, the surviving SEALs and controllers sped toward the island at high speed in one boat. When they encountered a Grenadian patrol craft, they cut their engine to avoid detection. The whaler swamped in the strong wind, and the men were forced to return to the destroyer. A second attempt to go ashore the next night met the same fate; consequently, the beach reconnaissance was never accomplished. The Delta Force and Rangers were required to land blind.

The marine helicopter assaults began at 5:00 A.M. on October 25. Two marine AH-1 Cobra gunships from the USS *Guam* led a force of CH-46 Sea Knight helicopters carrying men of the Second Battalion's E Company. They flew without lights to their objective at Pearls Airport. The Cobras immediately drew antiaircraft fire from the surrounding hills but suppressed it without difficulty. The marines landed just south of the objective and took it without a fight. They also took the town of Grenville without casualties.

The aircraft carrying the Rangers were delayed by thirty minutes because of a navigation error and arrived at Salinas at 5:30 A.M. After initially rigging for an assault with the aircraft landing on the runway, the Rangers were forced to reconfigure twice for a six-hundred-foot drop into antiaircraft fire. This was no easy task. With no reports from the SEALs who had failed to get ashore, the Rangers were forced to parachute in broad daylight on top of Cuban and Grenadian soldiers who were well entrenched and alert.

The Rangers' objective was to secure the airport and take the medical school campus located just to the east of the runway. At least one Soviet ZSU 23mm antiaircraft gun, located in the hills near the airport, fired at the Rangers as they approached. However, the antiaircraft guns had been set up to shoot at aircraft flying in at twelve hundred feet and were unable to lower their aim to shoot effectively at the Rangers jumping from six hundred feet, a bit of luck caused by changing the altitude of the drop. Incredibly, no men were lost to enemy fire during the airborne assault. However, two Special Forces Pathfinders, who had dropped in earlier, died in parachute failures. Five Rangers were killed and five wounded in the fighting on the ground as they cleared the airfield and the campus, an objective they achieved by 10:30. Within thirty minutes, two battalions of the Second Brigade of the Eighty-second Airborne Division began landing at Salinas in giant C-141 aircraft. The Eighty-second troopers were assigned the job of consolidating and occupying the entire island after the Rangers and marines had successfully taken their objectives and withdrawn.

In the northeast the marines from the Twenty-second Marine Amphibious Unit had taken their objectives of the town and port of Grenville by 7:30 with no resistance. By 8:00 there were eight hundred marines ashore who were being welcomed by the Grenadians. They also captured large numbers of Bernard Coard's soldiers and weapons. The marines were ordered to assist the lightly armed Rangers and SEALs in their attempt to secure the Governor-General's residence. F Company of the Second Battalion was to move by helicopter to the west side of the island to Mal Bay. Another company, reinforced with five M-60 tanks and thirteen amphibious tractors,

U.S. Marines board the *Mayaguez* from the escort ship USS *Harold E. Holt* to recapture the vessel on May 15, 1975. *(Courtesy of U.S. Navy)*

The seal from the U.S. embassy in Beirut after the April 1983 terrorist bombing. *(Courtesy of U.S. Marine Corps)*

Rescue workers at the U.S. Marine barracks in Beirut following the terrorist bombing on October 23, 1983.
(Courtesy of U.S. Marine Corps)

A poster distributed by the New Jewel Movement in Grenada showing, *left to right*, Daniel Ortega, Maurice Bishop, Fidel Castro.
(Courtesy of Department of Defense)

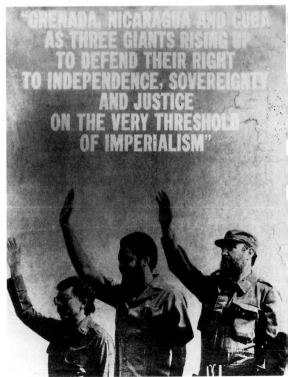

"GRENADA, NICARAGUA AND CUBA AS THREE GIANTS RISING UP TO DEFEND THEIR RIGHT TO INDEPENDENCE, SOVEREIGNTY AND JUSTICE ON THE VERY THRESHOLD OF IMPERIALISM"

(Above and below) UH-60 Blackhawks transported American medical students from Salinas Airfield to a waiting aircraft for return to the United States on October 26, 1983. *(Courtesy of U.S. Air Force)*

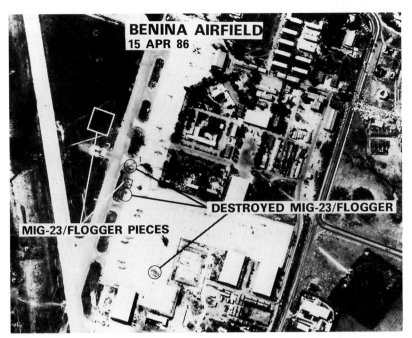

Aerial photos show some damage inflicted during the U.S. attacks on Libya on April 15, 1986. *(Courtesy of U.S. Navy)*

U.S. Drug Enforcement Administration (DEA) officers assist General Manuel Noriega into a C-130 cargo aircraft at Howard Air Base, Panama, for a flight to Homestead Air Force Base, Florida, for detention, on January 1, 1990.
(Courtesy of U.S. Air Force)

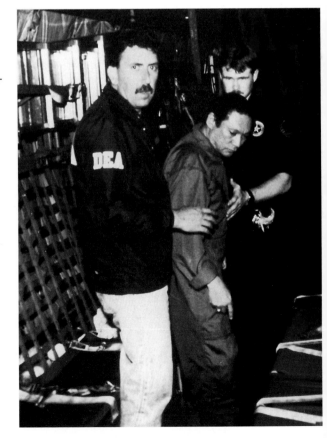

An Iraqi mine floats in the Persian Gulf near the battleship USS *Missouri* before being detonated by the Explosive Ordnance Disposal team during Operation Desert Shield. *(Courtesy of U.S. Navy)*

U.S. Marines awaiting action during Operation Desert Shield. *(Courtesy of U.S. Marine Corps)*

A U.S. Navy ordnance-disposal mine-clearing operation near Kuwait in February 1991. *(Courtesy of U.S. Navy)*

(Below) The highway west of Kuwait City heading north toward Basra is shown cleared of debris after it was bombed on February 27, 1991, by navy and marine aircraft in the final hours of the Gulf War. The "Highway of Doom" had been jammed bumper-to-bumper with Iraqi troops in civilian and military vehicles as they fled the city. *(Courtesy of U.S. Navy)*

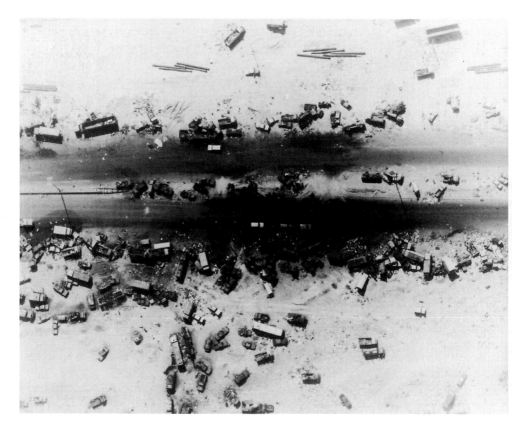

An F-14 Tomcat flies over burning oil wells in a field about ten miles west of Kuwait City following Operation Desert Storm. *(Courtesy of U.S. Navy)*

U.S. Marines, armed with M203 grenade launchers attached to M16A2 rifles, and with an AT8 light antitank weapon, run for cover from snipers as they attempt to secure Somali warlord General Aideed's weapon cantonment. *(Courtesy of U.S. Navy)*

A young Serbian boy reads a comic book about mine awareness distributed by the 315th Tactical Psychological Operations Company (PYSOPS).
(Courtesy of U.S. Army)

Serbian families gather items from humanitarian aid boxes in Kosovo.
(Courtesy of Department of Defense)

A U.S. Navy helicopter crewman hands out food rations to Bosnian children in Glamoc, Bosnia, in June 1996.
(Courtesy of U.S. Navy)

was sent around to Mal Bay aboard two amphibious ships and prepared to land by 6:30 P.M. the same day, October 25.

The assault on the Governor-General's residence did not go as planned. A team of navy SEALs flying in by helicopter came under intense antiaircraft fire while landing. In the ensuing firefight the SEALs were unable to get all their weapons and communications equipment out of the helicopters, and as a result they entered the battle too lightly armed and with marginal communications. They gained access to the mansion but were subsequently surrounded and pinned down by Grenadian army forces with heavy weapons. Four marine Cobra gunship helicopters were summoned to assist, but two were immediately shot down by heavy antiaircraft fire. After an early-morning landing in the dark on the twenty-sixth, marine forces from G Company of the Second Battalion advanced on the residence and just shortly after 7:00 rescued Governor-General Sir Paul Scoon, his family, and the twenty-two-man SEAL team pinned inside the residence. According to Admiral Metcalf, the SEAL commander's decision to restrict fire at the surrounding Grenadian forces was a brilliant deception that concealed the fact that the SEALs had only light weapons. There were no casualties from the fight at the residence.

The special operations assault on Fort Rupert on the twenty-fifth went badly. The attacking Delta Force in MH-60 Black Hawk helicopters flew into heavy machine-gun fire and were driven off. One helicopter on the mission took forty-seven hits from a 23mm antiaircraft gun and still continued flying. The Delta Force troops were unable to land at Fort Rupert, Fort Frederick, or the Richmond Hill Prison, and the postponement of their missions until after dawn had caused them to lose the essential element of surprise. Since the gunners on the ground defending the prison and forts relied solely on optics for their weapons, they would have been ineffective in darkness. According to retired Brigadier General David Grange, who was the Delta squadron commander leading the assault on Richmond Hill Prison, the failure to attack in darkness caused the problems. Grange said:

> As we flew across the island in morning light, some people waved, some shot at us with AK-47s. It was confusing at

first from what we expected of the attitude of the people. As I listened to the Grenadian local radio, I heard a spokesman tell all to "come out and defend your country from the Yankee imperialists." That is when I ordered my men to return fire against all identified threats. . . . . This was our country's first Black Hawk combat air assault. If we had used the old Hueys [UH-1 helicopters] on this mission, we would have lost every aircraft. We had one Black Hawk go down. Almost all the MH-60 door guns jammed as we tried to suppress enemy fire while attempting to land. Coming in, we caught a lot of air defense artillery fire from .51-caliber, 23mm, and small arms—thank God for the self-sealing fuel tanks. Every aircraft had no less than forty holes when we all finally landed on Salinas Airfield, after getting shot off the proposed landing zones at the prison and after dropping off our wounded on various navy ships off the coast. I had seventeen wounded in my force of forty-four. The mission was not very clear, nor were the rules of engagement. We were not sure who we were supposed to rescue from the prison.[10]

Learning rather late that Fort Frederick was the main military headquarters, Admiral Metcalf ordered an air strike. During that attack, navy aircraft flying from the *Independence* attacked the headquarters, and the defending forces fled. However, during that air strike, a civilian mental hospital, adjacent to the headquarters was mistakenly bombed and destroyed, with heavy loss of life. The same afternoon of October 26, the marines from G Company of Second Battalion attacked the headquarters of the PRA at Fort Frederick and took it unopposed; the remnants of the Grenadian army fled. Large quantities of weapons and ammunition were found there.

That afternoon, Vice Admiral Metcalf learned that there was a second group of American medical students at Grand Anse located northeast of Salinas. Acting on recommendations from his temporary army staff officer, Major General Schwarzkopf, he ordered a marine helicopter squadron to transport Rangers of the Second Battalion,

Seventy-fifth Ranger Regiment to the second campus where four CH-53 Sea Stallion helicopters evacuated 224 more American students on October 26. A total of 599 American and 88 foreign nationals were safely removed without a single civilian casualty.

By the morning of October 30 the marines turned over their areas of responsibility to the Eighty-second Airborne Division. At that time 6,140 troops of the Eighty-second had landed on the island to complete the sweep for remaining enemy resistance. By the evening of October 31 all marines were back aboard their amphibious ships, and the island reverted to its normal peaceful state. The crisis in Grenada did not result from American covert action or any other grand strategy to unseat Bishop or redirect the course his regime was taking, attractive though that might have been to the U.S. government. Grenada became the only Marxist regime in history to be replaced by force of arms by Caribbean nations cooperating with Western military power.

Just before the landings began, Admiral Metcalf was ordered by the Atlantic Fleet commander in chief to exclude the world press from the island until it was safely secured.[11] The order was based on the lack of an organized censorship program similar to the one in existence during World War II, the fact that so little time and few transportation assets were available, and, most important, the fear of compromising the element of surprise. The American commanders (including Metcalf) felt that the presence of a large number of press in the area of operations, each trying to scoop the other by broadcasting news from the ground, would endanger friendly forces. After the exclusion order was given, the press made numerous attempts to squeeze by the embargo. U.S. Navy aircraft once intercepted a high-speed craft carrying newsmen trying to approach the island. Another group of seven newsmen, including five Americans, succeeded in sneaking ashore but were picked up and flown to the *Guam*. They were held on board until the island was reopened to travelers. Understandably, any attempt by the armed forces to contain or otherwise restrain the press generates an antimilitary reaction in a democratic society. In the case of Grenada, Defense Secretary Weinberger told Admiral Metcalf to allow the press on the island on October 27, after the fighting was mostly over. On October 30, 167 reporters flew in from Barbados; however, the damage had already been done. The press coverage that followed lashed out bitterly at the military commanders and highlighted every shortcoming and accident that inevitably accompanies such operations, especially when hurriedly mounted.

U.S. casualties in the action were 19 American military dead and 89 wounded, including 3 dead and 15 wounded marines, 12 dead and 71 wounded army soldiers, and 4 dead and 3 wounded navy seamen. In one accident a navy aircraft killed 1 army man and wounded 15. No Caribbean security troops were wounded. Grenadian casualties included 45 killed and 337 wounded. Twenty-four of the total killed were civilians, 21 of whom were killed in the accidental hospital bombing. Cuban casualties were 24 killed in action and 29 wounded. Six hundred Cuban construction workers were taken prisoner. By November 9, most Cubans, 17 Libyans, 15 North Koreans, 49 Soviets, 10 East Germans, and 3 Bulgarians were returned to their countries.[12]

The results of the invasion were unquestionably supported by a congressional investigation, although the view of the media was understandably critical. The main reason for the failures of some of the most highly trained U.S. Special Forces was hasty planning. The ultimate success of the operation depended on the element of surprise and the secret movement of troops in order to minimize casualties among the invaders and civilians. Postponing the first assaults several times due to loading delays and navigation errors forced many of the attacks to occur in broad daylight. It was later learned that General Austin and the Cuban military on Grenada knew in advance that the invasion was to take place, and Radio Free Grenada had called all the island's militias to arms before the first landings were made. The Rangers who parachuted onto Salinas took an excessively long time—ninety minutes—to drop six hundred men. Luckily, the only casualties were from malfunctioning parachutes. Had there been determined resistance the results might have been horrendous. The six hundred Rangers from the Seventy-fifth were to land at Salinas after the airfield had been cleared by a team of thirty-seven men from

Delta Force, six of whom were killed and seventeen wounded in their attempt to clear the runway for the Rangers. The assaults by the Delta Force, SEALs, and other Special Forces against Forts Frederick and Rupert, Richmond Hill Prison, and the radio station were not crucial to the overall invasion and appear to have been ordered merely to ensure that these forces had a piece of the action—why they failed is another story.

In retrospect the intervention in Grenada was a job done at the right time, although in haste. Had it been necessary to wait a year, the task of taking the island by force would have been much more difficult and costly. It is clear from documents and material found during the post-intervention mop-up that within a year the PRA would have possessed a daunting array of Soviet armor and heavy weapons, sufficient to have equipped a sizable army. From captured documents dated July 2, 1982, it was learned that the country's armed forces planned to develop into an eighteen-battalion force that would have put between seven thousand and ten thousand men and women under arms by 1985. As it happened, the possibility for intervention occurred because of a squabble on the island between two Marxist-Leninist political factions—one close to Moscow, the other to Havana, yet both on a similar track of expanding an already serious impediment to stability and security in the region.

On December 19, 1983, free elections were held in Grenada, and independent political parties were able to choose their candidates. Four days before the elections the remaining U.S. forces left the island. A year later President Reagan was invited to attend the first anniversary of the invasion, and an estimated one hundred thousand Grenadians turned out—nearly the entire population—to cheer his speech. Undersecretary of Defense Dov S. Zakheim said it well: "The cumulative impact of Grenada on America's self image should not be underestimated. It represented a clear-cut military success—something that the American public had not witnessed since before Vietnam. It marked the expression of American vigor in foreign policy, and signified an understanding of the role of force as a vehicle for the support of U.S. foreign policy objectives when all other options are closed except passive resignation to the whims of fate."[13]

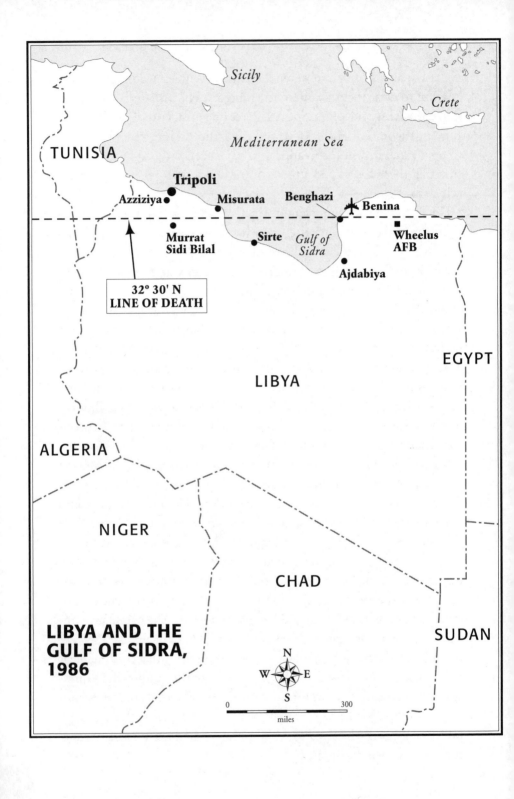

Sicily

Crete

Mediterranean Sea

TUNISIA

Tripoli

Azziziya

Misurata

Benghazi

Benina

Murrat
Sidi Bilal

Sirte

*Gulf of
Sidra*

Wheelus
AFB

**32° 30' N
LINE OF DEATH**

Ajdabiya

EGYPT

LIBYA

ALGERIA

NIGER

CHAD

SUDAN

**LIBYA AND THE
GULF OF SIDRA,
1986**

N
W   E
S

0   300

miles

CHAPTER 6

Retaliatory Attacks on Libya

The Gulf of Sidra, March–April 1986

In December 1985 the United States was again confronted by belligerent forces in the Middle East. This adversary was considerably more substantial than the Muslim factions faced in Lebanon. Not only was Libyan dictator Muammar Qaddafi espousing similar anti-American and anti-Israeli causes, but he was challenging the freedom of international airspace and the seas, a far more potent threat to the world's premier naval and air power and one much more likely to provoke a forceful response. Just as Britain had upheld its free access to international waters throughout the nineteenth century, so would the United States respond with significant force to any such provocation in the twentieth. The U.S. government had done so before by sending warship squadrons to the Mediterranean shores of Tripoli during the naval campaign against the Barbary pirates in 1803 and against the British during the War of 1812.

Muammar Qaddafi seized power in Libya in a 1969 coup against King Idris I, the ruler who had governed since the country gained independence in 1951. In a situation similar to that in postwar Iran, both Britain and the United States, in a effort to secure their military bases in Libya after World War II, had assisted Idris, a promising local strongman, to gain and retain power. Qaddafi, the young revolutionary coup leader, was not only a Bedouin tribesman but also a disciple of Egyptian president Gamal Abdel Nasser, who dreamed of pan-Arab unity. He was also allegedly a devout Muslim and anti-Communist. Nevertheless, his virulent anti-Western attitude rooted in the Israeli-Palestine rift drove him to the Soviet Union for arms and modern military technology.

Soon after taking power, Qaddafi demanded that the Americans and British return their bases to Libya; they complied. The United States turned over Wheelus Air Force Base, which had been used for decades by the Sixth Fleet and the air force as a major Mediterranean training base. The loss of this base was a significant blow to the forces of NATO's southern flank, whose position in the busy confines of the Mediterranean had depended on the use of training bases in the remote North African desert and in the large basin off the Libyan coast called the Gulf of Sirte, or Sidra.[1]

After Nasser died in 1970, Qaddafi sought to fill his shoes as the leader of a pan-Arab movement. He began to receive large amounts of Soviet arms. Much of the modern armament, however, proved far too complex for his small population of five million with a literacy rate of roughly 64 percent. Qaddafi realized he would be unable to prevail in a military confrontation with the West and instead chose the more expedient weapon of terrorism to further his political and religious goals.

Terrorists who received Qaddafi's active support and training have left a long and bloody trail. Throughout the 1970s the West reeled under a wave of gory actions beginning with the kidnappings of Israelis at the 1972 Olympic Games in Munich, followed by a rash of airline hijackings and car bombings carried out by a score of different factions supported by Qaddafi. The Soviet bloc nations were pleased to provide arms to Qaddafi's terrorists for hard currency, while the West was paradoxically supporting his activities by purchasing Libyan oil.

The frustrating years of failure to deal effectively with terrorist killings, compounded by the inability of the United States to free the hostages in Tehran, had precipitated the end of the Carter presidency after a single term. When President Reagan took the reins in Washington in 1981, he promised severe retaliation against terrorists.

Meanwhile Libya continued to be a source of state-sponsored terror-ism, not only invading its neighbor Chad and supporting guerrilla ac-tions in Sudan but also openly opposing Egyptian President Anwar Sadat's deliberate move toward peace with Israel. These activities brought Libya still closer to the Soviet Union, despite the religious and ideological divide between the two nations.

Ratcheting up his blatant challenges to the West, Qaddafi openly claimed the entire Gulf of Sidra to be Libyan in 1979. This gulf formed a basin penetrating the North African coastline that was flanked by Libya on three sides but was far deeper than the twelve-mile territorial water limit set by international law. Qaddafi declared the "Line of Death," delineating the extension of Libya's territorial waters south of a latitude line thirty-two degrees, thirty minutes north in the Gulf of Sidra. Qaddafi's line encompassed an area that extended as much as one hundred miles off the coast of Libya and was unmistakably intended as a further challenge to the United States. Because the gulf lies away from crowded shipping lanes, the U.S. Sixth Fleet had used it as one of the few remaining places in the Mediterranean to conduct live-fire exercises. Despite the major con-cern this caused the navy, the United States showed restraint and did nothing to challenge the Line of Death except to carry on with rou-tine aerial reconnaissance flights that sometimes included areas over waters claimed by Libya.

This extension of territory was far in excess of normal interna-tional practice. It would probably have gone unchallenged had it not brought about a further serious loss to the combat readiness of NATO and U.S. forces. When Qaddafi threatened several times to use force to defend his claims against interfering nations, the United States still did not immediately challenge his assertions of ownership and merely prohibited the Sixth Fleet from penetrating south of the line. In 1979 several Libyan MiG fighters sent from bases near Tripoli into the Gulf of Sidra harassed and then fired an air-to-air missile at a U.S. Air Force EC-135 aircraft on an unarmed reconnaissance flight in the area. It missed, and the United States still took no action.

Shortly after the Reagan administration took office, the U.S. Navy renewed its request to the National Security Council to challenge

Qaddafi's claims. The navy recommended an incursion called a Freedom of Navigation Operation. The United States had exercised a program of actively asserting navigational rights and freedoms since 1979. These operations deliberately challenged the claims of countries like the Soviet Union and Libya to territorial waters far in excess of what was established by international law. Some of these countries used a "baseline" method of measurement to determine their territorial waters, thereby seeking to close off vast ocean areas. Libya's line in the Gulf of Sidra was similar to that of the Soviet Union between the Sea of Okhotsk and the Bay of Vladivostok.[2]

One of these operations involved a demonstration by the U.S. Navy of its right of innocent passage—going from one point in international waters to another while passing through claimed territorial waters in the process. The planning of such operations often caused friction between the State Department, which usually wished to avoid souring relations even with belligerent countries, and the Defense Department, which claimed its freedom to operate was an essential policy instrument that was seriously restricted by excessive claims to territorial waters. The concern of American diplomats over this particular type of probe was the choice of location and timing. In August 1981 the new administration authorized the navy to penetrate the area below Qaddafi's line of demarcation.

The Libyan air force had by this time grown to a significant strength, equipped with modern Soviet Su-22s and French Mirage 100 fighters. The American force nevertheless crossed the Line of Death with a carrier battle group and conducted a fleet exercise. In the midst of the maneuvers, two F-14 Tomcats from Fighter Squadron Forty-one of USS *Nimitz* were confronted by Libyan air force SU-22 fighters piloted by non-Libyan pilots. While the navy F-14 fighters were flying protection for their ships, the SU-22s tried repeatedly to maneuver into advantageous positions. During the encounter navy ships and aircraft intercepted voice orders transmitted to the opposing SU-22s to fire on a flight of F-14 Tomcats. Under the rules of engagement, the U.S aircraft could not defend themselves unless fired upon first. While conducting a head-on intercept, the

Libyans fired a missile; the Tomcats evaded the missile and downed both SU-22s with Sidewinder air-to-air missiles.

Immediately after the air engagement, tensions heightened. Given Qadaffi's record, the Sixth Fleet and Americans abroad watched Libyan forces carefully for a reaction. After the downing of the two Libyan aircraft, Qaddafi remained passive for several years. On June 14, 1985, TWA flight 847 was hijacked and forced to land in Beirut, and an American sailor on board was murdered. On October 7 Palestinian terrorists seized the cruise ship *Achille Lauro* at sea, killing an aged and crippled American passenger. Later in October the military shopping mall at a U.S. Army base in Frankfurt was bombed, and twenty-three Americans were wounded. On November 24 an American air force civilian employee was shot by terrorists on an airliner that was hijacked and landed in Egypt. An Egyptian commando raid on the stranded aircraft failed. Fifty-eight people and all but one hijacker were killed. Airports in Rome and Vienna were attacked on December 27; five Americans were among those who died.

Interpol, the CIA, the FBI, and many other agencies soon linked these terrorist actions to Libya. Americans in Libya were ordered to leave, and in 1986 Qaddafi's actions were denounced by the U.S. State Department as unusual and extraordinary threats to the national security and foreign policy of the United States. Two and a half billion dollars of Libyan assets were frozen in America. European states had already taken measures against Libya: France had ceased arms sales and assisted Chad in repelling a Libyan invasion in 1983; Britain had stopped arms sales in 1984 after the murder of a British policewoman by Libyans outside their London embassy; and Italy banned further arms sales in January 1986.

Following the December 1985 terrorist attacks on the airports in Rome and Vienna, the Joint Chiefs of Staff developed a plan for an attack on Libya should it be involved in future terrorist actions against the United States. Chief of Naval Operations Admiral James Watkins proposed to the Joint Chiefs of Staff that the next round of Sixth Fleet Freedom of Navigation exercises include a challenge to Qaddafi's declared Line of Death in the Gulf of Sidra.

In 1986 President Reagan authorized the navy to again assert the right to operate across this line.

There was unusual agreement between the State and Defense Departments for this operation against Libya. Admiral William J. Crowe, Jr., the chairman of the Joint Chiefs of Staff, proposed new rules of engagement. The previous policy for such operations had been that participating ships and aircraft could respond with "appropriate force." For example, if a ship in the challenging force were attacked by an opposing aircraft, the ship would be authorized to destroy the aircraft, but the airfield from which it was launched would be safe from retaliatory action. These rules had been written to prevent the commander from taking action that might escalate into a major confrontation. However, it was no longer reasonable to insist that an American commander wait for an attack and significantly increase the risk to American lives. The recent experience in Beirut had been a shocking demonstration of what could result from such rules. The marines there had been so tightly limited to protection that their sentries were required to patrol with the ammunition removed from their weapons. Admiral Crowe proposed that the forces participating in the operation against Libya be allowed to respond immediately when a threat was detected and not to wait to see if it qualified for an appropriate response. The Crowe proposal was approved by Secretary of Defense Weinberger and President Reagan. But as Admiral Crowe pointed out in his memoir, *The Line of Fire*, old habits die hard. Commanding officers had not been given this much discretion since World War II and the Korean War. Despite the new rules of engagement, most American commanders, suffering from years of enforced hesitancy, probably wondered whether their actions would be supported if they responded forcefully.

The Freedom of Navigation exercise began on March 22, 1986, after a one-week delay to wait for a third aircraft carrier to arrive in the Mediterranean. The carriers USS *Coral Sea*, USS *Saratoga*, and USS *America* would participate together in the operation. One hundred and twenty-four smaller ships were in the fleet, including the Aegis-class cruisers USS *Ticonderoga* and USS *Yorktown*. This large force was mustered to ensure that there were enough ships present to handle a sizable response. Weinberger always insisted that the size of the force recommended by the military be doubled to ensure superiority and thereby avoid a repeat of the Iran hostage-rescue debacle.

By 1986 the Libyan air force had more than 500 Soviet and French aircraft, including the supersonic MiG-25. The size of the U.S. force clearly intimidated Qaddafi, and initially his aircraft and ships stood clear of the challenging armada. Two days into the operation, however, Libya fired two Soviet SA-5 surface-to-air missiles at two navy F-14 fighters. Although the missiles were fired at extreme range and fell harmlessly short, the act was sufficient under the new rules of engagement to authorize the Americans to return fire. Two navy A-7 aircraft attacked and destroyed the two air-defense radar sites, while the rest of the American forces began to search for Libyan ships and aircraft inside the Gulf of Sidra below the Line of Death. By the end of March 24 the navy had damaged a single Libyan patrol craft. The Sixth Fleet force withdrew on March 27 after crossing the line and countering the Libyan claim.

One week later, a terrorist bomb in West Berlin destroyed the La Belle disco, which was popular with Americans. One American serviceman and a Turkish woman were killed, and 230 other people injured. Evidence gained through intercepted communications showed that the Libyans were directly involved. Then on April 8 an explosion aboard a TWA flight from Rome caused by a terrorist bomb killed four more Americans. Those two actions set in motion a complex planning process to select targets for a significant punishment of Libya. The United States was ready to send a grave signal to the world that it would not tolerate any more acts of terrorism. The objective was to select targets in Libya that would not only emphasize this message and convey the full measure of ferocity but also keep civilian casualties near the targets low and minimize damage to U.S. forces.

To achieve these objectives, the Joint Chiefs of Staff decided to launch a short nighttime air strike with no second wave. To inflict less damage on noncombatants, American planners chose targets that had fewer homes nearby—in case the bombs missed their targets. Self-imposed restrictions forced the selection of targets that would have less psychological impact than those in the center of Tripoli, which limited the effectiveness of the retaliation.

Selected as targets were a headquarters compound at Azziziya, near Tripoli, and a confirmed terrorist training facility at Murrat Sidsi Bilal, where Yugoslav instructors were training Libyans for underwater sabotage. The Joint Chiefs of Staff selected two other clusters of targets for destruction, one near Tripoli and the other around Benina Airfield in eastern Libya. Navy carrier aircraft were to be augmented by twenty-four U.S. Air Force F-111 all-weather bombers based in Lakenheath and Upper Heyford in England. Six EF-111 electronic countermeasure aircraft and thirty KC-10 and KC-135 airborne tankers would participate—a considerable force for an air operation in peacetime. The addition of the F-111s was designed to catch the Libyan air defenses off guard, since they would be expecting any strike to come primarily from the carriers in the Mediterranean. Owing to the lack of overt allied support for the strike, the F-111s would be required to detour around French and Spanish airspace and enter the Mediterranean via Gibraltar, a route requiring five in-flight refuelings conducted at radio silence.

There were serious concerns about the ability to keep the operation secret. The recent experience in Grenada, where the press had been kept off the island until the initial assault was complete, had not endeared the military to the media. Furthermore, vocal opposition to Reagan's sharp response, if made known in advance, posed a serious risk of compromising the surprise attack. If news leaked to the Libyans and they increased their air-defense readiness, the strike aircraft would suffer significant losses. In addition, the War Powers Resolution Act of 1973 required President Reagan to confer with Congress before committing U.S. forces to combat. Incessantly hounded by the media, members of Congress are often unable to keep a military plan secret. Therefore, Reagan planned to wait until the last minute to seek the required congressional approval. The president called a meeting with congressional leaders in the Executive Office Building for 4:00 P.M. on April 14, the day of the strike, after the long-range F-111 bombers had already begun their seven-hour flight to Libya. The opposition, voiced by Senator Robert Byrd of

West Virginia, was primarily aimed at the lack of prior consultation in accordance with the War Powers Act. Although technically the action could be recalled, the die was cast, and the strike went ahead in spite of the congressional complaints.

The air force F-111 bombers were supported by Navy EA-6B electronic jammers, EA-3 intelligence aircraft, EA-2C radar-control aircraft, and A-7 and F-18 antiradar missile attack aircraft to suppress antiair defenses. Additional navy F-14 and F-18 fighter-bombers from all three carriers provided air cover and support for the F-111 bombers. The two groups of attacking aircraft met within three seconds of the planned times and flew to the target areas. Simultaneously, navy A-6 bombers flew in from two carriers, the *America* and the *Coral Sea,* and attacked separate targets in the Benghazi area, 450 miles to the east of Tripoli.[3]

The American participants knew that the Libyan air-defense systems—consisting of a wide spectrum of Soviet hardware, including surface-to-air missiles, from the SA-2 through the SA-9, and the formidable ZSU-23 radar-guided antiaircraft guns that had shot down many American aircraft and helicopters in Vietnam and Grenada—were among the most advanced in the world and comparable, on paper, with those in the Soviet Union and the Warsaw Pact countries. An estimated three thousand Soviet air-defense technicians were thought to be in Libya, along with some Yugoslavs and other advisers from North Korea, Vietnam, East Germany, and Syria.

The strike was scheduled for midnight Tripoli time, or 7:00 P.M. on April 14 in Washington, D.C. Because of radio restrictions by the participating forces, news of the raid would come only after the strike was over, when all the aircraft had cleared the coast off Tripoli. Tension was high in Washington. Although the inevitable rumors of a retaliatory strike had sent reporters scurrying to Tripoli, from where they were reporting on live television, the fact that the lights were still on in that city at 1:30 A.M. proved that there had been no advance warning of specific plans.

Not a single Libyan aircraft reacted in defense against the U.S. force, although a few antiaircraft missiles streaked harmlessly through the night skies. Navy aircraft returned to their carriers with minimal losses; one air force F-111 crashed while flying over the coast toward the targets and the two airmen were confirmed dead. Early damage assessment by reconnaissance was difficult because of cloud cover but eventually confirmed that some of the targets had been destroyed. Qaddafi later claimed he had been wounded and his adopted daughter killed, but there was never any proof that either claim was true.

This strike promoted the concept that if aircraft carriers and land-based strike aircraft were available nearby, the United States could use its technological superiority to carry out attacks with few losses. The close coordination and nearly flawless integration of air force and navy aircraft during this operation was a great improvement over the slipshod approach taken in Iran and Grenada. The attack had the desired effect. Because the personal impact on Qadaffi was evidently so great, his overt support of terror attacks ceased. The raid demonstrated that the United States could respond effectively to the terrorist menace if it used swift and decisive force.

CHAPTER 7

Escort and Retaliation in the Persian Gulf

1986–1988

In 1908 the Anglo-Iranian Oil Company discovered the first major oil deposits in southwest Iran. Britain, still the dominant world power, recognized that oil from these vast fields would soon be critical to the Royal Navy's new fleet of oil-burning supercombatants like the *Dreadnought*. Just as tall New England white pine for masts and royal oak for keel timbers had been necessary in previous centuries, the newly discovered Persian oil fields would become crucial to the continued rule of the seas.

Vast quantities of oil were discovered in Iraq in 1923 but were exploited at a slower pace than in Iran. Although oil was discovered in Kuwait in 1938, it wasn't produced in large quantities until after World War II; however, from the early 1950s Kuwait was the largest oil producer in the Persian Gulf until it was surpassed by Saudi Arabia in 1963. Oil production in the gulf region was dominated by British companies until after World War II, when American firms became more involved. By the end of the war American Standard Oil of California and Texaco had gained control of all foreign oil concessions in Bahrain and Saudi Arabia. In 1947 an economic watershed occurred: U.S. oil consumption exceeded domestic production for the first time, and America became an oil importer.

In July 1947 Admiral Chester Nimitz, the chief of Naval Operations, ordered contingency plans to be made for the defense of

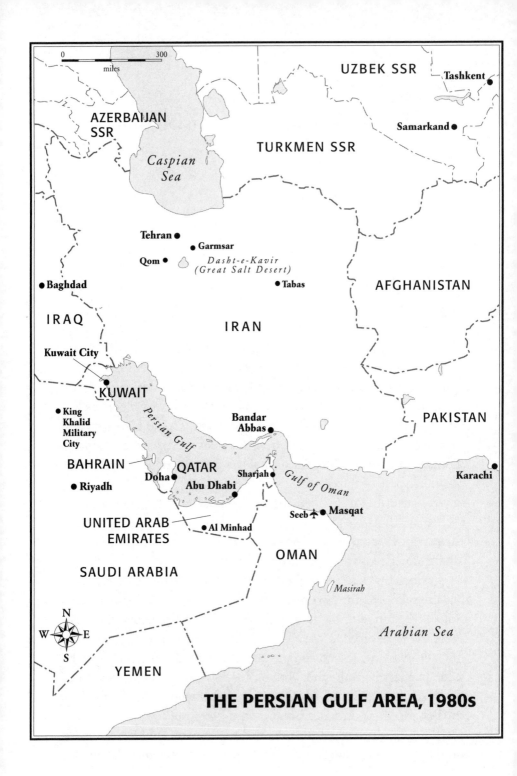

THE PERSIAN GULF AREA, 1980s

Bahrain. On January 1, 1949, President Truman established the Persian Gulf Area Command, which included the Arabian Peninsula, the Indian subcontinent, the Red Sea, the Persian Gulf, and the Indian Ocean north of the equator. The U.S. Navy established a permanent flagship with two destroyers as escorts and began what would become a long-standing continuous maritime presence. By 1956 the U.S. Navy was conducting joint military operations with Iran. The modest mission of the newly christened commander, Middle East Force, was coordination and communications: "With the development of the petroleum industry in the Persian Gulf area there has been a significant increase of shipping, particularly tanker; in order to coordinate ship movements and to provide adequate communications facilities, it has become necessary to maintain a station ship in this area."[1]

In the 1960s under the Central Treaty Organization, which had been expanded to include Britain, Iran, Pakistan, and Turkey as members, the United States was conducting annual naval maneuvers designed partially to fill the vacuum created by the British withdrawal from east of Suez. At this juncture the United States had two options: (1) to fill the power vacuum and assume the British role of protecting the Persian Gulf states or (2) to remain peripherally involved with a lesser security commitment. The choice initially fell to President Richard M. Nixon, who had already inherited an overextended security role in Southeast Asia. The Nixon Doctrine called for the United States to strengthen and support regional powers and not to assume direct security responsibility for any region in the world.

In the Persian Gulf region the Nixon Doctrine took the form of the "two-pillar" policy, whereby the United States labored to build regional security through vigorous defense of friendly regimes in Iran and Saudi Arabia. Under this doctrine America unabashedly poured sophisticated arms into both of these oil-rich countries. The collapse of the Iranian shah's regime in 1979 caught America by surprise and ended that doctrine with a sharp blow. The seizure of the American embassy in Tehran and the long hostage crisis that followed resulted in a bolstering of the naval presence in the area; in 1979 the U.S. Middle East Force was enlarged to a permanent deployment of five warships supported by the occasional surge to two aircraft carrier battle groups in the northern Arabian Sea. President Reagan not only supported but also reinforced the Carter Doctrine that called for war to save Persian Gulf oil if necessary.

When the Iran-Iraq War erupted in 1980 and the Soviets increased their forces in Afghanistan, President Reagan reaffirmed the Carter Doctrine and accelerated the buildup of the U.S. Rapid Deployment Force. America strengthened its military position by improving the base on the British island of Diego Garcia in the Indian Ocean and put on the fast track negotiations with the states of Oman, Egypt, Kenya, and Somalia for communications and logistic access to facilities for future contingencies in the region. On January 1, 1983, Reagan created a new joint military command called Central Command, with headquarters in Tampa, Florida, which would command all U.S. military forces earmarked for the Persian Gulf region, including the long-established Middle East Force. President Reagan further expanded the Carter Doctrine by declaring that any threat to the friendly Saudi Arabian government was a peril to U.S. interests. He further declared that America intended to keep the Strait of Hormuz open against any threat to international shipping.

The American perception of the threat depended on two main contingencies: (1) an outside power intervening in Iran either directly or by encouraging the establishment of a Soviet puppet state and (2) one of the regional powers—such as Iran in 1979 or Iraq in 1990—running amok in the region. The initial Reagan plan had a goal of building a capability to introduce five U.S. ground divisions, or one hundred thousand troops, into the region within one month, to be fully instituted by 1987.

Two fundamental policy factions divided the Reagan administration: One viewed the gulf problem primarily as a cold war, East–West confrontation. The other interpreted the primary threat to stability as an indigenous problem of the dynamics of the Persian Gulf States' social, political, and economic interests. As it turned out the latter was indeed the lasting issue—the former disappeared with the demise of the Soviet Union.

The Iran-Iraq War stretched through eight years, a vast bloody slaughter gradually edging the region to the brink of chaos. Kuwait, Saudi Arabia, and other Persian Gulf States were aiding Saddam Hussein financially by covertly shipping Soviet arms to Iraq; a number of unscrupulous Western businesses were doing the same. To further complicate the situation, arms from Eastern Europe and the Soviet Union were unloaded in the Red Sea port of Jidda, Saudi Arabia, and in the Persian Gulf port of Kuwait City and taken by truck into Iraq. Quite predictably, Iran reacted by accelerating attacks on and harassment of all gulf merchant ships, including neutral merchantmen from states overtly helping Iraq. Occasional raids on merchant ships had been occurring since 1983, but in 1986, the sixth year of the war, the attacks increased drastically.

The Iranian navy was well equipped with ships and weapons that had been supplied during Iran's days of romance with the West. Their inventory included small, heavily armed Swedish Boghammer patrol boats operated apparently autonomously by zealous revolutionary guards, a paramilitary force more fanatical and ideologically pure than the regular Iranian military, with little government control. Kuwaitis and Saudis were suffering more and more at the hands of Iran, but they did not fight back. They seemed content to absorb losses for fear of further alienating Iran. Iran began to attack all merchant ships trading with Kuwait to intimidate that country and punish its neighbors for providing political and financial support to Iraq. At the time Kuwait was the third-largest oil producer in the world, behind Saudi Arabia and Iraq.

Iraq, too, escalated the violence with attacks on merchant shipping in the gulf to counter Iranian interests. During 1986 Iraq attacked sixty-six ships in the gulf, twice as many as the total during the previous year, and Iran struck forty-one, which was three times the previous year's number. As the shipping security situation deteriorated, concern for the continued safe flow of oil to the world increased proportionally.

During this increase in hostilities, the U.S. Middle East Force, permanently stationed in the Persian Gulf, found itself in a war zone, but forced to stand by as unarmed merchant ships of all nations were struck repeatedly. Usually the Iranians attacked in such a manner as to maximize casualties among the crew and not necessarily to sink the ships. While the ships of the Middle East Force watched over American-flagged and -owned vessels, their rules of engagement allowed them to use force only in self-defense.

Kuwait expressed concern about its losses and risks at sea to the Gulf Cooperation Council. Its members were not happy about inviting a superpower into their circle, but recommended that Kuwait ask the United States rather than the Soviet Union for assistance. In an act of desperation, after a year of suffering unrelenting attacks, Kuwait requested in December 1986 that the United States escort its tankers under the American flag for protection. Unlike the other gulf nations, the Kuwaitis had up to this point continued to use their own flag on the tankers rather than reflagging them with neutral colors to protect them from increasing strikes by the Iranians or Iraqis. The Kuwaitis also quietly requested help from the Soviet Union.

The American relationship with Kuwait had been ambivalent prior to this time. Kuwait's free-market economy and heavy investment of its oil profits in Europe and America made it economically aligned with the West; however, its political hostility to Israel caused disruptions, some mandated by Congress, in the modest U.S. assistance program to Kuwait. Since the 1970s the United States had been quietly providing a specially built Skyhawk bomber, the Hawk air-defense system, vehicles, and other logistic systems to Kuwait. The situation was complicated by the almost 80 percent Palestinian population in Kuwait, and Congress was reluctant to authorize the sale of the more sophisticated arms that Kuwait requested. The Soviets, on the other hand, were gladly selling arms to all buyers.

Secretary of Defense Weinberger supported the reflagging and escort scheme largely as a measure to prevent the Soviets from gaining influence in the area. For clearly economic reasons it was not in America's interest to see the Iran-Iraq War widen. The United States found Iraq useful in checking Iran's export of revolution. However, while there was little popular sentiment in America for Iran after the

hostage ordeal, the Soviet Union's massive military equipment shipments to Iraq put the United States in an awkward position. Iraq was
a Soviet client; therefore, U.S. leaders did not wish to overtly support
Iraq, even though Saudi Arabia was already doing so. Still, the increase of attacks on merchant shipping was certainly contrary to
America's historical interest in freedom of the seas, and countering
this terrorism at sea offered a way to strengthen U.S. influence in the
region.

Thus the American rationale for entering the fray was twofold:
One group, led by Weinberger, claimed that the overriding issue was
the enforcement of freedom and security of the seas and the mini-
mization of Soviet influence in the area. The other side reflected the
philosophy of Admiral William J. Crowe, Jr., the chairman of the
Joint Chiefs of Staff, who was an experienced Arabist and former
commander of the Middle East Force. He said: "[I]t seemed to me
that reflagging would go a long way toward mending our fences in
the region. . . . My conclusion, then, was that we should go into the
Persian Gulf, not because of freedom of the seas, and not because we
didn't want the Soviets there, but because it was the best chance we
had to repair our Arab policy and to make some significant headway
in an area where it was absolutely crucial for us to forge the strongest
ties we could manage—despite the congressional undermining."[2]

If the United States turned down the Kuwaiti reflagging request,
the Soviet Union could end up as the sole guarantor of security of
the Persian Gulf States. When U.S. officials learned that Kuwait had
also asked the Soviets for help, they realized that the request may
have been a clever ploy to ensure U.S. cooperation. The Soviet Union
could quietly agree to assist without suffering through endless congressional discussions and front-page publicity. As self-sufficient oil
producers, the Soviets could be expected to respond to the reflagging
request strictly in the role of spoiler. In early March 1987 the Soviet
Union agreed to lease three of its oil tankers to Kuwait.

The U.S. Congress also had difficulty facing up to charges that
American arms policies usually favored Israel against the Arab states.
Congress was worried that reflagging and escorting would enmesh

the United States in the larger Iran-Iraq War. President Reagan nevertheless agreed to the Kuwaiti request on March 10, 1987, and set in action Operation Earnest Will under Marine Corps General George B. Crist, commander in chief of the Central Command area. Kuwait agreed to pay for a portion of the fuel the United States would use during the reflagging operations.

The Goldwater-Nichols Defense Reorganization Act of 1986 had given the chairman of the Joint Chiefs of Staff and American Unified Commanders the authority to tailor command and control to fit special circumstances. Admiral Crowe put that authority to work and organized a force tailored for use in the compact area of the Persian Gulf. It was no small undertaking. The organization and execution of offensive operations in this confined area of disparate political and religious factions called for new and unorthodox planning and initiative. It was fortunate indeed that the United States had a maritime innovator and a man experienced in that area at the helm of the Joint Chiefs of Staff. Admiral Crowe not only was an Arabist but also had experience working with unorthodox military formations when he commanded the American Riverine Forces in Southeast Asia.

On May 3 one of the Soviet tankers leased to Kuwait hit a mine. An Iraqi aircraft attacked the destroyer USS *Stark* with two French Exocet missiles on May 17, killing thirty-seven American sailors. But for the extraordinary battle damage-control measures taken by the surviving crew, the ship would have sunk. Although the strike was an apparent case of misidentification, the event outraged America and sparked renewed interest in protecting all gulf shipping from the increased threat. In mid-June President Reagan predicted that if the United States failed to act promptly to protect shipping in the Persian Gulf, the Soviet Union certainly would increase its support. Within one week the United States informed Kuwait that it would escort Kuwaiti tankers, which would be reflagged with the American colors, an extremely complex and hazardous mission in the midst of a full-scale war. During this period Iraq was attacking oil refineries and major cities in Iran, including the capital, Tehran, while Iran launched repeated ground offensives against the Iraqi army; both sides suffered massive casualties on the scale of a world war. Iraq was using chemical weapons against Iran, and both countries continued attacks on shipping in the Persian Gulf.

In May 1987 the merchant ships *Ethnic* (Greek) and *Marshall Chuykov* (Soviet) struck mines, and in June *Primrose* and *Stena Parker* (both American owned and Liberian registered) struck mines near Kuwait. In August the unescorted *Texaco Caribbean,* carrying a load of Iranian oil under a Panamanian flag, struck a mine in the Gulf of Oman. That year Iraq struck seventy-six ships in the gulf; Iran attacked eighty-seven, which was more than twice the number during the preceding year.

The United States needed to overcome major obstacles while preparing for intervention in the Persian Gulf. The navy was equipped and trained to fight in open waters, yet the gulf was extremely confined. Radar and communications were compressed because of the small operating area. As shown by the *Stark* incident, the situation demanded rapid response and a set of concrete rules of engagement that precluded the slightest indecision or hesitation. Distances were short, missile warning times were brief, and endless vigilance was extremely vital. A moment's hesitation in reacting to an inbound air threat could result in a disastrous encounter with an Iranian, Iraqi, or other fanatical terrorist attacker.

The legal aspects of reflagging were also complex. The predominant assessment by American intelligence was that intervention would infuriate the Iranians and possibly result in an outbreak of worldwide terrorist attacks against which American forces were ill defended. Many in Congress feared the gulf would erupt into unbridled chaos. The vast American intelligence bureaucracy was slow to accept that Iran might be undergoing a radical change in policy, and analysts tended to parrot the opinions of the large number of disaffected Iranian exiles.

In late July 1987 the commander of the U.S. Middle East Force requested naval special warfare support. Central Command approved and brought in forces from the newly formed Joint Special Operations Command, which had been established on April 13, 1987. Six Mark II patrol boats, two SEAL platoons, and other Special Boat teams arrived in August. At the same time, six new sound-quieted army MH-6 and AH-6 special operations helicopters with thirty-nine men were deployed. These units began to operate immediately from the helicopter decks of navy ships in support of the convoy operations. Later the Middle East Force converted two oil service barges named the *Hercules* and the *Wimbrown VII* to serve as mobile sea bases, avoiding the need to station men and equipment ashore and subject them to the threat of terrorist action. This arrangement also avoided practical obstacles. The Special Forces operated from the mobile sea platforms together with the conventional U.S. naval forces in an attempt to clear the convoy routes from covert Iranian mining and attacks by the numerous small Boghammer patrol craft. Each mobile sea platform housed 150 men, 10 small boats, and 3 special helicopters, with fuel, ammunition, equipment, and workshops to support the operation. Fully operational by October 1987, the barges were donated without cost by Kuwait. Stationed between Bahrain and Kuwait and just off the Saudi Arabian coast in an interlocking system for convoy protection, they virtually ended Iranian small-boat activity in the northern Persian Gulf.

A carrier battle group was stationed outside the Strait of Hormuz under the the U.S. Middle East Force commander. The convoying operation would be the first for the U.S. Navy since the early days of World War II. During this entire escort period fewer than half of the warships in the Persian Gulf were from the United States. The British escorted more British-flagged ships than the Americans did, and each of the European countries that assisted did so with a larger percentage of its navy than the United States used. At the height of the convoying campaign there were generally forty U.S. warships, fifteen French, ten Soviet, eight Italian, and twelve British, as well as assorted Belgian and Dutch minesweepers, operating within the gulf. During the fighting to come, the Iraqis relied primarily on airpower while the Iranians used a mix of ships, including two missile frigates and fifty Boghammer patrol boats, and occasionally aircraft—usually U.S. F-4s or F-14s.

The escort operations began on July 23, 1987. A convoy of reflagged ships entered the Strait of Hormuz headed north with the cruiser USS *Fox*, the destroyer USS *Kidd*, and the frigate *Crommelin* escorting three empty tankers and the four-hundred-thousand-ton *Al Rekkah*, renamed the *Bridgeton*. Saudi Arabia had agreed to support the convoy operations with Airborne Warning and Control System (AWACS) aircraft. As the convey passed northbound through the strait, it was detected and tracked by Chinese-made Iranian Silkworm missiles. Two U.S.-built Iranian F-4 fighter-bombers approached the convoy and circled at five thousand feet. The escort *Kidd* tracked the missile launchers with its missile radars, and, in accordance with the rules of engagement, warned them off. When the Iranian fighters approached within three seconds of the firing arc, they disengaged and withdrew. The next day the *Bridgeton* struck a mine.[3] Although there were no casualties and the ship made it to port, the dangers were now evident.

The first American-escorted convoy used Saudi minesweepers, Kuwaiti helicopters, and American divers to clear the channel to Kuwaiti waters, but Iran kept on laying new mines. The navy employed two Kuwaiti tugs and a cable to clear mines until more minesweeping equipment arrived. The continuing threat of Iranian mines caused the U.S. Navy to deploy its own minesweeping ships. The Middle East Force announced that any ships caught laying mines in the Persian Gulf would be destroyed. The British, Dutch, French, Italian, and Belgian navies all sent minesweepers.

On August 8 the new army helicopters escorted the third convoy of merchant ships. Iran attacked the Italian *Jolly Rubino* on September 2 and shortly afterward the British *Gentle Breeze*. U.S. special operations patrol boats began escort missions on September 9, and on September 20 intelligence reported that the *Iran Ajr*, an Iranian coastal shallow-water cargo ship, was leaving Bandar Abbas heading south in shipping lanes where convoys were working every two or three days. The destroyer USS *Jarrett* entered the area with special operations helicopters aboard and sighted mines on the Iranian ship's deck. As the Iranian crew began launching them by hand, American sailors watched from a silent helicopter. The next night the helicopters attacked while a platoon of SEALs from the USS *Guadalcanal* moved in and captured the boat. After boarding they found documents indicating where the crew had laid mines. In the brief action three Iranian crewmen were killed and two drowned. The navy returned the bodies to Iran with the help of Oman and the International Red Cross and later sank the boat in deep water.

After the mobile sea platforms went into operation in October 1987, their crews quickly determined the Iranians' pattern of activity: Iranian boats hid by day near oil and gas separation platforms inside Iranian territorial waters and by night ventured into the Middle Shoals near the tanker navigation aids, awaiting prey. On October 8, in their first action against the Iranians from their platforms, special operations helicopters followed by patrol craft successfully ambushed the Iranian boats, sinking three. On October 16 the reflagged tanker *Sea Isle City* was struck by an Iranian Silkworm missile near the oil terminal outside Kuwait City, injuring seventeen crewmen and the American captain. Four American destroyers attacked the missile site and wrecked it and two oil platforms in the Rostam oil field.

The struggle within the confined gulf waters continued, but the scales began gradually to tilt in the favor of the intervening allied forces. On April 14, 1988, approximately sixty-five miles east of Bahrain, the frigate USS *Samuel B. Roberts* struck a mine that blew a hole thirty by twenty-three feet in its hull; ten sailors were injured. In retaliation the United States attacked and sank the Iranian frigate *Zahan* and damaged a second frigate. During the battle an Iranian missile patrol boat from the port of Bushir launched a missile against the cruiser USS *Wainwright*. The cruiser sank the attacker.

The American forces watched for further Iranian reactions to the attacks and sinkings. After a period of relative quiet in July, a grand crescendo to the entire conflict ended in one less-than-glorious detonation. While patrolling in the Strait of Hormuz, the American frigate USS *Montgomery* went to the aid of a freighter that had been attacked by Iranian gunboats. Shortly after responding, the *Montgomery* was suddenly engulfed in the midst of a group of thirteen Iranian Boghammers that had been harassing several other merchant ships sailing through the strait. The cruiser USS *Vincennes* heard the report of the *Montgomery*'s encounter with the patrol boats while passing through the strait en route to Bahrain. The *Vincennes* abruptly returned to the vicinity and launched her helicopter to assist the *Montgomery*. When the helicopter came in sight of the gunboats, the Iranians opened fire. The two American ships pursued the gunboats and in the ensuing melee, which took place in and out of Iranian territorial waters, the *Vincennes*'s radar suddenly detected an aircraft taking off from an airfield in Bandar Abbas, Iran, that was used for both military and civilian flights. Knowing that Iranian F-14 Tomcats were located there, the commanding officer of the *Vincennes*, Captain Will Rogers, grew concerned and prepared to fire on the aircraft should it approach his ship. As the aircraft lifted off, it began to approach the cruiser at high speed. The *Vincennes* challenged the still-unidentified aircraft and warned it repeatedly to turn away, but, as was discovered later, neither the pilots nor the Iranian air controllers were tuned in to the same radio frequencies as the U.S. ships. As a result, the aircraft was never fully identified, nor did its pilots hear the American warnings. Believing that the swiftly approaching aircraft might have been an Iranian fighter mounting a suicide attack, Rogers stood ready to shoot but waited, even though still taking fire from the Iranian patrol boats. When the approaching aircraft was nine miles from his ship, he gave the order to shoot and downed the airplane with two Standard surface-to-air missiles.

The aircraft turned out to be a civilian Iranian Airbus en route to the United Arab Emirates with 290 passengers and crew; all were lost. American forces also damaged five of the attacking gunboats and struck two oil platforms in the Sirri and Sassan oil fields during the engagement. The shootdown was regrettable but unavoidable. However, unfortunate as the incident was, the United States had taken drastic action and unintentionally had scored a major blow against Iran. After the very heavy and no doubt demoralizing loss, Iranian attacks against gulf shipping dropped precipitously.

On July 18, 1988, Iran finally accepted the United Nations–brokered cease-fire, and on August 20 the Iran-Iraq War ended. The U.S. escort operations in the Persian Gulf, coupled with intervention by other Western countries and the Soviet Union, were successful,

PART FOUR

George H. W. Bush: Using a Big Stick

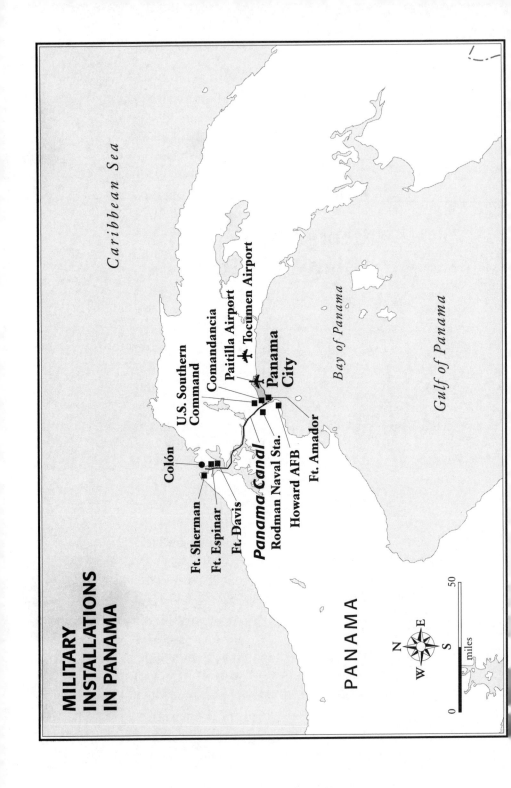

MILITARY
INSTALLATIONS
IN PANAMA

Caribbean Sea

Colón

U.S. Southern
Command

Comandancia

Paitilla Airport

Tocumen Airport

Panama
City

Ft. Sherman

Ft. Espinar

Ft. Davis

Panama Canal

Rodman Naval Sta.

Howard AFB

Ft. Amador

Bay of Panama

Gulf of Panama

PANAMA

N
W E
S

0   50
miles

CHAPTER 8

Storming Panama

December 1989

The U.S. military intervention in Panama in December 1989 was a unique departure for Americans from the long-standing cold war role of containing the Soviet Union. During the final months of that year the world had witnessed the sudden fissures rending the Iron Curtain. The Berlin Wall was down. East Germany's leaders were losing confidence in the survival of their regime. With their ally imploding, the Soviets were losing a base from which their nineteen crack army divisions had been poised as the main threat against the U.S. military and NATO for nearly forty-five years. Elsewhere, the invasion of Panama came to constitute the prototype for military action that America would be using in the coming years: small, highly mobile armed forces tailored to resolve policy disputes rapidly and cleanly with decisive force.

The American intervention in 1989 was precipitated by the collapse of law and order inside Panama and by genuine concern for the well-being and security of more than thirty-four thousand Americans who resided there. Unlike the events that catapulted U.S. forces to intervene in Grenada in 1983, the prelude to the Panama invasion extended over a longer period, which permitted more careful planning and the honing of intervention strategies already in existence. The operation integrated conventional forces with the new Joint Special Operations Command in a single successful effort. The long period

of distrust between these forces was finally overcome, and this operation would set a pattern for successful cooperation in the future.

In 1510 Vasco Núñez de Balboa, a Spanish adventurer, landed in
Panama and founded the first successful Spanish settlement there.
Panama became a part of the Spanish Viceroyalty of New Grenada,
which also included what is now Colombia. Since its independence
from Spain, Colombia had never been able to rule Panama effectively. During the nineteenth century, Panamanians revolted more
than fifty times against their Colombian masters. On two occasions,
in 1855–1856 and 1885, when Panamanian rebels were close to success, the United States intervened militarily to protect American interests, ending the revolts. After a vicious civil war in 1899–1902
seriously weakened Colombia, the Panamanians again prepared to revolt. With assistance from the United States and a Frenchman named
Philippe Bunau-Varilla, the Panamanians staged a successful uprising
and gained independence in November 1903. They entrusted Bunua-
Varilla to negotiate with the United States for the Panama Canal
Concession. He signed a treaty that gave the United States control
over the ten-mile-wide Panama Canal Zone as a protectorate. The
United States would have the use in perpetuity and would occupy
and control the Canal zone for an initial payment of $10 million and
an annual fee of $250,000. The arrangement continued for the con-
struction of the canal and until 1977, when President Carter negotiated the transfer of the canal to Panama in a treaty ratified in 1978 by
the U.S. Senate. Under that treaty, by the year 2000 the United States
would withdraw all military troops from the canal zone and transfer
all control of the canal to Panama.

The U.S. military involvement in Panama had intensified since
1903 when the government sent marines to guard the railroad across
the Isthmus of Panama. The marines remained and, when reinforced
in 1911 by the U.S. Army's Tenth Infantry Regiment, provided security for the construction of the Panama Canal. The troops were stationed in Fort Otis on the Pacific side of the isthmus. In 1915 the

army formed the Panama Canal Department, which was headquartered on Ancon Hill in Panama City. The headquarters was eventually moved to Quarry Heights, where it remained until 1989. Over time the headquarters also came to include the U.S. Southern Command, which was responsible for the activities of the U.S. armed forces working on various projects and plans in Latin America.

During World War II more than sixty-eight thousand troops were stationed in Panama to defend the canal, which was of major strategic importance to the United States for its role in both commerce and the movement of naval forces between the Atlantic and Pacific Oceans. Despite intrigue and rumors of invasion by the Japanese, the canal remained intact, unharmed, and safely in American hands throughout the war. After the war, the large U.S. military presence was reduced; by 1959 the total had dropped to just over six thousand troops. Many of the bases outside the canal zone that had been used by the Americans during the war were returned to the government of Panama. By 1963 the joint Southern Command maintained an average strength of about ten thousand troops in the entire canal zone. The primary mission of the headquarters was the defense of the canal, but it had gradually taken on the added tasks of providing security assistance to other Central and South American countries and designing and running training and education programs for their military forces. The mission had also expanded to include interaction with Latin American officers intended to encourage support of U.S. objectives in the region, including those in the sensitive areas of human rights and narcotics.

As in many small postcolonial countries, strong nationalism began to sprout in Panama. The Panamanian Guardia Nacional, a local military security force, had become the hotbed for a new Panamanian political movement. The Guardia had developed a unique identity and autonomy from the aristocracy that had originally supplied its senior and controlling leadership. Since the end of the war, tensions had grown between U.S. forces and the Guardia. These reached crisis levels in 1964 when American soldiers fired into a crowd, killing twenty-eight protesters and wounding three hundred, during a civil disturbance. The Guardia, having adopted a growing animosity toward the U.S. military presence, were suspected of having encouraged the riots.

The longtime Panamanian President Arnulfo Arias was toppled in 1968 in a military coup led by Omar Torrijos, a popular military leader supported by a young and mercurial officer named Manuel Antonio Noriega. Noriega was aggressive and soon muscled his way into the leadership of the Guardia and consolidated his influence over all the Panamanian military and police. He had worked with the U.S. Army for many years as an intelligence officer and later as a Central Intelligence Agency source providing information against the Nicaraguan Sandinistas. Torrijos ran the country with a military junta and in 1977 successfully negotiated the turnover of the Panama Canal and Canal Zone by the end of the century. After Torrijos died in a plane crash in 1981, the government of Panama endured a period of dynamic struggles with the Guardia, of which Noriega had become commander in 1983. Noriega renamed the guard the Panamanian Defense Force, or PDF. Six months after he assumed control over the new military formation, Noriega amassed significant political and military power, yet always maintained a civilian representative in the political front. When the government called for elections in May 1983, Noriega's PDF controlled most of the election apparatus, and his front man, Nicolás Ardito-Barletta, won the presidency handily. During this period of political intrigue the Reagan government was focused primarily on containing the perceived Communist threat embodied in the Sandinistas in Central America and viewed the de facto control by Noriega and Barletta as a known quantity and not a significant threat to regional stability. By 1983 the PDF had controlled Panamanian political life for more than twenty years, and although it had been created as a solid institution, over the intervening years Noriega had transformed it into an instrument of criminal activities.

Noriega and Barletta soon parted ways, and Noreiga began to run seriously afoul of U.S. interests in Panama. He became deeply involved with the illicit drug trade and formed a strong alliance with some of the most notorious Colombian cartel leaders, including the drug lord Pablo Escobar Gaviria. Dr. Hugo Spadafora, a respected Panamanian politician who openly opposed Noriega, began to speak out publicly against his blatant drug trafficking, focusing worldwide attention on Panama and its shadow dictator. When Spadafora was found brutally murdered, the event triggered a long and complex power struggle culminating with Noriega's emergence as de facto dictator. Over time his conduct grew more and more distasteful, and eventually he unleashed an anti-American movement reminiscent of the 1964 period: Demonstrations and open harassment of American citizens reached an alarming level. As the situation in Panama deteriorated and one failed coup attempt followed another, U.S. Army General Maxwell Thurman, the commander of the Southern Command, began to update plans for intervention. He picked U.S. Army General Kurt Stiner, commander of the Eighteenth Airborne Corps, to lead a strong Joint Task Force and directed him to prepare a plan for possible intervention in Panama that could take place anytime prior to the turnover of the canal in 2000.

The mission to unseat the Noriega regime was unique among other recent American interventions. More than thirty-four thousand U.S. citizens resided in Panama, and the United States had many large military bases inside the canal zone and combat units already on the scene. The U.S. military had also enjoyed a long-standing relationship with Noriega's PDF: Many PDF soldiers had attended American military schools, and many Americans had been involved in the training and equipping of the Panamanian military.

The proposed intervention in Panama was designed to achieve three vigorous objectives: to protect Americans and property; to capture Noriega, who had already been indicted in the United States as a drug dealer, and deliver him to legal authorities; and to immobilize the PDF.

More than a year earlier, on February 4, 1988, the U.S. attorney general had obtained from a grand jury in Tampa, Florida, an indictment naming the PDF as a criminal enterprise and Manuel Antonio Noriega specifically as a defendant. By April 1988 the Reagan administration had also imposed economic sanctions in an effort to create public pressure on Noriega. The sanctions succeeded in damaging the economic lot of ordinary Panamanians, but Noriega was unmoved by their suffering. With a U.S. federal indictment over his head, he was not about to leave office to face trial in the United States. Probably inadvertently, the U.S. government thus raised the stakes and reduced its options in Panama to one: the use of military force.[1]

The idea that the United States would take the drastic action of mounting a full-scale invasion of a country to capture its leader, however illegally he had come to power, may in retrospect seem absurd. However, after a series of attempted coups by disgruntled Panamanian military officers, President George H. W. Bush decided it was time to act. Noriega's indictment in Florida for drug offenses rendered intervention more palatable to those who might otherwise be opposed outright to the action; the report that Noriega was planning urban guerrilla attacks against Americans in Panama further justified taking decisive action. As the situation deteriorated and real concern for the safety of Americans in Panama increased, President Bush quietly took action. He ordered nineteen hundred army troops and marines sent to Panama as a show of force. He then sent the U.S. Army Delta Detachment and U.S. Navy SEAL Team Six, both antiterrorist units, into the area to be in place to respond to anti-American actions by the local Panamanian forces. The Southern Command began moving convoys throughout Panama in a deliberate show of force and to exercise U.S. rights under the Panama Canal Treaty.

The secondary objectives were to replace Noriega's ruling clique with a democratically elected government. Finally, the last phase was to reconstruct the PDF with a viable and acceptable leadership. In May 1989, despite the presence of a group of international monitors, Noriega, who had a long history of opposing free elections, had simply terminated the election when it appeared that the opposition had won more than 75 percent of the vote. Noriega ordered his forces to harass and beat the opposing candidates and finally declared himself the winner.

General Stiner's plan called for attacking seventeen objectives simultaneously. The forces intended for the intervention relied heavily on the troops already in the country who were experts on Panamanian geography and society. They included the U.S. Army 193d Light Infantry Brigade, a battalion of mechanized infantry from the Fifth Infantry Division, a platoon of Sheridan light tanks, and two companies of marines. Reinforcements to be flown in during the intervention included three battalions of the Seventy-fifth Ranger Regiment, the entire Eighty-second Airborne Division, a battalion of the Seventh Infantry Division, and a brigade of Military Police. Additional forces from the Joint Special Operations Command would include two SEAL teams and two units from the Seventh Special Forces Group. Air transport, tactical fighters, bombers, gunships, and helicopters would support the forces under the command of U.S. Air Forces Panama. An extraordinary number of aircraft would participate in the assault flying in an extremely high-density environment at night without running lights. The bulk of them would be ferrying troops for landing and parachute drops without radar. General Thurman's planners devised a complex airspace control plan in which fixed-wing aircraft, helicopters, and missiles and projectiles were given different designated altitudes during entry and exit routes. This would be one of the most high-density air operations in the history of the American military, and there would be little room for mistakes.

The Delta and SEAL commandos were poised to respond forcibly in case the PDF took any action to block or in any way harass the convoys, or, in the worst case, take Americans hostage. The previous decade had witnessed the proliferation elsewhere of brutal terrorist acts and kidnappings often aimed at the United States. President Bush was intent on preventing such actions on America's own doorstep. Bush had occupied senior government positions during most of the military engagements since the *Mayaguez* seizure, when he was an envoy in China. During the Beirut intervention and Grenada invasion he was vice president. He had a strong sense that America should apply swift retribution in such situations, and a group of senior defense and national security advisers shared his readiness.

Reagan's use of force in the past decade, sometimes less than a model of precision and efficiency, had succeeded in honing the military into an experienced and aggressive force consisting of a highly motivated and mobile light infantry and an effective conventional heavy armored and mechanized infantry. Bush's commitment of these revitalized units in Panama and later in the Persian Gulf would restore the dignity and pride of the U.S. armed forces.

The American invasion of Panama was unusually delicate and complex, but its execution finally showed that the American armed forces were incorporating all the lessons learned in the short but vicious interventions since the end of the Vietnam War. The concept was straightforward. A single commander on the ground would use overwhelming force and employ conventional and special operations troops to the full extent of their capabilities. The one lesson seared into the minds of all military commanders was the nearly impossible task of mounting a significant military force without having the fact trumpeted widely in the headlines of every American newspaper and on TV news programs. America's military actions had become a victim of its own free press. Unlike the experience in Grenada, the invasion of Panama would commence in total darkness to ensure that surprise was not compromised; it was not easy.

As the political situation in Panama deteriorated, final planning began for a military operation. The new chairman of the Joint Chiefs of Staff, U.S. Army General Colin Powell, had his own criteria for committing American troops to action, and once those standards had been met, he would not hesitate to use decisive force. Powell's experience on the National Security staff during the Reagan years had provided him with a superb background for taking the post as America's senior fighting man. With him at the helm, America could once again field the world's best-trained and -equipped fighting men with a new purpose and, above all, a clear understanding of the mission.

The immediate trigger for initiating action in Panama was the rapid increase in the harassment of American residents, including the wounding of one marine and the detention of a naval officer and the molestation of his wife by the PDF, which culminated in the shooting death of another marine, Lieutenant Robert Paz, on December 16, 1989. This series of incidents by the Panamanian military police and members of Panama's Dignity Battalions, essentially bands of thugs granted policing authority, brought the situation to a head. When Noriega was suddenly named supreme head of state by the Panamanian government, he declared that an open state of war existed with the United States. The wheels began to turn for a forceful U.S. takeover.

The plan called for augmenting the U.S. troops already in Panama, which had been quietly reinforced to a total of thirteen thousand over the weeks during the buildup of tensions. The Eighty-second Airborne Division, additional units from the Seventh Infantry Division, and Special Forces would also be brought in. A U.S. Marine company already in place in Panama was poised to take and hold the Bridge of the Americas over the Panama Canal. Special operations troops would track down and seize General Noriega, and the Delta Force would assault the Modelo Prison in Panama City to free Kurt Muse, a radio broadcaster who had been arrested and jailed there. Muse, a forty-year-old American citizen from Washington, D.C., who had been raised in Panama, had become disenchanted with the lack of freedom and poor human rights record of the regime and had begun a series of antigovernment radio broadcasts in Panama City called the Civic Crusade. Noriega had accused Muse of operating an underground propaganda radio station that had assisted his opposition during the election. Muse had been arrested and charged with crimes against security and of being an agent of the Central Intelligence Agency.

The U.S. takeover operation was set for 1:00 A.M. on December 20, 1989. The air force had assembled an armada of 285 aircraft for transporting the troops from the United States mainland and refueling the carriers en route. The new F-117 Stealth bomber made its combat debut by dropping two large bombs near a Panamanian barracks to intimidate and stun, not to hit, Noriega's troops as the operation's opening blow, and they were precisely on target. Before the

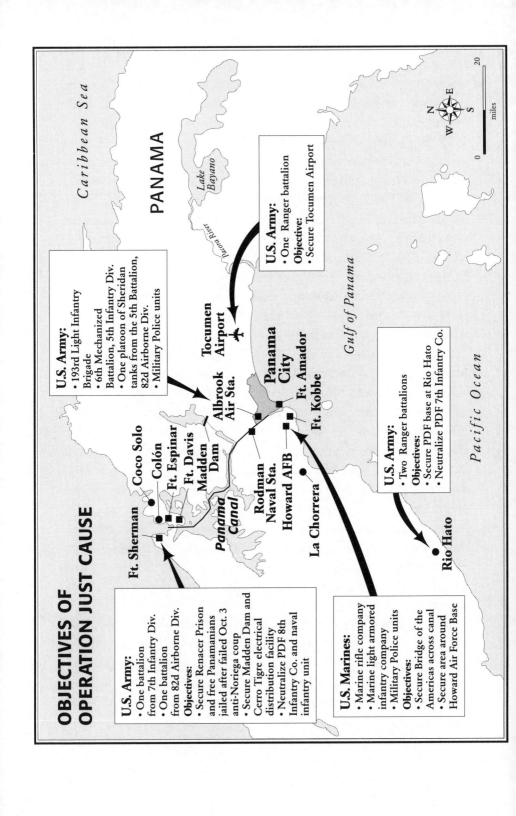

OBJECTIVES OF OPERATION JUST CAUSE

U.S. Army:
• One battalion from 7th Infantry Div.
• One battalion from 82d Airborne Div.
Objectives:
• Secure Renacer Prison and free Panamanians jailed after failed Oct. 3 anti-Noriega coup
• Secure Madden Dam and Cerro Tigre electrical distribution facility
• Neutralize PDF 8th Infantry Co. and naval infantry unit

U.S. Army:
• 193rd Light Infantry Brigade
• 6th Mechanized Battalion, 5th Infantry Div.
• One platoon of Sheridan tanks from the 5th Battalion, 82d Airborne Div.
• Military Police units

U.S. Army:
• One Ranger battalion
Objective:
• Secure Tocumen Airport

U.S. Marines:
• Marine rifle company
• Marine light armored infantry company
• Military Police units
Objectives:
• Secure Bridge of the Americas across canal
• Secure area around Howard Air Force Base

U.S. Army:
• Two Ranger battalions
Objectives:
• Secure PDF base at Rio Hato
• Neutralize PDF 7th Infantry Co.

Caribbean Sea

PANAMA

Lake Bayano

Bayano River

Gulf of Panama

Pacific Ocean

Ft. Sherman
Coco Solo
Colón
Ft. Espinar
Ft. Davis
Madden Dam
Panama Canal
Albrook Air Sta.
Tocumen Airport
Panama City
Ft. Amador
Ft. Kobbe
Rodman Naval Sta.
Howard AFB
La Chorrera
Rio Hato

N
W — E
S

0   20
miles

main assault more than one thousand special operations troops from all three services went into action against airports and key media and transportation sites.

Operation Just Cause was the first American military intervention to completely integrate conventional and special operations forces. Troopers from the line infantry units, such as the Panama-based 193d Infantry Brigade and the Fifth Infantry Division, went into combat simultaneously with special operations forces, each understanding the other's mission. When the first troops of the 193d swept out of their barracks after midnight on the day of the intervention, they went into action with members of the elite Delta Force. Armored personnel carriers of the Fifth Infantry Division ferried the Delta commandos into the heart of town, while the 193d Brigade and Fifth Division stormed Noriega's headquarters, the Comandancia.

The airborne assault consisted of two Ranger battalions parachuting from five hundred feet onto the Rio Hato Airfield to the south of Panama City. A third Ranger battalion dropped and secured Tocumen Airport to the east of Panama City. One battalion of the Eighty-second Airborne Division and the Seventh Infantry Division landed from helicopters on Fort Sherman on the north Atlantic side near Colón. The 193d Infantry Brigade, together with the Sixth Mechanized Battalion of the Fifth Infantry Division, a Sheridan tank platoon from the Eighty-second Airborne, and assorted Military Police units permanently stationed in Panama, attacked multiple targets in and around Panama City. One battalion of the Seventh Infantry and one battalion of the Eighty-second Airborne attacked Renacer Prison to free the political prisoners jailed there after the October 3 anti-Noriega coup. One marine rifle company and a light armored infantry company secured the Bridge of the Americas across the canal and Howard Air Force Base. The remainder of the Eighty-second Airborne arrived as reinforcements with the Sixteenth Military Police Battalion at Tocumen Airport after its capture by the Ranger battalion. The SEALs assaulted and blocked Paitilla Airfield, where Noriega kept a private Learjet.

The first-wave parachute drop of the Eighty-second Airborne began at Tocumen Airport at 2:11 A.M., twenty-five minutes later than planned. Icy weather had delayed the takeoff from Pope Air Force Base at Fort Bragg, North Carolina. The second wave arrived at 3:30 and the third at 4:30, both on time. They dropped without casualties from five hundred feet. The airborne troops achieved their objective even though 50 percent of their heavy equipment dropped by parachute, including tanks and other vehicles, landed in ten-foot-high elephant grass or in a swamp and was unusable.

Delta Force and other Special Forces teams went after Noriega, and one Delta unit forced its way into Modelo Prison to rescue Kurt Muse in an M-113 armored personnel carrier driven by members of B Company, Fourth Battalion, Sixth Infantry Regiment, Fifth Infantry Division. They easily freed Muse from the cell and planned to escape via the roof in an AH-6 Little Bird helicopter, but the helicopter was shot down and fell into the street below. A second armored personnel carrier rescued them. A SEAL team destroyed the high-speed naval patrol boats moored near Fort Amador in Balboa Harbor to prevent their use by Noriega to escape and to silence their large cannons. The SEALs swam in and placed explosive charges on their propeller shafts and blew them up at 1:00 A.M. in a spectacular explosion that rocked the downtown Panama City area.

A six-man team from the Central Intelligence Agency and the National Security Agency had set up a twenty-four-hour watch to follow the daily activity and movements of Noriega. The team reported directly to General Thurman in Panama. They successfully tracked General Noriega until 6:00 P.M. December 19, the day before the attack. He departed from Colón, on the Atlantic side of the canal, then went underground and disappeared. The Delta Force commandos raided all of Noriega's hideouts and villas on the night of the invasion but missed him by mere minutes. Noriega was a master at deception and apparently threw off the tracking team by transmitting decoy messages. When traveling, he would split his convoy, with one part heading off in one direction while the other took a different way. Although Noriega evaded the special operations forces for almost five days, moving an average of five times per night, his flight kept him from personally coordinating the PDF in reaction to the invasion. On December 24, four days after the invasion began, he turned himself in to the papal nunciature, or Vatican embassy, wearing running shorts and a T-shirt and carrying two AK-47s over his shoulders. Special Forces had mounted more than forty operations, in an attempt to catch him. At times they were within twenty minutes of his last position, even once bursting into a hideout to find his coffee warm and cigarettes still burning.

The Rangers parachuted successfully onto Rio Hato Airfield and the SEALs attacked Paitilla Airport while the Eighty-second Airborne dropped onto Torrijos International Airport. The smooth flow of the action, exactly as it was planned, was spoiled only by the frustrating failure to apprehend Noriega himself. The SEALs lost four men and thirteen were wounded during their assault on the airfield where Noriega kept his escape aircraft. A communications misunderstanding and a lucky burst of automatic weapons fire by a single PDF guard disrupted an almost perfect operation. This time the successful use of night landing and parachute drops had caught the enemy unable to respond, even though they were expecting some kind of attack.

One factor that contributed to the operation's success was the overwhelming support of the local population, who were grateful to be out from under the repressive control of Noriega and his PDF. Although there was a great deal of damage in the urban areas, large numbers of Panamanian troops surrendered when called on the telephone by U.S. Army psychological warfare propaganda teams. Most officers fled as soon as the U.S. forces began their assaults, leaving their men to fight alone. Although some resistance was fierce at the Comandancia, most attacks overwhelmed the resistance after brief exchanges of fire. The total special operation forces committed, including Delta, navy SEALs, Army Special Forces, Rangers, and air force Special Forces, reached 4,150. Eleven men of the Special Forces were killed. Of the remaining twenty-three thousand soldiers, twelve were killed. A total of 23 Americans soldiers and 3 civilians died, and 324 were wounded in the action. At least 314 Panamanian troops were killed and about 300 civilians died.

The invasion of Panama not only demonstrated U.S. resolve to pursue policy using military intervention but also reinforced the long-standing American efforts at containing Communist-inspired insurgency in Central America. Three months after the Panama invasion the Communist-supported Sandinista Party in Nicaragua was ejected from power at the ballot box, a remarkable event given the nature of the protracted struggle. While many Latin Americans understandably opposed U.S. intervention anywhere in the region, many leaders of the area quietly expressed satisfaction that Noriega was no longer in power. In a CBS News poll, 92 percent of Panamanian citizens supported the American intervention. As the New Year dawned, Noriega left Panama in custody and in disgrace, and America's support for its military reached a new post-Vietnam high.

CHAPTER 9

The Gulf War: Desert Shield

1990–1991

Not since the Grand Alliance of World War II has the modern world witnessed as full an array of allied democracies, assorted kingdoms, and principalities as the Americans amassed against Iraq in 1991. The impressive host of allies, all with widely divergent ideologies, pulled together painstakingly by President George H. W. Bush and the royal family of Saudi Arabia in the months following the invasion of Kuwait in August 1990, is not likely to be duplicated again. Today the polarization in the Middle East has split traditional allies so much that America's 2003 move against Iraq found fewer participants.

In 1988 Iraq had emerged more or less the winner from the bloody eight-year war with Iran, but its victory had been costly. Iraq had suffered roughly 350,000 casualties, and an additional 60,000 Iraqis had been taken prisoner by Iran. The Iraqi army, one of the world's largest, still had more than a million men in uniform and maintained a significant air force with modern equipment, including the French F-1, Soviet MiG-29s, and Soviet Su-24 fighter-bombers. Iraq possessed an extended-range surface-to-surface missile capability and a fondness for using it indiscriminately. The missile threat was limited to a crude Soviet-built system called the Scud, enhanced with a known arsenal of chemical weapons that Iraq had proved ruthless enough to employ in combat during the war against Iran. The Iraqi ground army, the largest in the Persian Gulf, was a considerable force, including the elite Republican Guard, the regular army, and the Popular Army, with five thousand main battle tanks, five thousand armored infantry vehicles, and three thousand artillery pieces larger than 100mm.

Iraq was $90 billion in debt after its war with Iran. Its leader, Saddam Hussein, was bitter against his neighbors Kuwait and the United Arab Emirates for compounding Iraq's debt by exceeding oil quotas set by the Organization of Petroleum Exporting Countries (OPEC) and thereby driving down the price of oil. Hussein also believed that Kuwait had cheated him of billions more in oil revenues by siphoning off more than $2.5 billion in oil from the shared Rumaila fields, which straddled the border between the countries. On February 23, 1990, during a meeting in Amman, Jordan, of the Arab Cooperation Council, which Egypt, North Yemen, Jordan, and Iraq had formed in February 1989 to create a unified bloc to resist Iranian hegemony, and again at an Arab summit in Baghdad, the Iraqi leader sought to gather support by accusing the United States of trying to dominate the Persian Gulf by supporting Israel. To oppose the United States and Israel, he called for a united Arab front and openly castigated Kuwait's Emir Jaber al-Ahmad al-Sabah for his stance on OPEC oil prices and quotas. Hussein also appeared to have already decided to move to seize Kuwait and to expand his coastline from 37 to 225 miles, gaining a major deepwater port in the process. The Iraqi leader had hinted earlier at his plans to isolate Kuwait by buying off other Arabs. Hussein offered Egyptian President Hosni Mubarak a part in a military coalition consisting of Iraq, Syria, Egypt, and Jordan, which would take over and divide up Kuwait and Saudi Arabia, awarding Egypt $5 million in spoils. Mubarak declined.[1] At the same time Hussein offered to give Jordan and Yemen portions of Saudi Arabia after he carved it up.

In early July 1990 Iraq began to deploy three divisions close to the Kuwaiti border. The world watched and wondered: Was Hussein up to his usual posturing, or was he preparing to strike? His behavior had been erratic over the years, and he was growing more and more unpredictable. He had surprised many analysts earlier when he unleashed chemical weapons against Iranian units on the front and again on his own people in the northern areas where Kurds had risen in defiance of his rule. When Hussein gave an address in Baghdad on July 17 in which he accused Kuwait and others of cheating Iraq out of oil revenues and of occupying Iraqi territory, his Republican Guard divisions were already poised on the border just north of Kuwait. By July 21 Hussein had more than three thousand military vehicles on the road heading toward the Kuwaiti border.

On August 1, when Kuwaiti and Iraqi leaders were discussing the issues again, in a last effort at reconciliation in Jidda, eight Republican Guard divisions—two armored, one mechanized, one special forces, and four infantry—were already positioned between the town of Basra on the Euphrates River and the Kuwaiti border. A total of 140,000 troops supported by fifteen hundred tanks and air force assets were ready to cross into Kuwait. U.S. intelligence had detected these movements, and the president was well aware of the proximity of these forces to the Kuwaiti border. Some analysts saw it as a bluff; others surmised that the deployments meant certain invasion. Although no one could predict Iraq's true intentions, the obvious deployments, difficult to mask in open desert terrain, triggered a reaction by senior American commanders in Tampa, Florida, at Central Command, which was responsible for American military forces in the Persian Gulf area. The command dusted off existing plans for responding to a crisis in that theater.[2] General Colin Powell, the chairman of the Joint Chiefs of Staff, directed General H. Norman Schwarzkopf, the commander in chief of Central Command, to update existing contingency plans for retaliation against Iraq and the defense of Kuwait or, worse, Saudi Arabia, home of 25 percent of the world's oil reserves. In June and July of 1990 the U.S. Central Command had run a complex war game with Iraq as the assumed enemy. The exercise had led the army to conclude that it would need more than four divisions of U.S. ground troops to defend against Iraq.

An early version of Operation Desert Shield grew out of the exercise and later evolved into the complex plan used to defend Saudi Arabia and other friendly Gulf States from attack by the Iraqi army. America's posture at the time was one of guarded concern. The United States had been hearing from many Arabs that Saddam

Hussein was just saber rattling and would do no more than threaten, while the Israeli government reported that it anticipated the worst: a full-scale attack against Kuwait.

On August 2, 1990, Iraqi forces attacked on a broad front and took Kuwait with little effort. The invading forces murdered and tortured many citizens and burned the Dasman Palace of the emir, who fled to neighboring Saudi Arabia. The closest American forces at the time were the Middle East naval force in the Persian Gulf and four military cargo ships moored in Diego Garcia, the island base in the central Indian Ocean.

The United Nations quickly provided legitimacy for the formation of a coalition of nations opposing Iraq. On August 2 the United Nations Security Council unanimously passed a resolution (with Yemen abstaining) condemning the invasion of Kuwait as a violation of the UN Charter and demanded that Iraq withdraw. Four days later the Security Council passed Resolution 661, which imposed a trade and financial embargo on Iraq and established a special sanctions committee. Only Cuba and Yemen abstained.

President Bush authorized the deployment of 150,000 U.S. troops into the area on August 6. The next day Central Command began the military movements, and Bush acted in the political realm. He faced the immediate problems of forming a coalition of allies to oppose Iraq and freeze all its assets abroad, restraining Israel from taking retaliatory action, and gaining the support of a Soviet Union preoccupied with its own disintegration. President Bush quickly summarized America's interests: preserving oil supplies, containing Iraq's program to develop nuclear weapons, supporting the security of Israel, and maintaining the credibility of America as the sole remaining world military power. Secretary of Defense Richard Cheney and General Powell met with Prince Bandar Bin Sultan, Saudi Arabia's ambassador in Washington. In that meeting the two Americans assured the Saudis that they had a contingency proposal for protecting the kingdom against Iraq, a plan to deploy one U.S. brigade, an air wing, and a carrier battle force immediately if needed. The prince immediately approved of the plan, which became the beginning of Desert Shield, a much revised and beefed-up scheme to defend Saudi Arabia. The president and many of his advisers were convinced that Saddam Hussein planned to invade Saudi Arabia before the United States could deploy enough troops for a meaningful defense. President Bush declared that for Hussein to attack Saudi Arabia, he would have to attack U.S. forces, and the president deployed the first American troops and aircraft to the area to form a "trip-wire force."

The United States quickly sent the 2,300-man alert brigade of the Eighty-second Airborne Division from Fort Bragg, North Carolina, which would be protected by two aircraft carriers and air force F-15 fighter-bombers already en route. A 16,500-man Marine Amphibious Brigade immediately began moving to the area from the U.S. East Coast; its heavy armor was already in the theater aboard the large prepositioning cargo ships. These troops would be followed by 19,000 more from the 101st Air Mobile Division tank killers and an advance brigade of 12,000 soldiers from the Twenty-fourth Mechanized Infantry Division, a heavily armored force trained in desert warfare, all coming from bases in the United States. Special operations forces from Central Command deployed to Riyadh, Saudi Arabia, on August 10 and established a base at King Fahd International Airport. The Fifth Special Forces Group deployed two battalions to King Khalid Military City, while army aviation helicopters from the 160th Special Operations Aviation Regiment joined them. These initial units were used to form the first line of defense, or trip wire, to sound the alarm should Iraqi forces move into Saudi Arabia before more American and coalition forces were in place fully to defend that country.

Meanwhile, in a press conference on November 8, President Bush outlined the national objective of the American response: the complete and unconditional withdrawal of Iraqi forces from Kuwait; restoration of Kuwait's legitimate government; the security and stability of Saudi Arabia and the Persian Gulf; the safety and protection of the lives of American citizens abroad. When American defense leaders first met with the leaders of Saudi Arabia, they reached agreement very quickly on the terms for victory over Iraq, but they signed no agreements or treaties and exchanged no written agreements. Secretary of Defense Cheney merely said that America would come if asked and would leave when asked to depart. The quest began for ways to cobble together a coalition. Each state to join had its own interests for doing so, of course, and fifty nations contributed in some fashion to the coalition. Thirty-eight of them deployed military forces, together contributing more than 200,000 troops, 60 warships, 750 aircraft, and 1,200 tanks. The participants came from all parts of the world, including Arab and Islamic states. Others donated financially, contributing billions of dollars in cash to the United States and billions in economic aid to the countries most touched by the crisis. Saudi Arabia and the United Arab Emirates agreed to pay a good part of the costs of the American intervention. Still other nations provided valuable in-kind support, such as construction equipment, heavy vehicle transporters, chemical-detection vehicles, food, fuel, water, and air and sea transport. The man picked to lead the American and coalition troops could not have been more perfectly suited for the job. General Norman Schwarzkopf was a proven product of America's military schools, a graduate of Valley Forge Military Academy in Pennsylvania and the U.S. Military Academy at West Point, who from travels with his father was well acquainted with the gulf region and its people.

At the time Iraq invaded, there were three thousand Americans citizens living in Kuwait, making the protection of Americans a real issue. Within one week after their invasion, Iraqi forces rounded up and detained most westerners and Japanese nationals in Kuwait. A few managed to escape or go into hiding. Taken to hotels in Kuwait City or to Baghdad, the detainees were permitted to contact their respective embassies, but the threat of the Iraqis' using them as hostages was for a while a real concern.

The European allies all responded with determination. The British prime minister, Margaret Thatcher, immediately froze all Iraqi and Kuwaiti assets. Britain deployed warships to augment its single ship already on station in the gulf. France ordered ships to reinforce its two already in the gulf, and President François Mitterrand announced his intention to commit ground units and advisers to Saudi Arabia. Italy, Spain, and Germany approved the use of their bases by American forces. Canada also dispatched three ships to the gulf. In an unusual show of unity all the Eastern European countries that were Iraq's creditors complied with the economic sanctions, thereby forfeiting substantial funds. Poland, Czechoslovakia, Romania, Bulgaria, and Yugoslavia all granted overflight rights to the allies, while Hungary and Czechoslovakia contributed humanitarian assistance.

Turkey played a vital role throughout the crisis. It shut down the Iraqi pipeline that had been pumping 50 percent of Iraq's oil exports to the Mediterranean port of Ceyhan. Turkey also deployed air force fighters and more than fifty thousand troops to its border with Iraq, a move that forced Iraq to retain a sizable force on the northern border, away from the anticipated ground fight against the coalition forces. The allies were authorized to station forces at Turkish bases.

The Soviet Union, then in its last confused months of existence, was not a member of the coalition but called for Iraqi withdrawal from Kuwait and declared the invasion to be an action detrimental to stability in the Middle East. President Bush was able to persuade the Soviet Union to denounce Iraq and to cut off weapons supplies, a feat that would have been impossible during the Reagan administration. More important, the Soviet Union supported all the UN Security Council resolutions against Iraq.

Within the region, the Gulf Cooperation Council also reacted quickly. This consultative defense grouping formed in 1981 during the Iran-Iraq War consisted of Saudi Arabia, Bahrain, Qatar, the United Arab Emirates, Oman, and Kuwait, and represented those countries most threatened by their proximity to Iraqi forces. After the Kuwaiti ambassador to the United States requested American military assistance, the other council states also committed troops and logistic support to the alliance and began sending in their forces in early September.

Egypt reacted quickly by condemning the invasion. President Mubarak regarded Iraq's attack as a direct breach of faith, since Saddam Hussein had personally promised Mubarak in July not to use force to settle his dispute with Kuwait. Thus Egypt, the most powerful member of the Arab Cooperation Council, became the leader of the Arab/Islamic contingent opposing Iraq, dispatching more than two heavy divisions to Saudi Arabia. Cairo also became the leading home for Kuwaiti exiles who had escaped during the invasion. Kuwaiti radio, television, and newspapers relocated to Cairo and continued to report to citizens at home on the progress of the crisis.

Syria also condemned the invasion, spoke out publicly in support of the Kuwaiti royal family, and deployed two army divisions to its undefended border with Iraq. In mid-August, at Saudi Arabia's request, Syria dispatched a special forces regiment to help shore up Saudi Arabia's defenses, and by October Syria had sent a full armored division. Morocco's King Hassan also sent troops to defend Saudi Arabia. While the other states of North Africa—Libya, Tunisia, and Mauritania—did not support Iraq's invasion, they did not join the coalition and from time to time spoke out against foreign intervention in general.

Iran condemned the invasion but immediately declared itself neutral. Iran supported the UN responses against Iraq but was openly opposed to the presence of American military forces in the region, claiming that the United States was using the situation to establish permanent bases. In a move that made the coalition forces nervous, Saddam Hussein gave up much of the territory he had occupied on the Iranian border during the eight-year war. The coalition worried that Iraq was seeking a way around sanctions by using Iranian ports to funnel weapons and supplies into Iraq. However, throughout the crisis period, the only significant contraband known to have passed through on the ground from Iran to Iraq was smuggled food products. During the period, and until the end of the Gulf War, the Iraqis moved more than 130 military and civilian aircraft to Iran, where they were impounded.

Jordan remained loyal to Iraq primarily from economic necessity. The sole port left open for Iraq was the Jordanian Red Sea port of Al-Aqabah, which Jordan allowed Iraq to use for arms imports in return for low-priced Iraqi oil. This port was closely monitored by the coalition, whose maritime interdiction effort mostly sealed its use, although some smuggling continued. The PLO, Yemen, and Sudan were vocal supporters of Iraq throughout the crisis, although they contributed no serious military assistance.

At the time of the invasion, a critical issue at hand for American military leaders was what size U.S. force to commit to the defense of Saudi Arabia. They recognized that it would take months to move enough troops into the area to confront Hussein on the ground without suffering inordinately high casualties in a protracted standoff. More than a few naval ships showing the flag would be necessary to dislodge the Iraqis from Kuwait. Defense experts feared that the United States might sustain heavy casualties in containing Hussein, but in a show of support for the Arab allies decided to deploy massive air, naval, and ground forces to the area to do the job. Although President Bush realized it might take a war to eject Hussein from Kuwait, he continued to seek diplomatic and economic sanctions while steadily building up American forces in the area.

In the weeks after the invasion of Kuwait, the allies' most urgent objective issue was to place some nominal forces on the ground in support of the Saudi Arabian forces, to show that determined support would be forthcoming. Until then, there existed a "window of vulnerability" during which an Iraqi attack would have a good chance of succeeding. Iraq already had eleven divisions inside Kuwait before the initial U.S. ground forces began to arrive in the area, and Iraqi reinforcements continued to pour into Kuwait. According to American military planners, the United States would require seventeen weeks to have sufficient ground forces in place to deter Iraq from attacking Saudi Arabia. While the Saudi ground forces had set up along a thin defensive line, the first American ground troops would be spread out among several locations to defend entry-point facilities for American and other coalition forces.

The first American units, consisting of the light infantry of the Eighty-second Airborne Division, landed on August 9 and immediately prepared to defend ports and airfields on the gulf coast at Al-Jubayl and Dhahran, along the primary corridor the Iraqi forces were expected to use if they attacked; thus, the Iraqis would be forced to confront U.S. forces soon after they began any invasion. These light forces would be supported by tactical aircraft from USS *Eisenhower* and USS *Independence,* the two navy aircraft carriers on the scene shortly after Iraq invaded Kuwait.

The gargantuan repositioning of ships containing equipment for the Marine Expeditionary Forces began as the ships sailed from Diego Garcia and Guam, where they had been stationed for such contingencies. U.S. Air Force fighters and the advance brigade of the Eighty-second Airborne were the first to arrive in Saudi Arabia. The two carrier battle groups, each with more than one hundred combat aircraft, and ten other navy surface ships had been ordered into the area on August 2. The Middle East naval force was already on station, patrolling actively as part of the Maritime Intercept Operation to enforce the UN-ordered embargo against Iraq. Within several days air force F-15C fighter aircraft from the First Tactical Fighter Wing arrived in Saudi Arabia from Langley Air Force Base in Virginia. These aircraft had flown nonstop with multiple air-to-air refuelings and began to patrol over the Saudi Arabian border areas as soon as they arrived. They had very little ammunition in place.

On August 11 B-52G bombers with full weapons loads arrived at air bases within striking range of Iraq and were placed on alert. On August 12 the 101st Airborne Division, an air-assault unit with its own integral lift helicopters and antitank weapons, began to deploy from Fort Campbell in Kentucky. By August 13 two brigades of the Eighty-second Airborne were in defensive perimeters around the air base in Dhahran. The next day the Seventh Marine Expeditionary Brigade began unloading at Al-Jubayl. This marine brigade was a combined-arms force with armor, helicopters, and fixed-wing attack aircraft. During these deployments, Iraq's ground forces moved closer to the Saudi border, and its air force was flying brief incursions in and out of Saudi airspace to test the resolve of the defenders. President Bush ordered a complete naval blockade around Iraq and Kuwait as a way to enforce the UN sanctions. At this point in the deployment, the allies tested the Iraqis to see if they would fight. When the first U.S. Navy patrols stopped Iraqi ships it was a tense moment, but Hussein hesitated and did not attack.

The main U.S. objective at the time was to get the full-strength Twenty-fourth Mechanized Division into the theater as soon as possible; its 216 Abrams M1A1 tanks were superior to the Soviet-built Iraqi tanks. While the original plan called for 120 days to deliver all of the Twenty-fourth Mechanized's cargo, the sea-lift command completed the task in just 95 days. General Schwarzkopf then asked that all available antitank units be poured into the area as soon as possible. Air force fighters, A-10 ground-support aircraft, Apache helicopters, and Hellfire antitank missiles were rushed in to protect the growing number of troops arriving each day. The general also obtained more Patriot antiaircraft missiles to defend against the Iraqi air force's Soviet-built Scud missiles.

Before the Grenada and Panama incursions, which had required secrecy, the media had been purposely kept in the dark, but now the Pentagon made daily announcements listing the units being deployed. Since Iraq had virtually no strategic or tactical reconnaissance capability, it was easy to mask the slowness of the deployments. Camera crews from all major news companies were invited to broadcast the arrivals of the giant C-5 and C-141 transports at Saudi airfields to emphasize the size and speed of the American buildup. Televised news of the massive movement of men and machines enhanced the psychological message aimed at Iraq and the world: The military power amassed by America and the coalition in the gulf area was formidable.

Desert Shield was more demanding logistically and larger than any other operation in military history, including the Normandy landings in 1944. The distances were greater, the cargoes were bigger, and there had been little time to prepare. By the end of August, three hundred cargo missions a day were arriving in the Persian Gulf. By the first of September the United States had already shuttled in seventy-two thousand troops and one hundred thousand tons of cargo. Within three weeks of the approval to deploy on August 6, the U.S. Central Command had in place a total force of seven brigades of ground troops, three carrier battle groups, fourteen tactical fighter squadrons, and four tactical airlift squadrons for local transportation. A strategic bomber squadron and a Patriot ground-to-air defense missile system had been relocated to a country that was more than eight thousand miles from the United States. The window of vulnerability had been reduced; however, although these forces could put up a significant fight, they lacked the strength to stop a full-scale attack by the Iraqis, whose forces included three full-armored and two

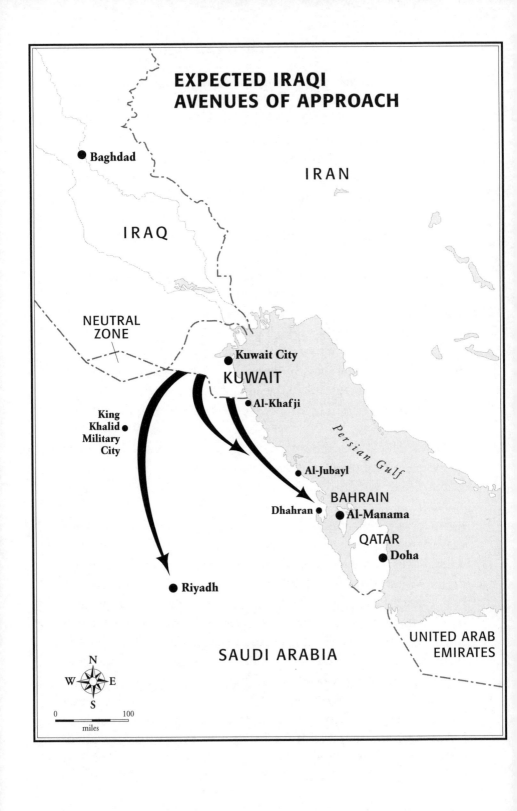

EXPECTED IRAQI AVENUES OF APPROACH

Baghdad

IRAN

IRAQ

NEUTRAL ZONE

Kuwait City

KUWAIT

Al-Khafji

King Khalid Military City

Al-Jubayl

Persian Gulf

BAHRAIN

Dhahran

Al-Manama

QATAR

Doha

Riyadh

SAUDI ARABIA

UNITED ARAB EMIRATES

N
W E
S

0   100
miles

mechanized divisions plus a score of smaller armored, mechanized, and infantry formations—all experienced combat veterans of the war with Iran.

The American troops took up defensive positions along the most likely corridor of Iraqi approach. Intelligence showed that Saddam Hussein was poised for an advance into Saudi Arabia with three main thrusts: an eastern thrust along the gulf coast down the Al-Khafji–Al-Jubayl route to Dhahran, and a western thrust passing King Khalid City and merging with a center thrust heading directly to the capital, Riyadh. There was significant uncertainty whether Iraq would employ chemical and biological weapons and whether it would use its still-notable air force. The Americans anticipated having to fight shortly after landing in Saudi Arabia, and the adequate logistic means of support for them were still not in place. Despite this uncertainty and a feeling of impending threat, U.S. ground troops continued to arrive in the area throughout September and October. They vigorously dug in and prepared for the worst. The Iraqis still did not attack.

An additional U.S. Marine Expeditionary Brigade, the Fourth, arrived and was positioned off the gulf coast to be rushed ashore to reinforce those thinly spread forces already in place. By September 12 the First Marine Expeditionary Brigade arrived to flesh out the First Marine Division. By September 15 most of the remaining brigades of the army's Twenty-fourth Mechanized Infantry Division arrived with their M1 heavy tanks and M2 series fighting vehicles in the port of Ad-Dammam. By the end of September the remainder of the division arrived and moved north, joining with the First Marine Expeditionary Brigade northwest of Al-Jubayl. The Third Armored Cavalry Regiment arrived and was attached to the Twenty-fourth Mechanized, giving it a reinforced antitank unit. In the first week of October the remainder of the 101st Airborne Division had arrived along with the Twelfth Aviation Brigade, which was equipped with the formidable AH-64 Apache attack antitank helicopters. In early October the First Cavalry Division began to arrive, and by the third week in October it was in place in the gradually forming defensive line.

Additional air reinforcement arrived the same month, raising the total combat strength to more than one thousand American combat aircraft, including elements of three tactical fighter wings. Five squadrons of ground-support aircraft, including F-16Cs and A-10s, arrived along with the Third Marine Aircraft Wing. Two attack carriers remained on station and ready, one in the Red Sea and the other in the Arabian Sea. All of this had been completed in two months.

As additional coalition forces continued to arrive, they were fitted into the basic scheme. Significant new forces included the French Sixth Light Armored Division and a Syrian special forces regiment backed by their Ninth Armored Division, which patrolled the Iraq and Kuwait borders. To their right flank was the Egyptian Ranger Battalion and Third Mechanized Division.

When these forces were in place, General Schwarzkopf felt that the window of vulnerability had been narrowed so that coalition forces could sufficiently defend against an Iraqi invasion. By this point the sanctions and naval blockade had already reduced Iraq's imports by roughly 90 percent. But the long war with Iran had made Iraqis used to war and misery, and they seemed unhurt by the sanctions. By the end of September the CIA estimated that the sanctions alone would not be sufficient to drive Iraqi forces from Kuwait before the international coalition began to take action.

The proposal for the defense of Saudi Arabia called for deterring an Iraqi attack as far north as possible while the combined coalition airpower inflicted maximum damage. The U.S. forces arrayed behind the static defenses along the coast would remain mobile, with the capability to react and hit Iraqi forces wherever they attacked and to defeat them before they reached Al-Jubayl, the first coastal town.

Coalition warfare brought with it a new mission for American Special Forces. The need for smooth liaison among the great variety of foreign units demanded that well-trained and language-capable teams be assigned to all non-American units to assist in the delicate and precise air and artillery support and communications coordination, a role filled by units from the U.S. Joint Special Operations Command consisting of army, air force, and navy Special Forces. Naval Special Warfare Units assigned SEALs initially near the border areas for early warning and reconnaissance until the larger units arrived from abroad. The SEALs were linked by radio to air-defense units standing by on alert. The naval units also trained Saudi naval forces and helped reconstitute remnants of the Kuwaiti navy that had escaped from their homeland. The U.S. Army Special Forces trained Saudi engineer units to clear minefields using the latest equipment. During the valuable time when coalition forces were cementing their defenses, special operations teams were training and coordinating for future combat and search-and-rescue missions, anticipating that air forces would be used over the vast and open desert terrain. The search-and-rescue training would prove invaluable when the defensive operation turned into an offensive campaign.

On November 29, after the UN resolutions failed to induce Iraq to comply and withdraw, the Security Council authorized the coalition to use "all means necessary" to enforce the previous resolutions if Iraq did not depart Kuwait by January 15, 1991. The deadline had been set.

CHAPTER 10

The Gulf War: Desert Storm

February 24, 1991

At the beginning of the buildup to defend Saudi Arabia, military experts had estimated that to shift to the offense, should that be an option, would require one hundred thousand more troops than would be needed for defense. The planners initially anticipated that the U.S. Marines and allied formations would keep the Iraqis pinned to the border, expecting coalition ground attacks and amphibious landings, while the U.S. Eighteenth Corps, with some of the more mobile European units, would carry the attack around the flank to surround the Iraqis.

By October Saddam Hussein had moved most of his forces from the Iranian border into Kuwait. He also erected elaborate defenses within Kuwait for his tanks and antiaircraft artillery and missiles, built enormous minefields, and rigged the Kuwaiti oil fields and refineries with explosives in case they were attacked. Hussein withdrew his elite Republican Guard units to southern Iraq and reinforced them with 150,000 troops formerly on the Iranian border. He backed up his poorly trained forces on the Saudi border with more experienced armored forces and additional Republican Guards, thus setting up a layered array against the coalition forces.

Saddam Hussein entertained the idea of dragging out a costly war in an attempt to weaken the resolve of America and the other allies by inflicting casualties so numerous that public support at home would be eroded. For their part, American leaders were determined that if it came to fighting a war, a quick finish to the combat, achieved with overwhelming force and decisive action, was imperative. For General Schwarzkopf's plan to outflank the Iraqis to work he needed additional NATO forces from Germany, namely the Seventh Corps of 21/3 armored divisions, one more armored cavalry regiment, plus the First Mechanized Infantry Division from Fort Riley in Kansas. This plan, known initially as the "enhanced option," was kept secret for some time. The formula was then increased by three additional carrier battle groups, the battleship USS *Wisconsin*, the Second Marine Expeditionary Force (MEF), and the Fifth Marine Expeditionary Brigade. That escalation would add two hundred thousand troops and would take until January 15, 1991, to complete. President Bush approved the enhanced option on October 30, 1990, after other coalition members and congressional leaders had been consulted. On November 8 Bush announced a doubling of U.S. forces to be committed to the Persian Gulf to create an offensive military option. Congressional leaders were dissatisfied with the White House's advance consultations, which they saw as inadequate. In the ensuing months, Bush grappled with the problem of winning congressional support for the offensive option. In the end, Iraq's public intransigence convinced enough congressmen and senators to support the president.

In early January 1991 President Bush decided to shift to the offensive. So far all diplomatic efforts to get Hussein to withdraw from Kuwait had failed. Following a last futile attempt at accommodation by the Russian envoy Yevgeny Primakov, the senior commanders in the field were given the attack order just four days before the January 15 UN deadline for Iraq to withdraw from Kuwait. In order to prevent Iraq's detection of a surge of allied air activity that might disclose the timing for beginning an attack, the Central Command air force leaders mounted an intensive series of daily air exercises.

The offensive campaign named Desert Storm was designed in four phases. The first three made up the air offensive and the fourth was the ground offensive. The air offensive would start with the heavy bombing of Iraqi strongholds, followed by the suppression or destruction of ground-based air defenses in Kuwait, then direct air attacks against ground forces in Kuwait. The air campaign began early on January 16, when the initial B-52G Stratofortress bombers, most of them more than thirty years old, took off from Barksdale Air Force Base in Louisiana on round-trip missions. Twelve hours before the full force of the air attack began, these bombers flew to points from which they launched their AGM-86C air-to-surface cruise missiles against eight key Iraqi communications, power, and transmission facilities and returned to their bases. At 2:20 A.M., still forty minutes before the main attack was set to commence, a special task force called Normandy streaked across the Saudi Arabian border into Iraq. This combined force of long-range and heavily armed MH-53J Pave Low II and AH-64 Apache helicopters flown by Special Forces, along with air force F-117 Stealth fighter-bombers and Navy Tomahawk cruise missiles launched from the battleship USS *Wisconsin*, all headed into Iraq. The Pave Low helicopters, acting as the navigation pathfinders for nine Apache gunships, swooped low over the desert and in a spectacular display of precision obliterated the Iraqi early-warning radar sites and returned without a loss.

The entire massed strength of the coalition air forces flew through the newly created hole in the radar coverage and began forty-three days of continuous and devastating air strikes against targets in Iraq. The warship-launched Tomahawk cruise missiles and F-117 Stealth strikes were the first to hit key military targets in Baghdad and were followed by a mix of allied air force aircraft and navy aircraft from carriers in the Persian Gulf and Arabian Sea. Also employed were electronic warfare jammers, the EF-111A Ravens and navy EA-6B Prowlers, and the little-known EC-130H aircraft. There were F-4G Wild Weasels firing antiradiation homing missiles and F/A-18 Hornets looking for surface-to-air missile sites. British Tornadoes and F-111F and A-6E bombers attacked key Iraqi airfields and Scud missile sites, and air force F-15Cs and F-16s, British Jaguars, and navy F-14s suppressed air defenses and protected the bombers. During the first hours of the air offensive approximately four hundred attack aircraft from the coalition struck targets in Iraq while hundreds of others supported their attacks. On the first full day of the air offensive allied airmen flew more than thirteen hundred combat missions.[1]

The air campaign continued throughout Desert Storm and the allies quickly achieved air superiority. U.S. and coalition bombers repeatedly stuck the primary Iraqi nuclear facility on the target list, the Baghdad Nuclear Research Center at Tuwaitha, and seven additional targets suspected to be key nuclear weapons construction sites. Attacks against these nuclear targets continued until the end of the war.[2] Suppression of the Iraqi Scud surface-to-surface missiles proved the most difficult air objective, and the air forces never fully achieved their destruction, primarily because the Iraqis kept the Scuds constantly on the move. During the Gulf War, 2,780 coalition aircraft, 75 percent of which came from the U.S., flew more than twenty-three thousand sorties against Iraqi ground forces who proved to be a predictable enemy on open terrain. The results were devastating to Iraq.

The coalition commander used a number of factors to decide when to begin the ground offensive, including the successful deployment of forces, the prepositioning of supplies, favorable weather forecasts, the readiness of the coalition, and the results of the air campaign strikes. General Schwarzkopf was seeking to reduce the Iraqi army's effectiveness by 50 percent before committing the ground troops to action. Once the air campaign had begun, it was possible to better assess the capabilities of the enemy by observing his conduct in action. The opportunity for such an assessment finally came on January 29. On that day the coalition's attention was suddenly deflected from the air campaign by two Iraqi ground probes across the border from Kuwait. A battalion-sized armored force led by units from Iraq's Fifth Mechanized Division, equipped with the obsolete Soviet T-55 medium tanks, moved against Khafji, a city of forty-five thousand inhabitants, from which all civilians had been totally evacuated. The attacking Iraqis faced only twelve marines of the First Marine Expeditionary Force who had remained in the city as artillery observers. As the Iraqis advanced across defensive earthworks southwest of the town of Al-Wafrah, one marine scored a direct hit on the lead tank with a wire-guided TOW antitank missile. That hit blocked the Iraqi's advance. At Khafji, Arab forces, helped by U.S. Marine forward observers calling in close air support and artillery, stopped the Iraqi's advance in the town and pushed them back toward Kuwait. At Al-Wafrah the Sixth Marine Regiment came forward the next day and dug in around the town, which ended the offensive. That action gave the allies their first indication of how the Iraqis would fight: The performance was not impressive.

During the tense days and nights before the ground offensive began, Saddam Hussein pursued his strategy based on trying to divide the large and unlikely coalition. To do this he appealed to the Arab distrust of the West and hatred of Israel. He tried to draw Israel into the fray by indiscriminately launching his long-range Scud missiles into Israel. Most of the Scuds landed harmlessly, but some caused horrible civilian casualties. At one point on the second day of the air offensive, Iraqi Scud missiles struck Tel Aviv and Haifa, slightly injuring a few civilians. Then on January 19 allied air forces responded to another Scud attack with a fierce and precise strike against the launchers by F-15Es from the Fourth Tactical Fighter Wing, which resulted in massive damage and large secondary explosions, and there followed a pause of more than three days before additional Scuds would be fired. The Iraqis then shifted the firings from fixed to mobile sites, making them more difficult to attack from the air.

By the end of January the pressure to halt the Scud strikes had intensified to the point that General Schwarzkopf ordered special operations teams across the borders into Iraq to seek out the missiles and destroy them. On February 7 the allies launched the first Special Forces anti-Scud raid: More than a dozen personnel in two high-speed desert vehicles with Black Hawk helicopter escorts crossed the border into Iraq. The teams hid by day, conducted reconnaissance forays by night, and laid mines to limit the Scud's mobility. At one time there were as many as four Special Forces teams roving inside Iraq, seeking Scud missiles. The exact number of missiles destroyed has never been disclosed, but some favorable direct attacks were made against the launchers. The greatest effect of these cross-border raids proved to be psychological, as they undermined the confidence of Iraqi soldiers in their homeland.

Before the ground offensive began, roughly two hundred thousand coalition combat troops were quietly repositioned to the west

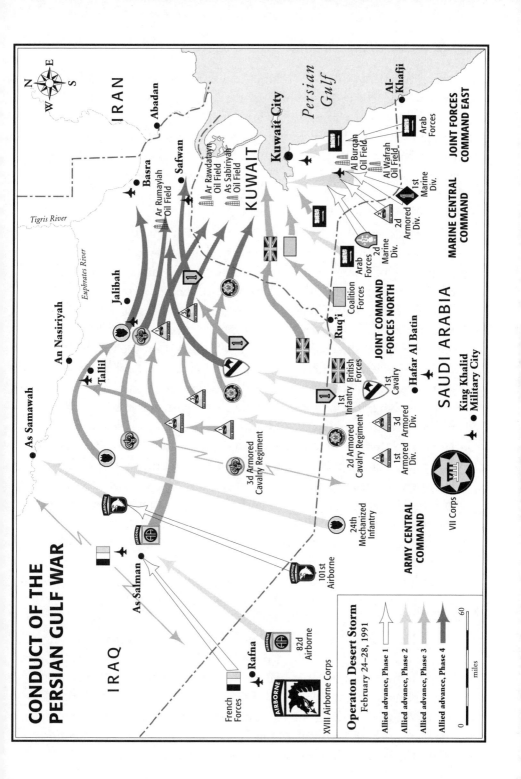

CONDUCT OF THE PERSIAN GULF WAR

Operaton Desert Storm
February 24–28, 1991

Allied advance, Phase 1
Allied advance, Phase 2
Allied advance, Phase 3
Allied advance, Phase 4

0 miles 60

IRAQ

IRAN

KUWAIT

SAUDI ARABIA

Persian Gulf

Tigris River
Euphrates River

As Samawah
An Nasiriyah
Tallil
Jalibah
Basra
Abadan
Safwan
Ar Rumaylah Oil Field
Ar Rawdatayn Oil Field
As Sabiriyah Oil Field
Kuwait City
Al-Khafji
Al Burqan Oil Field
Al Wafrah Oil Field

As Salman
Rafna

XVIII Airborne Corps
French Forces
82d Airborne
101st Airborne
24th Mechanized Infantry
3d Armored Cavalry Regiment
2d Armored Cavalry Regiment
1st Armored Div.
3d Armored Div.
1st Infantry
British Forces
1st Cavalry

Hafar Al Batin
King Khalid Military City

ARMY CENTRAL COMMAND
VII Corps
JOINT COMMAND FORCES NORTH
Coalition Forces
Arab Forces
2d Marine Div.
1st Marine Div.
2d Armored Div.
MARINE CENTRAL COMMAND
Arab Forces
JOINT FORCES COMMAND EAST
Ruq'i

where they were poised to commence a flanking run into Iraq. Their mission was to cut off the bulk of the best Iraqi forces in southern Iraq and the north of Kuwait. This was done in a perfect maneuver completely masked from the enemy by the furor of the ongoing air campaign and Iraq's lack of reconnaissance capability to detect this massive shift of allied forces. The allies moved the equivalent of seventeen divisions hundreds of miles west over the desert and the limited road network. The vehicles used for this massive feint came primarily from U.S. military units augmented by allied civilian firms. The allies set up forward logistics bases, which placed thousands of tons of supplies—water, food, ammunition, fuel, and spare parts—in the path the attacking units would follow in their sweep.

A simulated amphibious invasion designated Desert Saber, conducted by the Fourth Marine Expeditionary Brigade and supporting naval forces off the coast to the east of Kuwait, kept the bulk of the Iraqi troops and fortifications anxiously looking east for an assault that never came. Naval Special Warfare troops on board amphibious ships in the gulf conducted frequent reconnaissance missions close to the Kuwaiti shoreline in support of the deception strategy. From January 29 until February 16 these missions continued nonstop. The deception culminated in one large-scale operation that simulated beach reconnaissance and clearing operations on the night of February 23–24, the eve of the ground offensive. This strategy bewildered the Iraqi army and prevented Iraqi units at the beaches from leaving their positions to reinforce those that would come under attack in the west when the critical offensive began.

Following more than 180 days of maritime blockade and 38 days of aerial and naval bombardment, the final phase of Operation Desert Storm began on February 24. The political objectives of the ground operations were to eject Iraqi occupation forces from Kuwait and to restore the government there. A southern force—consisting of U.S. Marines from the First Marine Expeditionary Force; a British armored division; and Egyptian, Saudi Arabian, and Syrian divisions—attacked together along the Kuwaiti–Saudi Arabian border and held the forward Iraqi divisions in place. Two U.S. Army corps made up of the Eighteenth Airborne and Seventh Corps, augmented by British and French divisions, swept west of the Iraqi main defenses, severed Iraqi communications lines, and began to destroy the Republican Guards. The speed and overwhelming force of the units advancing from the west across the breadth of Iraq, combined with the rapid and well-orchestrated advance through the southern Kuwaiti border, made short work of the offensive.

The well-coordinated thrusts bewildered the Iraqis, and their soldiers surrendered in droves. By the morning of February 28, the Iraqi army, including the Republican Guard, was routed and either fled Kuwait or surrendered. Apart from several daring attacks made against the advancing coalition units, it was a near-total capitulation and defeat. The ground offensive was over in one hundred hours. Fears that the Iraqis would resort to house-to-house fighting as the coalition forces entered the capital city were allayed when the Iraqis merely piled their loot onto stolen vehicles and fled. U.S. Special Forces assisted the returning Kuwaiti troops in liberating their once-besieged capital city and reestablishing Kuwaiti authority. When allied forces reached the outskirts of Kuwait City, Special Forces soldiers flew into Kuwait City Airport on February 27 with the Third Special Forces Group A Teams, but the Iraqi forces had already abandoned the city and there was little organized resistance. Acting on the assessment of General Powell that the Iraqis had been defeated, President Bush announced a cease-fire at midnight Washington time on February 27—at the end of the ground offensive: "Kuwait is liberated, Iraq's army is defeated. Our military objectives are met."[3] Coalition military losses during the entire war were 240, including 148 Americans; total U.S. wounded were 278. The number of Iraqi military killed varies from initial allied estimates of 100,000 to Iraqi figures of 20,000. The actual total of Iraqi civilians killed was remarkably small, given the large-scale bombing. The Iraqis claimed that 2,278 civilians were killed and 5,965 injured.[4]

Some of the American losses came on February 25, when an Iraqi Scud missile struck a U.S. barracks in Dhahran, Saudi Arabia, killing twenty-eight and wounding one hundred.[5] By the end of the war the allies determined that Iraq had launched eighty-eight Scuds against Israel and forty-six against Saudi Arabia and other Gulf

States. In Israel two civilians were killed by Scud missiles, and eighteen died from heart attacks and gas-mask malfunctions. The greatest threat posed by the Scud missiles was the continuous uncertainty of what type of horrible warhead these missiles might contain. At one point during this period, after President Bush had dispatched Deputy Secretary of State Lawrence Eagleburger to try to restrain Israel, the Israelis were ready to conduct their own air strikes into Iraq. At one moment they even requested that the commanders of the coalition pause in the air campaign for four hours to permit Israeli aircraft to conduct their own raids without interfering with allied aircraft. The primary fear not far from the minds of world leaders about the Israelis' retaliation was the expectation that they might launch a nuclear attack against an Iraqi city. In the end Israel restrained its reaction after the deployment of additional American-built and -operated Patriot antimissile systems and the acceleration of the Scud-busting attacks by coalition aircraft and Special Forces racing in desert vehicles inside Iraq. The tactic of provoking Israeli retaliation was most likely an attempt to rupture the coalition. However, the Scuds caused few casualties, and the Israelis were restrained. The Arab coalition partners were determined not to fall for this tactic, and the war ended quickly before the coalition could fracture.[6]

One effective tactic employed by Saddam Hussein was delay. By stringing out negotiations and holding his forces in place he attempted to convince the coalition that the heavy cost in casualties should deter them from a final offensive. But Iraq's stream of propaganda, including bellicose threats interspersed with conciliatory gestures, failed to break the resolve of the allies. How long this resolve might have held up under Iraqi pressure is unknown, but the highly effective air campaign followed by the swift end run and advance into Kuwait rendered Hussein's delaying tactics ineffective.

The dark fears of a long and protracted fight against large numbers of Iraqi troops equipped with chemical and possibly germ weapons vanished in a few hours of swift-maneuver warfare. The highly effective air campaign of forty-three days proved far too costly for the Iraqis, and they soon agreed to meet to fulfill the victors' conditions. It was at this point, with total victory in the coalition's grasp, that the ultimate result—whether the war had achieved its goals or not—passed from the hands of the soldiers to the politicians, leaving the media squabbling over whether they had missed the chance to march on to Baghdad. The massive Iraqi capitulation and surrender gave the coalition the feeling that it could retire and go home after a job well done. And whatever the political and diplomatic failures of the Gulf War, the coalition won an overwhelming military victory. The objectives were met. Kuwait was liberated, and the bulk of the Iraqi army was destroyed or rendered ineffective.

The Gulf War was not about ethnic divisions within a national boundary, nor was it about independence for Kuwait. The issues were territory, ground taken and targets destroyed, troops on the battlefield, and decisive victory. This was a major conflict by pre–cold war standards of combat. The U.S.-led coalition engaged Iraqi forces on flat, open expanses, ideal for the highly mobile heavy armor and tactical airpower the United States and allied armies had been training with for fifty years in anticipation of Soviet armies' attacking Europe from the east. This conflict would, in Henry Kissinger's words, "mark the glorious sunset to the Cold War world. . . ."[7]

Although U.S. military power had been used decisively and with overwhelming force in December 1989 in Panama, the Gulf War was warfare on a grand scale with a tightly knit coalition of many unlikely allies. Operations Desert Shield, Desert Saber, and Desert Storm required the largest mobilization of U.S. Reserve and National Guard components since the Korean War. The Gulf War promised to mark the end of an era for the U.S. military. For the first time since World War II the United States had achieved a massive victory and was looking ahead to a new role as the world's sole military superpower in an extended peace. However, in the ensuing years military personnel would face eruptions of nasty little wars, called "operations other than war" or "civic actions" or "peacekeeping missions." They would also continue to die in high-technology standoff bombing or in violent urban clashes. Ten years after the Gulf War, American soldiers and their allies would be waging a different war in the mountains of Afghanistan, and then would return to battle in Iraq, in classic maneuver warfare in the open desert, and in hand-to-hand urban combat.

CHAPTER 11

The Rescue of the Kurds in Northern Iraq

March 1991

In March 1991 the Iraqi army was greatly diminished from its prewar strength of fifty-eight divisions; just thirteen divisions remained intact. Iraq's air force had lost more than 250 of its best planes while more than 130 had fled to Iran and were impounded. The Iraqi navy had been annihilated. In March the Iraqi army faced two major postwar problems: a Shiite revolt in the southern marshlands around Basra and shortly afterward a Kurdish uprising in the north near Mosul. These two events posed a major threat to Saddam Hussein's internal hold on power. He was limited in his military response to these uprisings by the terms of the cease-fire with the coalition. UN Security Council Resolution 686 of March 2, 1991, set forth the conditions of the cease-fire, which had gone into effect on February 28. Major terms were the release of prisoners, return of loot and abducted citizens from Kuwait, and cooperation in clearing mines and booby traps. Iraqi generals had managed to exempt the use of their helicopters for internal policing from the list of restrictions on the post-cease-fire use of their air forces. With that exemption in hand, Hussein then went about a methodical suppression of the two revolts. The one to the south was put down without interference from the coalition forces, who were in the process of returning home. To the north, however, his brutal attempts to quell the Kurdish revolt met with allied resistance that must go down in history as one of the most successful humanitarian operations in modern times.

The American and allied ground forces had stopped at the Euphrates River and remained in an arc around Basra, holding Kuwait and all the territory of the southeastern fifth of Iraq. The Gulf War cease-fire was agreed to at Safwan, where General Schwarzkopf and his generals met with the Iraqi army leaders. The agreements at Safwan set up a demarcation line limited by the coalition's forward area and stipulated that each group would remain on its side of the line. At the talks the senior Iraqi general requested that Iraq be allowed to operate helicopters in areas where roads and bridges had been severely damaged. The coalition agreed, provided that the operation of helicopters was inside Iraq and not connected with the allies' front lines. The provision was carefully limited to helicopters only and did not include fixed-wing military aircraft.

With the Shiite and Kurdish revolts in full swing, the Iraqis attempted to move the Hammurabi Armored Division, one of their Republican Guard units, through some of the forward positions of the U.S. Twenty-fourth Mechanized Infantry Division and to escape to the north. On March 2, in a fierce action, the American forces stopped the Iraqi breakout and destroyed thirty tanks and more than five hundred vehicles, inflicting enormous casualties on personnel.[1] The engagement had been a turkey shoot for the American gunners as they cut down the Iraqis, forcing their infantry to retreat by foot back into the "Basra Pocket." The goal of the Iraqi's breakout had been to reposition their forces to the area of the Kurdish uprising and to quell that threat against Hussein.

The seemingly minor concession at Safwan allowed the Iraqis to initiate helicopter-borne military suppression of the Shiites in the south, who were put down with a bloody vengeance by the Republican Guard. The allies watched helplessly as the Iraqis massacred thousands of their own citizens. Although some allied forces still in position created safe havens for the those Shiites who managed to flee, there was little else they could do.

To the north, however, the plight of the Kurds was different. Taking advantage of the weakened state of the Iraqi military and helped by the defection of several local Iraqi army units including the Iraqi Twenty-fourth Infantry Division, the Kurds in northern Iraq revolted. While Saddam was moving the battered remnants of his army south to clean up the Shiite rebellion, in the north the Kurds had succeeded in gaining control over half of Kurdish Iraq. In mid-March the Kurds captured the large oil center of Kirkuk, which was the eastern end of the Iraqi oil pipeline passing through Turkey.

The Kurdish population inside Iraq was considerably smaller than that of the Shiites; roughly eighteen million Kurds live in a "home-land" composed of the corners of six separate countries—Turkey, Armenia, Azerbaijan, Iran, Iraq, and Syria. Their native tongue is an Indo-European language that closely resembles Farsi, the language of Iran; their written language dates back to the Middle Ages. Predominantly Sunni Muslims, they have a tradition of being fiercely independent and vicious fighters. The Kurds for decades had been hated, abused, distrusted, and even prohibited from serving in the Iraqi military. Although the Kurds were usually left alone and ignored by their neighbors, there have been exceptions. During the heyday of the Ottoman Empire they were hired by the Ottoman armies and were, like the Nepalese Gurkas in Queen Victoria's time, granted limited autonomy for their service as fighters. After the fall of the Ottoman Empire each of the six host countries at various times staged its own anti-Kurdish campaigns. Immediately following World War II, the Soviet Union briefly supported a Kurdish uprising in northern Iran. Iran's instigation of several Kurdish uprisings in Iraq, first under the shah and then under Khomeini, was one of the primary causes of the long Iran-Iraq War of the 1980s. Saddam Hussein granted limited autonomy to the Kurds and left them in relative peace until the Iran-Iraq War, when entire Kurdish villages in northern Iraq were destroyed by chemical weapons and firebombing.

By the end of March 1991 most of the coalition forces still inside Iraq at the cease-fire had left. Emboldened by their departure as well as the allied inaction during his suppression of the Shiites, Hussein turned north and began to attack the Kurds, using helicopter-borne troops to break the rebellion. By March 29, after a short fight, the

Iraqis recaptured the Kirkuk oil terminal and began to smash the Kurdish settlements northward to the Turkish and Iranian borders, where the winter snow remained deep. More than a million Kurds fled to the mountains, roughly one-third going toward Iran; the remainder sought refuge in Turkey.

Among Turkey's persistent problems was a hundred-year-old insurgency in the rural southeast near the border with northern Iraq. The arrival of more than six hundred thousand Iraqi Kurds in this border region alarmed the Turks, whose first reaction was to force the refugees back into Iraq. Meanwhile, the plight of the Iraqi Kurds won the attention of the media in the United States and Europe. To cope with the refugees inside Turkey, the government of Turkey appealed for help. In Britain, where the outcry in the press and on television was incessant, the government favored intervention. The Americans, who were likewise influenced by the riveting media images of starving and freezing Kurds huddling in desolate mountain camps, realized that helping Turkey at this point could prevent the Turks' anti-Kurdish reflexes from making the situation worse. Turkish President Turgut Ozal, who had allowed American airmen to fly more than fifty-five hundred air strikes from Incirlik during the Gulf War, suggested as a solution the establishment of safe-haven enclaves in northern Iraq.

Furthermore, United Nations Resolution 688, issued on April 5, 1991, denounced Iraq's repression of its Kurdish population, called for dialogue to be opened with the Kurds and Shiites, and compelled the contribution of member nations, including the United States. What followed was a large-scale and generally unknown but successful American-led military relief and peacekeeping effort that was to be a forerunner of and model for future peacekeeping ventures in Somalia, Bosnia, and Kosovo. It was called Operation Provide Comfort.

The Gulf War cease-fire of February 1991 was a month old, and roughly half of the deployed U.S. forces remained in the Persian Gulf area. Reacting to criticism that the allies had allowed Saddam Hussein to remain in power and were ignoring the plight of the

Kurds, President Bush responded: "We simply could not allow 500,000 to a million people to die up there in the mountains."[2] He ordered the operation to begin on April 7.

American contacts were already well established on the ground in northern Iraq. Several detachments of the U.S. Army Tenth Special Forces Group supported by the U.S. Air Force Special MC-130E Combat Talon transports and MH-53J Pave Low III helicopters had been operating a rescue-and-recovery system for downed allied pilots and aircrews during the Gulf War out of an airfield at Batman, Turkey. Men who had roamed the mountains of northern Iraq and had been in contact with many of the Kurdish camps became the backbone of the relief effort.

American aircraft began dropping food and relief supplies to the Kurds in the area on April 7. Initially U.S. aircraft dropped thirty to forty tons a day into the Kurdish camps. Recognizing how difficult it was for the Kurds to recover the dropped supplies, the Americans sent in teams of Special Forces to assist with the airdrops, organize camps, and help provide medical care and improved sanitation. The commanders of this operation realized that a significant combat force would be required quickly to confront Iraqi forces approaching from the south and to encourage the Kurds to return to enclaves inside Iraq and not to cross the mountains into Turkey.

To fend off advancing Iraqi ground forces spreading north in mid-April to quell the revolt, the United States repositioned a number of combat aircraft, including the A-10 tank hunters from Saudi Arabia, to the airfields in Incirlik, Turkey, from which they had flown in the Desert Storm air campaigns. Iraqi forces pushing north included three mostly unscathed infantry divisions and one Republican Guard brigade. By mid-June the allies had gathered a force of over a division, totaling about twenty thousand troops from eleven countries. The Americans included in this force were marines from the Twenty-fourth Expeditionary Unit, which had its own integral air support, and the 325th Airborne Battalion Combat Team from Vicenza, Italy, a well-trained and independent airborne unit. Britain provided a Commando Brigade, France sent its Parachute-marines, the Netherlands committed an Airborne Commando Group, and Spain and

Italy each sent an elite commando battalion. These troops represented the major forces that had been left in their barracks in Europe after other units had deployed for the Gulf War. They were backed up by a formidable air combat team, including aircraft from the carrier USS *Theodore Roosevelt*.[3] A large number of supporting units, including engineers and military police from all services, assisted in building transit camps from which to move the Kurds south and back into Iraq.

Lieutenant General John M. Shalikashvili, who was then the deputy commander of U.S. Army forces in Europe, took charge of the entire relief effort. Having been born in Poland of parents who fled the Russian Revolution first to Germany and then to the United States, Shalikashvili had a personal understanding of refugees. He quickly molded the elite European and American forces into an effective task force that headed south to prepare enclaves in northern Iraq for the Kurds to settle in. By early May the first groups of Kurds were headed to their new homes.

The first showdown with Iraqi forces occurred outside the nearly abandoned Kurdish city of Zakho. After a show of force, the determined allies forced the Iraqis to back down, and the return of the Kurds to Iraq continued. When the Iraqis demanded that their Special Police Battalion remain to supervise, the allied task force commander sent American, British, and Dutch marines with light armor into the city ahead of the Iraqis. After a few scattered skirmishes the Iraqis were forced to withdraw. The greatly relieved Kurds returned to safe settlements inside northern Iraq, escorted by highly specialized troops from eleven nations. The mission was so successful that by June 8 the allied task force announced that it was completed.

The American action in Turkey and Northern Iraq was the antithesis of the 1982–1984 Lebanon intervention, when U.S. armed forces proved unable to react to a dynamically changing situation and responded with hesitancy and serious inattention to security. The success of Operation Provide Comfort, although not widely proclaimed, showed how much a determined effort combining military forces with effective relief and aid organizations could accomplish. This success may have created a mistaken expectation that every similar situation could be rectified by the timely use of specially trained soldiers regardless of the complex nature of the civil conflict. The Kurdish relief operation came back to haunt U.S. and UN forces only two years later, when they tried to duplicate the action in Somalia.

For America, the Gulf War and the successful humanitarian action in Kurdistan that followed were the first real war in which U.S. troops fought using conventional arms, classic armored forces, and the full spectrum of air-delivered weapons, including Stealth bombers and long-range cruise missiles. It was the sort of war—neither small nor splendid but short—in which the United States performed at its best to achieve its objective and, most important, minimize casualties. It was the first time since Korea that U.S. forces in action were pitted against a foe who not only was visible on the battlefield but also acted as soldiers were expected to act. Although badly trained and demoralized, the Iraqis were equipped with modern weapons and were generally viable opponents.

The United States and its allies won the Gulf War in less time and with far fewer casualties than anticipated. America had gone to the aid of a small country that had been invaded and occupied, using overwhelming force, and emerged victorious. For the first time since 1945, a victory in war gave Americans a good feeling despite the survival of the dictator Saddam Hussein, who even with his diminished army remained a considerable threat long after his defeat.

PART FIVE

Intervention in Somalia

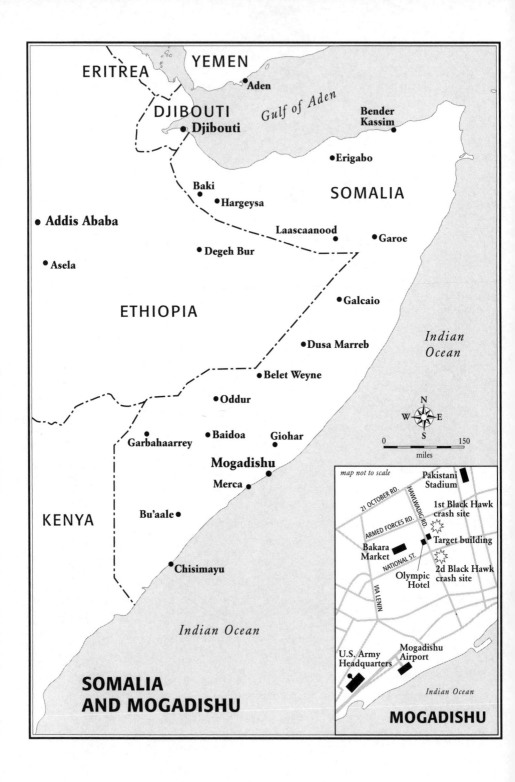

SOMALIA
AND MOGADISHU

CHAPTER 12

President Bush Responds to Starvation

1991–1992

The American involvement in Somalia from 1991 through 1993 fluctuated wildly from peaceful guarding of humanitarian aid to violent street fighting in the capital, Mogadishu. Somalia was a case in which absolutely no U.S. interests were involved beyond performing a purely humanitarian function—to allay the widespread starvation of a helpless populace. There were no hidden agendas, no black gold linking American interests to the region as in the Persian Gulf, and no vital allies in the area to bolster for future geopolitical reasons. The American government committed armed forces to protect the supply of emergency relief, but this soon failed because of the fierce civil war raging among scores of local Somali warlords. The Americans then restructured the armed force, but the effort failed again. Although it was evident that humanitarian aid could not reach the Somali citizens unless all the warring factions were disarmed, American leaders avoided tackling that option. Instead, they chose to apply force selectively in an attempt to remove the most dominant faction of the leadership. This strategy failed because the forces committed were woefully insufficient. The strongest Somali faction was led by a wily leader who cleverly manipulated UN and U.S. military and humanitarian efforts and solidified his followers into a violent antiforeign resistance focused primarily against the Americans. The violent incident he caused claimed so many American lives that a less-than-determined U.S. leadership quit the effort.

Some seven million people predominantly from the single ethnic group called the Samaal, mostly Sunni Muslims who speak multiple dialects of the same language, have inhabited Somalia for more than a thousand years. Throughout history many imperial powers have sought the people of Somalia as allies in order to advance their interests in Africa. Somalia is a land barely able to support human habitation, as severe drought is frequent. The Somalis experienced few tribal disputes and existed in relative harmony for many generations. However, fierce disputes, much like family feuds, have sprouted in recent generations, destroying the relative equilibrium among the six main clans and generally dividing the population into two major groups—the cattlemen and the farmers.

In the nineteenth-century scramble to gain new territory in Africa, Britain managed to assemble an impressive array of local allies in East Africa. By 1884 the east coast of British Somaliland was protected by a strong British garrison in Aden across the Gulf of Aden. The boundaries of Somaliland were fixed in 1897, and a separate British colony was set up in 1905 in the northern region. During the period of British control of the Horn of Africa, the landmass jutting northeastward into the Indian Ocean that includes areas of what is now Kenya, the British allied themselves in the north with the Ethiopians, who were among the earliest peoples to become Christians and who were archenemies of the Somalis. The Somalis were fervent believers in Islam and fiercely combative.

During the first decade of the twentieth century the British and Italians enjoyed a colonial entente in Africa and united in a common campaign against the Somali warlord Muhammad Abdulla Hassan, known as the "Mad Mullah," who threatened the peaceful colonial life of the British and Italian holdings in Somaliland. For more than twenty years the British pursued the wily Hassan, who, like the brilliant Muhammad Aidid in the 1990s, opposed foreigners in a protracted campaign of classic guerrilla warfare.

After six major campaigns against Hassan, the British were still unable to bring him to heel, just as the Americans would fail to topple the elusive Aidid in 1993. After eluding the British for decades, the Mad Mullah died a peaceful death in his bed; Aidid was eventually killed by his own followers and died in a hospital of gunshot wounds. Britain retained the northern region until 1960. After the British finally departed, their former colony merged with the Italian colonies that had been under UN protection since World War II to become an independent country, Somalia. The new country adopted a Western-style parliamentary system but failed to develop the art of democratic compromise. By 1969 a total of seventy politically active parties offered up nearly a thousand candidates for the 123-seat parliament. The election campaign soon deteriorated into a fraud-filled debacle, and the country descended into a period of protracted violence. After the newly elected president was murdered by one of his own bodyguards, a strongman named Muhammed Siyad Barrah, or Siad Barre, took power in a bloodless coup. Siyad Barrah's dictatorship took the form of a Stalinist regime, which offered handsome rewards to keep the support of his corrupt Darood henchmen. Unlike Stalin, however, he did not persecute the prevailing religion. He understood the strength of Islam among his people.

While locked in the cold war struggle, the United States backed Ethiopia and Kenya and the French backed Djibouti, thereby hemming in any Somali expansion. Siyad Barrah flirted with the Soviet Union, which lavished modern weapons, including tanks, artillery, and modern MiG-21 jet fighters, on his regime. Encouraged in his brief affair with the Soviets, Siyad Barrah began to foment insurrection in the Ogaden, a neighboring area partly in Ethiopia and Kenya, which was populated by some Somali clans who had been forced away. In an attempt to rally these clans to his country, Siyad Barrah launched the Ogaden War of 1977–1978. In 1974, the Soviet Union supported a coup in Ethiopia that successfully ousted the last emperor, Haile Selassie, a friend of the West, and the United States lost its foothold there. Subsequently the Soviet Union turned its back on Somalia, and with active Cuban support on the ground, the Soviets fostered the new Ethiopia. The Soviets were summarily ejected from

Somalia just a few short years after being ousted from Egypt. But in the end the Soviet-backed Ethiopians pushed back Siyad Barrah's expansion, after massacring thousands of Somalis. By 1981 Siyad Barrah's movement had failed, and he reluctantly renounced his claims on Kenya, Djibouti, and Ethiopia. Now seeing the Soviets and Cubans as his main enemies, Siyad Barrah turned to the United States, hat in hand, to request assistance, betting that America's cold war priorities would help him recover his elusive objectives. With some reluctance and a view primarily toward blocking the Soviets' expansion of their footholds in Ethiopia and Yemen, the Carter and Reagan administrations gave Siyad Barrah some support. The desire to gain allies in contested areas often forced U.S. presidents to choose the lesser of two evils, and thus America backed some convenient but shaky dictators, such as Shah Mohammad Reza Pahlavi in Iran.

In the interest of keeping the Soviets out of Somalia, the United States facilitated Somali access to soft loans and provided arms and advisers to Siyad Barrah in exchange for access to ports and the freedom to conduct military maneuvers on Somali territory. From 1983 to 1984 the United States provided $40 million in arms and military assistance, including heavy artillery, Vulcan air-defense systems, and small arms and ammunition. This material was added into a mix of arms furnished earlier by the Soviet Union, Italy, and even Germany, which had provided light armored vehicles and weapons for the Somali special forces and police. Soviet ambitions in the area were successfully thwarted by the growing American naval presence in Oman and on Diego Garcia and by its rights to use ports in Kenya and Somalia.

Eventually Siyad Barrah's atrocious human rights record caused the United States to cut off the arms flow. Siyad Barrah's unfortunate attempt to expand Somalia destroyed not only his army but also his country. Resistance and opposition began to form at home. A growing number of clans resisted his excesses, and some members of his own Darood clan turned against him. Several major power groups emerged. In the north Abdirahman Ahmed Ali Tur, leading the Somali National Movement, represented a remnant of the old Isaaq faction of the Mad Mullah who had opposed the British with such great persistence. In the south a smaller and less potent organization called the Somali Patriotic Movement claimed to be representing the Somali people abandoned in the Ogaden. This group was led by Omar Jess and Muhammed Said Hersi Morgan, both of the Darood clan. The third strongest group, the United Somali Congress, was led by Ali Mahdi Muhammed of the Hawiye clan and was not limited to any one region; its military commander was Muhammad Farah Aidid. By late 1989 these groups were fully engaged in an all-out, multisided civil war. The war in Somalia was approaching its climax in the closing days of 1990.

On January 5–6, 1991, while much of the West and the Arab world were focused on the Gulf War, a U.S. Navy and Marine rescue operation succeeded in evacuating four hundred civilians from war-torn Mogadishu, Somalia, in an extraordinarily complex mission called Eastern Exit that has gone relatively unnoticed. With no advance warning, on January 2, 1991, the American ambassador to Somalia, James K. Bishop, urgently requested the evacuation of Americans, allied nationals, Soviets, and others from the capital. In Mogadishu the situation in the streets had dissolved into near-total chaos. The U.S. Navy amphibious assault carriers USS *Guam* and USS *Trenton* were sent from the western Arabian Gulf shortly before midnight on January 2, carrying the First Battalion of the Second Marine Regiment and a SEAL team. Two CH-46 Sea Knight helicopter squadrons and a detachment of CH-53E long-range Super Stallion helicopters were aboard the *Trenton*. The amphibious force approached Mogadishu at top speed. At 466 nautical miles away, the helicopters, with sixty marines and SEALs aboard for ground security, were launched. The helicopter force reached Mogadishu at dawn on January 6 after twice conducting hazardous night refuelings in midair. The marines had no maps more current than 1969. They had difficulty finding the embassy compound, which had recently been moved out of the center of Mogadishu. The CH-53 helicopter pilots were guided to the embassy grounds by employees using strobe lights and white flags; they landed and deployed the marines and SEALs to protect the area. The sixty-man relief force threw a cordon around the embassy and repelled attackers and looters who were using ladders thrown over the fence to get onto the grounds. The marines held the compound while another team of marines and SEALs brought in the American and Kenyan ambassadors from a separate building nearby. The force eventually evacuated all the civilians to the ships in two loads, with only slight signs of resistance—some surface-to-air missile radiation alerts.

During the first two months of 1991, the battle for Mogadishu erupted into its full, horrible form. Aidid commanded the forces that unseated Siyad Barrah in house-to-house combat that is believed to have caused more than forty thousand civilian casualties. Siyad Barrah escaped to Nigeria, leaving a large portion of Somalia in ruins. The ten years of civil strife had virtually destroyed the country.

Educated in Italy and trained in the Soviet Union, Aidid was a cunning and able leader. He had served as ambassador to India under Siyad Barrah and then as the Somali army's chief of staff. One of his fourteen children was a U.S. Marine who served in a unit that would later support UN operations in Mogadishu. Aidid had no compunctions about killing his own followers; as the situation in Mogadishu deteriorated, he often staged ambushes of his own people and blamed the UN for the killings to develop a united front of hatred focused against foreign intervention.

After the civil war reached a stalemate in 1992, the country passed into a state of anarchy, as the temporary alliance of resistance to Siyad Barrah soon collapsed. The Somali National Movement controlled the north, and the Somali Patriotic Movement under Omar Jess occupied the southern port city of Chisimayu and the immediate surroundings, although he was still competing for control with other leaders of the same clan. In the capital region of Mogadishu both Hawiye clan leaders, Aidid and Ali Mahdi Muhammed, fought to control the city and the remainder of Somalia.

As these costly struggles spiraled downward, the people paid dearly. Warlords patrolled their areas in armed vehicles called technicals. This term was derived from the Somali word for bandit, which was similar in pronunciation to the local English colloquialism for security guard. The warring factions hoarded food and medical supplies for their own minions while a devastating drought struck from 1991 to 1992. Western television and print news editors, whose appetite for disaster stories had been whetted by the Kurdish refugee crisis, began to focus attention on Somalia, where millions were starving. Despite the attention being given to suffering elsewhere, the images of death and destruction on the ground in Somalia became compelling. Public concern grew vocal; politicians reacted. Recalling the Kurdish precedent, they turned to the United Nations. On April 27, 1992, the UN Security Council issued Resolution 751, granting authority for armed intervention to deliver relief supplies. The United Nations Operation in Somalia, or UNOSOM, was designed to be small, precise, and short. Initially the United States did not participate. First to enter was a team of fifty observers from Pakistan.

Despite the well-meaning intentions of so many, the first months of the operation were a dismal failure. The warlords brazenly stole the humanitarian aid at gunpoint for their own clans. Efforts of the small group of observers proved futile. The United Nations attempted to enlist the support of the clans by paying them to guard the food supplies in transit, but food was stolen outright by other armed bands that intercepted convoys, then diverted it to rival clan hideaways. In July 1992, two UN relief flights were stopped and looted by armed gunmen right on the runway at the Mogadishu airport.

Against this backdrop the United States was being pressured to do something. Ongoing relief operations at the time included Provide Hope in the newly independent Republic of Georgia, Provide Promise in beleaguered Bosnia, Southern Watch and Intrinsic Action in Kuwait, and Provide Comfort in eastern Turkey and northern Iraq for the Kurds. The Gulf War's success had instilled in Americans the confidence that they could indeed make a difference in cases of massive human suffering, even in Somalia, where no government, no state, and no order existed. The American effort to help, called Provide Relief, began with a modest airlift flying in via Mombasa, Kenya. The initial operation consisted of three C-141B Starlifters and a dozen C-130E Hercules transports from the 314th U.S. Air Force Airlift Squadron. Security at the airport was provided by a platoon of Military Police flown in from the U.S. Berlin Brigade and several A

Teams from the Fifth Special Forces Group. The operation came under the Central Command based in Tampa, Florida, headed by U.S. Marine General Joseph Hoar.

The operation was to be implemented by the Humanitarian Assessment Survey Team, a new interagency group made up of specialists in civilian emergency relief from the State Department's Office for Foreign Disaster Assistance and the Agency for International Development. The team was trained to conduct a survey of a disaster area with military escorts for security. The team had been tested in one exercise, but had not been used in a real crisis. General Hoar designated the First Marine Expeditionary Force as a standing Humanitarian-Peacekeeping Joint Task Force, which was designed and equipped to work in a hostile environment. When ordered on August 16, 1992, to begin Operation Provide Relief, General Hoar sent in an assistance team trained and commanded by U.S. Marine Brigadier General Frank Libutti. Unlike the many relief missions in the past for tornado or earthquake assistance, the operation was a delicate move in which U.S. military forces were being injected into a man-made calamity. Like the intervention in northern Iraq, this was direct involvement in a civil war.

While conducting the survey, the American team made its headquarters in Mombasa, which was not only more secure but also enjoyed better communications than any location in Somalia. The people of Kenya were not enthusiastic about the presence of Americans who were trying to assist the Kenyans' ancient rivals in Somalia and were less than helpful to the mission. In order to secure Kenyan permission to begin the relief flights from Mombasa, the United States had to agree initially to supply relief to the unwieldily large numbers of Somali refugees who had fled to refugee camps just inside the Kenyan borders. The assignment to command a relief-delivery force was demanding. Brigadier General Libutti had to appease the Kenyan government and get access to Kenya's airport. After that, his men had to get the material safely to the recipients and work outside normal command relationships with international aid workers.

The large air force C-141Bs could use only the long runway at Mogadishu, while the C-130Es could land at smaller, but barely safe, runways at Chisimayu to the south and Bale Dogle to the east of the capital. The military commander was forbidden by the International Red Cross to place security forces on the ground in advance for his airlifts. In desperation, he organized a quick reaction force made up of U.S. Army Special Forces and Air Force security police who would orbit overhead in helicopters in a holding pattern while the relief flights landed—in order to be able to come to their assistance and preclude the hijackings of cargo experienced by the initial UN relief efforts.

Relief flights began on August 28, 1992. Flights came in on a regular schedule and local Somali workers unloaded the aircraft. In September U.S. Air Force transports airlifted a five-hundred-man Pakistani light infantry battalion into Mogadishu. This was to be the initial element of a three-thousand-man UN peacekeeping force authorized by Security Council Resolution 751. The city was divided by a demarcation line reminiscent of the Cyprus Green Line, which had separated two (in that case Greek and Turkish) major warring factions. In Mogadishu Aidid was on one side and his archenemy Ali Mahdi on the other. By the time Brigadier General Libutti was replaced by U.S. Marine Brigadier General Paul A. Fratarangelo on November 11, 1992, the operation had already delivered fifty million meals and about fifteen thousand tons of other humanitarian cargo, but the situation in Mogadishu was not improving.

The American commander had hoped to be able to turn over a successful mission to UN-chartered civilian air transports by January 1993, but the aid material was still not reaching the people for whom it was intended; instead, all of it was snatched by armed clansmen within hours of delivery. By mid-November Aidid even began shelling merchant ships in the harbor, and his technicals basically closed the ports to shipping. The situation on the ground had deteriorated into disorder and sheer mayhem. The Pakistani battalion proved unable to enforce order on the ground and remained hunkered in billets in the port, outnumbered by the clan forces, who possessed more and heavier weapons.

CHAPTER 13

President Clinton Crosses the Mogadishu Line

1993

The situation in Somalia appeared dismal as 1993 began and President Bill Clinton took office. More than a half million Somalis had already died from war and starvation, and a million more were expected to die of hunger. One million had fled to either Kenya or Ethiopia, where they were suffering just as much. The famine had not abated despite the UN relief effort. The constant bombardment of gruesome pictures on American and Western television, showing starving children with distended stomachs and the marauding clansmen dashing around the capital stealing UN relief goods, proved too much for the West and the UN leadership. They wanted action. However, the senior military leaders in the United States were initially opposed to going in with significant ground forces. The success of the Gulf War had proved the now-accepted policy among military advocates that if one entered a conflict, no matter how benign it appeared, one went in only with decisive force and with clear and concise goals. Moral indignation was widespread, but a national policy was elusive. The American press had dubbed the military's hesitancy "the Powell Doctrine."

In this case the moral outrage of the American public was matched in kind by that of UN Secretary General Boutros Boutros-Ghali. He was the first to request directly that the United States provide a plan of intervention on the ground to enforce delivery of the badly needed relief material. At first his request appeared hazy; senior military officers asked what outcome would constitute winning. Involvement appeared to be endless. Although most military leaders still urged caution, General Powell's Joint Chiefs of Staff designed a plan to send two divisions—one marine, one army—to provide security for the distribution of relief supplies. The fresh effort would be called Operation Restore Hope. It seemed a simple and straightforward task: escort the relief shipments with a multinational force composed of armed formations of highly trained and disciplined troops with modern weapons and fend off theft by a mixed force of opposing rabble—poorly equipped and barely trained local Somali clansmen. The mission was envisioned as a limited armed operation to get humanitarian assistance to the people of Somalia using a massive show of force against those resisting the distribution of the relief.

The United Nations passed Resolution 794 on December 3, 1992, giving the United States the lead "to establish as soon as possible a secure environment for humanitarian relief operations." The UN resolution further authorized the use of force to defeat any threat to international security and "to restore peace, stability, and law and order with a view to facilitating the process of a political settlement under the auspices of the United Nations." No Security Council resolution had ever authorized such an extensive interference in a member state's internal affairs, not even the UN vote to enter the Korean War in 1950.

On December 4, 1992, President Bush announced that the United States would lead the intervention for the United Nations. Though the UN resolution was wide in its scope, the U.S. government chose to get the task done quickly. "This operation is not open-ended," Bush said. "We will not stay one day longer than is absolutely necessary. Let me be very clear: our mission is humanitarian, but we will not tolerate armed gangs ripping off their own people, condemning them to death by starvation. General Hoar and his troops have the authority to take whatever military action is necessary to safeguard the lives of our troops and the lives of the Somali people."[1]

Even before Resolution 794 passed, General Powell directed General Hoar to provide security to the transportation facilities in

Mogadishu on December 2. Within a few days a U.S. Navy amphibious squadron composed of USS *Tripoli, Juneau,* and *Rushmore,* with SEAL and Special Boat Units embarked, arrived off the coast of Somalia. The availability of the U.S. Navy to project such power on short notice paid off. One aspect of the situation was similar to what the Americans had faced in short-fused operations in Grenada and Panama: Satisfactory charts and beach studies of the Somalia coast were not available; therefore, the SEALs and Special Boat Units accompanying the force conducted a hydrographic reconnaissance to chart the beaches. First, they executed a preliminary reconnaissance, and then they swam into Mogadishu Harbor on December 7 through strong currents and raw sewage. The swimmers found the harbor suitable to support the large maritime prepositioning ships. The following night, they led the first wave of marines in their amphibious tractors to the beaches, only to be met by a large group from the news media who were quick to play up the combat readiness of the force as belying its benevolent mission.

Ten days later American SEALs swam out from the French navy frigate *Dupliex* and surveyed the port of Chisimayu to the south of the capital. This was the first mission during which American forces received hostile fire from local armed gangs. There were no casualties.

The Central Command order activating the operation read: "When directed by the National Command Authorities, Commander in Chief Central Command will conduct combined operations in Somalia to secure the major air and sea ports, key installations and food distribution points, to provide open and free passage of relief supplies, to provide security for convoys and relief organizations and assist UN/nongovernmental organizations in providing humanitarian relief under UN auspices." The directive said nothing about encountering or disarming the local gangs, but soon it grew clear that the United Nations wished the Americans to disarm the Somali warring factions. Although realizing the need for some disarming to ensure the safe flow of humanitarian relief, General Hoar did not envision rendering the entire scene safe for relief operations. There was a wide margin between what the UN resolution called for and what President Bush had ordered his military to achieve.

General Hoar focused the operation on the nine southern districts of Somalia, where the situation was the worst. The remaining seven northern regions, in what had been British Somaliland, were left to the UN to administer. There was initially no opposition. With remarkable skill and daring, U.S. Ambassador Robert Oakley, special envoy to Somalia, had done a superb job of entering the dens of both warring factions and had convinced them, at least temporarily, not to challenge the large-scale relief effort and not to antagonize the security forces involved.

U.S. Marine Corps Lieutenant General Robert B. Johnston was named to command the Unified Task Force (UNITAF). The lead assault element was the Fifteenth Marine Expeditionary Unit taken from the Third Marine Division in the Far East. The basic unit was formed around a battalion landing team of the Ninth Marine Regiment, the 164th Medium Helicopter Squadron, and the Fifteenth Marine Expeditionary Unit Service Support Group from the three-ship USS *Tripoli* amphibious group. The Fifteenth Marine Expeditionary Unit had the capability to take and hold the port and airport of Mogadishu but required reinforcements to stay on the ground for any extended period if facing combat against the warlords and their heavily armed factions.

After receiving their equipment from the maritime prepositioning ships that had moved to Mogadishu from Diego Garcia, the marines were reinforced by the Seventh Marine Regiment from the First Marine Division at Camp Pendleton in California. A total of approximately six thousand marines were eventually ashore in Mogadishu. The remainder of the American forces consisted of the U.S. Army Tenth Mountain Division, a light infantry division from Fort Drum in New York, which was not equipped with armor. U.S. Air Force Air Mobility Command C-141B Starlifters, KC-10A Extenders, and C-5 Galaxies with additional civilian charters brought in the twenty-four thousand U.S. Army troops and one thousand additional foreign troops. The USS *Ranger* battle group with the Aegis cruiser USS *Valley Forge* was on the scene in support and was later re-placed by USS *Kitty Hawk*. Their mission was to be ready to provide carrier air support until the intervention force was reorganized into the UNOSOM II in May 1993. Total American forces in Operation Restore Hope ashore in Somalia and Kenya and embarked in ships offshore reached a total of 25,426.

On December 28, 1992, the U.S. Special Forces units already in Kenya moved to Somalia and joined the operation. Their mission was to make initial contact with indigenous factions and leaders, to provide information for force protection, and to assess areas for fu-ture relief and security operations. The Special Forces were sent to di-rectly support the nine designated relief sectors. Between December 1992 and April 1993 these units captured 277 weapons and destroyed more than forty-five thousand pounds of ordnance from the warring factions. The Special Forces deployed a civic-action battalion and a psychological-warfare task force that produced a Somali-language newspaper called *Rajo,* meaning "truth," and set up a radio station in the U.S. embassy that broadcast in the Somali language. By January 1993 non-U.S. participation had ballooned to include troops from twenty-one countries, a total of thirteen thousand. The largest of these units were the First Battalion Royal Australian Regiment, the Belgian First Paracommando Battalion, the Botswana Task Force, the Canadian Airborne Battle Group, the French Foreign Legion Thir-teenth Demi-Brigade, the Italian Task Force, the Royal Moroccan Task Force, and the Pakistani peacekeeper battalion.

By May 1993, after the operation had eased the situation of the Somali population and ended the immediate starvation, the com-mand of UNITAF was transferred back to the United Nations and the intervention force was renamed UNOSOM II. The secretary gen-eral named Turkish Lieutenant General Cevik Bir as the overall com-mander. Boutros-Boutros Ghali's personal representative was retired U.S. Navy Admiral Jonathan Howe, and roughly thirty American of-ficers occupied senior positions in the UNOSOM II command struc-ture, including the deputy commander, U.S. Army Major General Thomas M. Montgomery, under whom all American combat units operated. He also held tactical command of the Quick Reaction

Force, which began immediately to conduct aggressive operations against the Habar-Gedir clan run by Muhammad Aidid. Recognizing the reality of the large coalition of American and other military forces, the clans initially upheld their promises to Ambassador Oakley. They all paused in their fighting.

Within several weeks of the transformation from UNITAF to UNOSOM II, some command problems arose, especially when the U.S. Marines were withdrawn. Their removal cut the force from a total of thirty-eight thousand to twenty-eight thousand men. Meanwhile, the international participation expanded from the initial seven countries to a total of thirty-one participating member countries. Many of the military elements were poorly paid and inadequately trained units from developing countries that participated mainly for prestige or financial reasons. While the initial function of the larger military formation was to provide a safe environment for the humanitarian relief distribution, the force was really unable to do so, since it had not disarmed the warring factions. It had been purposely avoiding that measure, since it would have meant opening hostilities against both sides in the ongoing civil struggle; moreover, the Americans had been neither tasked nor authorized to do that. Now, with a force of twenty-eight thousand men, primarily from Africa and Asia, and the American Tenth Mountain Division acting as the Quick Reaction Force, the United Nations set about to salvage the situation. It proposed (1) to disarm the factions on both sides, (2) to establish a police force and judicial system, and (3) to repatriate refugees and urge the country toward a national reconciliation. In other words, the mission had changed from providing security for humanitarian relief to "nation building."

On June 5, 1993, General Muhammad Farah Aidid's Somali National Alliance forces ambushed a detachment from the United Nation's Pakistani battalion. Twenty-four men were brutally slaughtered, some of them mutilated and skinned alive. In response to this provocation, General Hoar at Central Command immediately requested four AC-130 gunship aircraft to strike back at Aidid's gunmen. By

June 7 four U.S. Air Force Special Operations AC-130 Hercules gunships arrived. Using their rapid-fire machine guns, 105mm howitzers, and 40mm cannons, they carried out thirty-two missions against Aidid's factions beginning on June 12, eventually forcing him into hiding. The gunships demolished two weapons-storage facilities and an armored vehicle compound. The United Nations subsequently declared the Somali National Alliance an illegal faction, and the secretary general's representative, Admiral Jonathan Howe, offered a $25,000 reward for Aidid. The joint UN forces then raided his residence but did not capture him.

The campaign against the warlord soon took on the tone of a personal feud between Jonathan Howe and Muhammad Aidid that, ironically, took on the characteristics of a struggle by Somali clan chiefs. Howe requested the use of America's roughest men, its Special Forces, to go after the evasive clansman. The request was denied, and Howe pursued Aidid with the forces he had at hand. He sent helicopters with broadcast speakers to warn civilians of ongoing operations, a tactic that was soon ridiculed by the Somalis.

The American forces on the ground in Somalia were primarily conventional troops and did not have the capability for a smash-and-grab operation like the Delta Force, so Admiral Howe again sought approval from President Clinton to deploy and use Special Forces. The president again denied the request on the grounds that their deployment might derail ongoing diplomatic negotiations, and again the UN commanders on the scene took action with the forces they had on hand.

On June 17 a Multinational Force of Italian, Pakistani, French, and Moroccan soldiers attacked Aidid's compound and searched each building, to no avail. On July 12 the UN Quick Reaction Force launched 16 TOW antitank missiles from helicopters against the Abdi House, a major Aidid military command center. The attack was conducted without warning and caused heavy Somali casualties: 73 killed and 250 injured. Following that attack, four Western journalists who rushed in to cover the scene were killed by an angry mob. The journalists' deaths enraged the West, just as the missile attack had incensed the locals, whose fury was focused against the United Nations in general and the United States in particular. Open and vicious warfare soon developed on the streets of Mogadishu.

On August 8 a devastating Somali car bomb killed four American soldiers; two weeks later another injured seven more Americans. The troops assigned to the United Nations to provide humanitarian assistance to the Somalis did not have the muscle or the means to perform their mission. They were insufficient in numbers and backed with inadequate heavy weapons and armor. Furthermore, they lacked the special training and ability needed to conduct selective raids to neutralize the leaders of the warring factions.

The U.S. Special Forces did have that capability and could have been effectively employed had they been supported by the requisite armor. Although well-trained and well-equipped, the Tenth U.S. Mountain Division, the Pakistanis, the Italians, and the Malaysians were all light infantry. None possessed the heavy weapons or armor now needed to subdue the aroused Somalis arrayed against the United Nations. Their usefulness declined as the conflict escalated. The armor requested by General Montgomery, the American ground commander, was denied by Secretary of Defense Les Aspin and Chairman of the Joint Chiefs of Staff General Colin Powell.[2] Then, after more deaths of American troops, Chairman Powell reversed himself and requested the use of Special Forces, which President Clinton finally approved.

On August 22 Secretary of Defense Aspin directed the deployment of the Joint Special Operations Force to Somalia. Named Task Force Ranger, it was ordered to capture Muhammad Aidid. The command and control structure of this unit was unique. In accordance with the Goldwater-Nichols Defense Reorganization Act, which specified the functions of the unified commander, such a commander—in this case, General Hoar at Central Command, located at McDill Air Force Base in Florida—was entitled to organize his forces as he desired. General Hoar directed that the commander of Task Force Ranger, U.S. Army Major General William Garrison, report to him directly from Somalia. Task Force Ranger would not fall under the UN command and at all times would remain under U.S. operational command and control. General Garrison would coordinate his

Ranger operations with Major General Thomas M. Montgomery, the commander of all other U.S. forces in Somalia.

The American commander planned a three-phase operation. The first phase would be to quietly install Task Force Ranger in Mogadishu and get it operational. The second phase would be to find and localize Aidid. The third phase would be to target his entire command structure and to capture him dead or alive. The conflict was personal: Aidid became the political objective of the escalating American effort. Task Force Ranger arrived in Mogadishu on August 28, a force of 450 men, mostly U.S. Army Rangers with a detachment of army Delta Force operators, Navy SEALs, and air force special tactics personnel with their distinct helicopters. During late August and September 1993, the task force conducted six missions into Mogadishu, using helicopters and ground vehicles to reach their targets. All of these were tactical successes in which some of Aidid's close associates were seized. Although Aidid was not caught, his movements were severely restricted. Task Force Ranger's first success was the capture of Osman Ato, Aidid's chief arms supplier and finance man. As the missions continued, a growing number of captured Aidid men were taken to a confinement camp outside of Chisimayu.

Aidid's international relations adviser, Muhammad Hassan Awale, later admitted in interviews with westerners that the Somali forces chose to focus their increasingly violent action against the United Nations in general and against Americans in particular, since the latter represented the most visible arm of UN action. To incite the Americans to further actions they intensified their efforts to engage U.S. forces. After watching the initial Task Force Ranger operations, Aidid had concluded that the most vulnerable chink in the Rangers' armor was the helicopters upon which the majority of their operations depended. The use of Black Hawk helicopters in low-level flights over the city had given Aidid's men the idea that to exact a punishing ambush they need only shoot down one of these helicopters, which would then act as a magnet to draw in a sizable relief-and-rescue force against which the Somalis could concentrate their efforts. The idea of downing a helicopter had intrigued Aidid for some time, and his knowledge and understanding of the American fighting man's code of loyalty was key to his plan. He would draw the Rangers into a location of his choosing where he could concentrate a massive number of his rabble in arms and gain a major victory against the Americans.[3] Aidid's gunners began to concentrate on using rocket-launched grenades and heavy machine-gun fire to damage a low-flying helicopter. Aidid was aware that intelligence was being sent from the team employed by the Rangers and he did not try to stop it. Rather, he used it as a means to lure the Rangers so that his men could hit and, with some luck, bring down one or more of the Black Hawks.

In late August, following the initial Ranger missions, Aidid sent a personal letter to former president Jimmy Carter requesting that he intervene with an independent commission "composed of internationally known statesmen, scholars, and jurists from different countries," to investigate the claims that Aidid was responsible for the massacre of the twenty-four Pakistani soldiers. Aidid claimed that the mob action had been caused by the American gunship attack against his Radio Mogadishu. He asked for an independent mediator to settle the dispute with the United Nations. Carter obtained President Clinton's approval for the negotiations, and he began working quietly with the State Department to obtain intercession through the Ethiopian and Eritrean governments. Carter's plan sought an immediate cease-fire; Aidid was to leave the country until a multinational inquiry had been completed. The plan also proposed a series of reconstruction talks for November 1993. The Americans were certain that Aidid's new willingness to talk was based on the severe pressure exerted by Task Force Ranger. Thus, in the midst of the manhunt, the U.S. government opened secret negotiations with Aidid, and neither the U.S. military commanders in Mogadishu nor those at the Joint Special Operations Command in Florida were notified.

Working on the Carter plan to end the confrontation peacefully, UN special envoy Admiral Howe flew to Djibouti and Addis Ababa. He returned on October 3, 1993, the day that General Garrison's troops launched their seventh and last raid, one based on an unusually urgent intelligence report that Aidid and his two leading lieutenants were meeting in a building near the Olympic Hotel in the central district of the teeming Bakara Market in Mogadishu, the roughest center of Aidid's territory. At 3:32 P.M. Black Hawk helicopters carrying both assault and blocking forces took off from the Ranger base at Mogadishu Airport. Three minutes later a ground convoy made up primarily of Humvees and trucks departed the Ranger base. By 3:42 the ground convoy had arrived at the target location just as the air-dropped blocking force was setting up perimeter positions and the assault force was searching the building and taking twenty-four of Aidid's key supporters captive. The ground team came under fierce fire, more intense than any it had ever encountered on previous missions. While team members were loading the prisoners onto trucks, one MH-60 Black Hawk was hit and downed by a rocket-propelled grenade. Concentrated fire against the low-flying helicopter succeeded, and the Black Hawk crashed three blocks from the target building.

In a predictable move, the six-man element of the Ranger blocking force ran to the scene of the downed helicopter. Two additional helicopters, an MH-6 Little Guy and an additional Black Hawk carrying a fifteen-man search-and-rescue team, also hurried to the scene of the crash. The first to arrive was the MH-6, which, in a fierce firefight, collected two wounded crewmen and evacuated them to a military hospital. The six-man blocking element then arrived at the site of the downed helicopter with the search-and-rescue helicopter. As the last two men of the fifteen-man rescue team were sliding down their fast ropes, their MH-60 was hit by a rocket-propelled grenade. The two men on the ropes reached the ground safely, and the helicopter limped back to the airport. In the meantime, two more Black Hawks were hit, one crashing less than a mile from the first downed helicopter. Another Black Hawk was hit broadside by rocket-propelled grenades but returned successfully to the airport. A mob of Somali gunmen overran the second crash site and, despite an intense fight, killed all aboard with the exception of the pilot, U.S. Army Chief Warrant Officer Michael Durant, whom they captured. He was saved at the site by an elderly Somali man who spirited him away from the mob and took him to Aidid.

Meanwhile, after loading their prisoners onto the ground convoy while under a heavy fusillade of small-arms fire, the remainder of the assault force made their way on foot to the first crash site, where they set up defensive positions in surrounding buildings and held the Somali mob at bay while they treated their wounded and extricated the pilot's body from the wrecked Black Hawk. The truck convoy with the detainees aboard was unable to find the remainder of the Rangers at the crash site and, amid withering small-arms fire from all directions, finally returned to base, losing two five-ton trucks and sustaining numerous casualties and heavy damage to all vehicles. As the convoy was returning, it encountered another outbound convoy attempting to reach the second crash site. The wounded were transferred to vehicles that then returned to the airport, while the remainder of the group fought its way back to the second helicopter's crash site. A company from Quick Reaction Force's Tenth Mountain Division was pinned down by throngs of Somali clansmen during the attempt and forced to retreat to the airport base with support from two additional AH-6 helicopters.

The American crewmen and Delta operators holding the clansmen captive were pinned down and fought for the rest of the day—seventeen hours—trying to withdraw from the crowded city center. Between five hundred and one thousand Somalis were believed killed, and eighteen Americans, including two Delta operators, were killed. Michael Durant, the captured American pilot, was subsequently released. One Malaysian soldier and one Moroccan soldier who were part of the armored relief column that fought its way in to rescue the Americans were killed. Fighting an orderly withdrawal against heavy numerical odds is a very difficult thing, even for well-disciplined soldiers.[4]

The decision to attack had been made at the Joint Special Operations Command in Florida and relayed directly to Mogadishu. The UN commander, General Cevik Bir, was informed just before the strike was launched. Admiral Howe was not informed of the planned strike and was away conducting negotiations. Neither General Montgomery nor General Garrison was informed of the peace negotiations under way between Aidid and Carter. President Clinton's response to the new situation in Somalia was to withdraw the troops and cut his losses. He initially sent in substantial combat troops as short-term re-inforcements but declared that American troops were to be fully withdrawn from Somalia by March 31, 1994. The hunt for Aidid was abandoned, and U.S. representatives resumed negotiations with the warlord. Two weeks later, in a letter to President Clinton, General Garrison accepted full responsibility for what had happened in the battle. This incident resulted in Presidential Decision Directive 25 of March 1994, which stated that U.S. support for peacekeeping opera-tions must be contingent on a conflict's threat to international peace and security, or on a determination that the operation "serves U.S. interests."[5]

In Somalia, a loosely organized mob achieved astonishing success using their numbers and an assortment of knives and small arms against highly trained U.S. Special Forces. The Americans lost the fight in the streets of Mogadishu to a mixture of citizens and warlord gangs. Even though the Somalis suffered hundreds of casualties ver-sus eighteen for the Americans, the United States was forced to with-draw. The defeat doomed the entire UN intervention to certain failure.

PART SIX

William J. Clinton:
On the Edge of the Balkans

THE BALKANS

CHAPTER 14

Intervention in Bosnia

1991–1999

Historians, journalists, and experts disagree over the nature of the wars that have afflicted the Balkans during the past decade. There are in print hundreds of historical studies, articles, eyewitness stories, memoirs, analyses, and other accounts of the wars. Opinions about the roots of the conflict abound, and simple explanations—ancient ethnic hatreds, demagogues, the termination of Western loans—are incomplete. Complex explanations, which the Clinton administration embraced, tended to create paralysis in Washington, because they implied complex, messy solutions that were not implemented easily.

Perhaps a serviceable way to explain these most recent wars in the Balkans is to paraphrase Thucydides, historian of a war that took place twenty-four centuries earlier in the southern end of the Balkan Peninsula. What made the twentieth-century Balkan wars inevitable was the growth of Serb power and the fear this caused among the other peoples of Yugoslavia. The fears of Slovenes, Croats, Muslims, and Serbs who lived in minority clusters in the various republics accelerated the movement for decentralization when the Communist glue that had held the republics together for forty years of Tito's central control melted way.

In 1980, with the death of Tito (Josip Broz), ethnic hostility seemed tamed. Intermarriage between Catholic Croats, Muslim Bosnians, and Orthodox Serbs, while not commonplace, was widely accepted, reaching a total of one-fifth of the Yugoslav populace. But hungry power brokers caused more discord with hate propaganda in their relentless quest for political power. Slobodan Milosevic, the ambitious Serbian Communist apparatchik who became president of Yugoslavia in the late 1980s, deliberately reminded the Serbs of the terrible atrocities committed against them by the Croats during the Nazi occupation of the 1940s. Then, in a moment of virulent anti-Muslim hate-mongering, Milosevic yanked away the autonomous status of the Albanian-dominated Kosovo in 1989 and proclaimed his quest for a Greater Serbia. In early 1990, Croat leader Franjo Tudjman, a venomous nationalist demagogue, returned from exile. He adopted many of the fascist trappings of Croatia's recent past while building a corrupt nationalist one-party dictatorship in Zagreb. The Serb-Croat rivalry polarized the newly independent Bosnian Republic, and both factions turned against the Bosnian Muslims. Even moderates were compelled to accept the theme of Bosnian leader Alija Izetbegovic, who reminded all Bosnians of the Muslims' long-standing victimization at the hands of both Serbs and Croats.

By 1990, after Yugoslavia had achieved a better life for its citizens and an economy that approached European levels of free-market success, the new political despots reversed all their postwar gains. Each new tyrant surrounded himself with cronies who were outright criminals, and each sought to trump the others by seizing disputed territory for his cause. In a land steeped in a history of hatred and intolerance, these were not difficult tasks for new Balkan tyrants weaned on the unscrupulous methods of the Communist party. The collapse of Communist ideology and the subsequent vacuum of authority provided these despots with fertile fields for their work. The Yugoslav populace, content with the moderate economic success given to them by Tito's government, and still imbued with the Communist-imposed behavior of passive acquiescence, proved easily led.

While the world watched in horror, murder and mayhem in Bosnia accelerated to a level unknown in Europe since the years of the Nazis. Europe, the United Nations, and the United States wrung their hands in dismay but found it difficult to contemplate intervention until the flood of refugees and the sight of horrible suffering daily on the news reached unbearable levels. Overcome by the guilt of standing idly by, they finally took action. First under President George Bush and then under Bill Clinton, the United States had sought to avoid direct intervention in Bosnia. It was not our war, according to Bush's secretary of state, James Baker; the Europeans certainly had more interest than did the United States. As a candidate in 1992 Clinton promised to do more but was vague about the specifics. President Bush finally approved aid and assistance that year and sent naval and air forces to join the sea and air arms embargoes but refused to participate on the ground with UN peacekeepers. As the new president, Clinton hesitated to lead the introduction of robust combat forces in May 1993. Later he succumbed to the prevailing moral outrage and sent in a token ground force to join Scandinavian peacekeepers in Macedonia, where no fighting was going on, as a deterrent against spillover into that republic. In Bosnia two years of war followed.

In August 1995 a reconstituted Croatian army drove the last of the Serb forces out of western Croatia. The victorious Croats soon had the Serbs retreating in neighboring Bosnia. With this ad hoc ally on the ground willing to fight, President Clinton committed U.S. airpower to a NATO bombing campaign against the Serbs. This combined ground and air offensive forced the Serbs to the bargaining table in less than two months. The result was the Dayton peace accords, which ended open warfare and most of the bloodshed in Bosnia.

Tito's legacy of stability in Yugoslavia had already slowly begun to unwind following his death in May 1980. His masterfully crafted "All People's Defense" had held the disparate forces of the eight republics and autonomous regions together until 1991, when Slovenia and Croatia sought to extract themselves from Yugoslavia's federation, which they saw coming under Serb domination. The leaders of the republics of Slovenia, Croatia, and Bosnia, who predicted bloody results ahead, appealed to the United States to help them become independent peacefully. But President George Bush, who was already

trying hard to discourage the creeping nationalism that was fragment-
ing the Soviet Union, strongly favored preserving the integrity of
Yugoslavia to avert a similar splintering there. Yugoslav President Slobodan Milosevic interpreted that stance as a green light for unleashing force to keep Slovenia, Croatia, and Bosnia from seceding.

As the Yugoslav secession crisis loomed, the United States and the
European Union tried desperately to prevent bloodshed. President
Bush sent Secretary of State James Baker to try to hold things together. He flew to Belgrade on June 21, 1991, directly from a meeting
in Berlin of the Conference on Security and Cooperation in Europe
(CSCE), carrying with him a statement committing all thirty-six
CSCE members to unity, reform, human rights, and a peaceful solution of the crisis in Yugoslavia. Baker met with the Yugoslav prime
minister and foreign minister and the leaders of all six Yugoslav republics, as well as Vojvodina and Kosovo.[1] But his words fell on deaf
ears. The Belgrade leaders vowed to use the Yugoslav army to force
cohesion of the state. Baker appealed to Slovenian President Milan
Kuchan and Croatian President Franjo Tudjman. He pointed out
that the best way to preserve the rights of minorities in each republic was to remain a united Yugoslavia. He warned that the United
States would not recognize unilateral secession that would lead to violence.[2] The mission failed and the republics went their separate
ways. Kiro Gligorov, the leader of Macedonia, and Alija Izetbegovic
from Bosnia and Herzegovina tried in vain to hold Yugoslavia together, accurately predicting that if Slovenia and Croatia successfully
seceded, serious violence would follow in their own republics because of the large Muslim presence. Slovenia and Croatia declared independence on June 25, 1991, and two days later fighting erupted in
Slovenia in what was to become the first of three bloody wars that
cost the lives of more than one hundred thousand and drove millions
from their homes.

The Slovenes won their secession first, in July 1991, after a brief ten-
day fight and a standoff in which numbers, heavy weapons, and equipment greatly favored the Yugoslav army. Yugoslav troops had promptly
moved north to challenge Slovenian independence and to reinforce

their own units already stationed there. In a brilliant campaign, Slovenian territorial troops isolated the road-bound columns. They also surrounded and captured more than forty thousand Yugoslav army troops in their barracks and ended the fight with minimal casualties.[3]

The fight for Croatia with its large Serb minority was prolonged and more bloody. Milosevic claimed that the Yugoslav army had the right to intervene to protect Serb minorities there once Croatia decided to secede. After Croatia proclaimed independence, Yugoslav army and Serbian paramilitary forces were able to gain control over substantial chunks of Croatia, operating primarily with local guerrilla units, made up of Serb gangs living in scattered Croatian enclaves and gangs from Serbia. Vicious fighting continued in Croatia until early 1992. By then Croatia had lost a third of its territory, and Serbia had also become embroiled in Bosnia. The European Union and the United Nations finally negotiated a halt in the fighting. Veteran U.S. diplomat Cyrus Vance, working with the European Union, had managed to negotiate a cease-fire in the disputed regions of Croatia, calling for a temporary arrangement in which UN peacekeepers would protect the minorities. Led by Germany, which had a long, close association with Slovenia and Croatia, the European Union formally recognized the two newly independent states on December 16, 1992, and began to send in relief material. The precipitous European recognition of the new Balkan states hastened the Balkans' plunge into open warfare.

In Bosnia, elections in late 1990 had produced a parliament of ninety-nine Muslims, eighty-five Serbs, and forty-nine Croats, proportions that roughly matched the population as a whole. Bosnian Muslims made up roughly 44 percent of the Bosnian population and lived mostly in the urban areas of Sarajevo and larger towns. Muslims also dominated population centers in easternmost Bosnia, along the Drina River, which formed the border with Serbia. The Croats controlled much of the southern area of Bosnia and Herzegovina, making up roughly a fifth of the population. Much of the remainder of

Bosnia's rural area was inhabited by Serbs, who wasted no time linking up with their benefactors in Belgrade and fought tooth and nail to prevent Bosnia from becoming independent. The leader of the Muslims, Alija Izetbegovic, sought to form a government of national unity by including members of all three groups in major parties, even though he could have excluded the Serbs. It soon became apparent that the Serbs were intent on the partition of Bosnia and on seizing for themselves the lion's share of territory. Most of Bosnia's Muslims were fully secularized and therefore uninterested in a Muslim Bosnia based on Islamic principles. The Croats were not in favor of partition but reluctantly fell in with the Serbs. In March 1992, Bosnian President Izetbegovic, seeing little hope of a reconciliation with the Serbs, and despite U.S. State Department advice, declared Bosnia independent from Yugoslavia. The stage was set for a bloody three-way fight. The end of the fighting in Croatia meant that Serb strength in the region had increased. With Belgrade running the show, the Serbs took the initiative in Bosnia using the Yugoslav army—by this time made up almost entirely of Serbs—as the primary strike force. The role of the Yugoslav army in the strife that followed in Bosnia and eventually Kosovo is key to understanding the Balkan tragedy of the 1990s.

The Yugoslav People's Army was the third largest regular land force in Europe in 1948. At Tito's death in May 1980 it numbered 220,000, but it declined to 170,000 by 1992 following the loss of conscripts from the newly independent Slovenia and Croatia. Embodied for forty years within the Yugoslav army's officer corps was Tito's principle of proportional representation of the area's variety of nationalities. The Yugoslav army traditionally condemned nationalism and chauvinism in Yugoslavia, and many dedicated Titoists in the army were opposed to the rebirth of the Serbian nationalism that brought Slobodan Milosevic to power in the late 1980s. The army tried in vain to reverse the decentralization and disintegration of Tito's Yugoslavia, but in March 1991, the self-styled Staff of the Supreme Command of the Armed Forces of Yugoslavia issued its first decree, effectively shedding civilian control of the military. Following that decree the Yugoslav army began functioning openly as a fully autonomous entity of the only two remaining Yugoslav republics, Serbia and Montenegro. Then, to weaken national and regional identity, the predominant Serbs manipulated the army's transformation into a "Serboslav" culture. The Yugoslav army had been forced to reorganize quickly after its abortive campaign to keep Slovenia in the Yugoslav fold in June 1991. By December of the same year it had completed its transition to an all-Serb force and began to redeploy into Bosnia. Code-named Rahm by the Belgrade general staff, the plan was accomplished allegedly to protect all minorities in a possible future conflict should Bosnia break away from Yugoslavia and declare independence, which is exactly what happened.

During the redeployment process Belgrade covertly provided large quantities of arms to local Bosnian Serb forces. By early June 1992, the Yugoslav Federal Military Command officially adopted the goal of "protecting Serbs" and agreed to station its fourteen thousand peacekeeping personnel in the conflict areas.[4] The primary motive behind the Yugoslav army's initial seizure of large parts of Bosnia and Herzegovina in 1992 was to capture the enormous amount of heavy weapons and explosives there. Major parts of the Yugoslav army's arsenal were produced in defense factories in Bosnia and Croatia. Yugoslavia was among the world's ten largest arms producers, and the defense industry was the country's chief source of hard currency. The defeats suffered by the Yugoslav army in Slovenia and the agreed pullout from most of Croatia in 1992 represented a major loss to the Yugoslav defense industry. Nevertheless, the Yugoslav army managed to strip and evacuate large quantities of machinery, equipment, and technical documentation from many of the defense plants in those areas lost and to relocate them in Serbia and Montenegro. Since the summer of 1992, the Serbs had reestablished and in some cases strengthened their overall defense manufacturing capabilities.

The first clashes in Bosnia erupted in early 1992 among Serb, Muslim, and Croat fighters and quickly accelerated to open slaughter of unarmed civilians. Western leaders were unwilling to recognize that the action had been carefully planned and directed by the top Serb political and military leadership in Belgrade and carried out through the general staff of the Yugoslav army. The Bosnian Serbs, with the help of the Yugoslav army, gradually seized 70 percent of

Bosnia. Despite Milosevic's repeated denials of Belgrade's involvement, the Yugoslav army moved quietly into the Second Yugoslav Military District of Sarajevo just before the fledgling Bosnian Serb Republic declared its sovereignty on January 14, 1992. Without the preemptive move into Sarajevo the Serbs never could have conquered such a large part of Bosnia so quickly. In a 1993 judgment, the International Court of Justice in the Hague implicitly recognized that Belgrade was directing and supporting Serb military and paramilitary forces in Bosnia. The court issued strong legal words of censure against Belgrade but stopped short of taking immediate action for compensation. The court's findings reflected a strong worldwide consensus and damning evidence that the actions of the Bosnian Serbs were directed and controlled by Serbian President Slobodan Milosevic in Belgrade.

Bosnian independence was the last resort of most Muslims, not their first choice. The struggle between advocates of independence, dominated by the Muslim inner circle, and those opposed, Bosnian Serbs in the north and Bosnian Croats in the south, soon erupted into violent and vicious slaughter. The governments in Belgrade and Zagreb sent armed military factions and bands of paramilitary thugs into the contested areas to protect their ethnic populations and to grab more territory by evicting Bosnian Muslims from their homes. The strife continued for months while the United Nations and Europeans dithered in despair, wishing for a solution but not daring to intervene. The United States watched and took little action as the carnage in and around Sarajevo ebbed and flowed in bursts of murderous savagery targeted mostly against helpless civilians. In addition to Sarajevo, the Yugoslav army also encircled the Muslim towns of Banja Luka, Bihac, Gorazde, Tuzla, and Zepa. Further south in Herzegovina the Croats, assisted by their home forces from Zagreb, attacked and destroyed much of the ancient town of Mostar. Eighteen months of grisly killing gave birth to the term *ethnic cleansing*, which grew into a common practice in the Balkans for those who wielded the most firepower in a given area. When the Serbs and Croats were not busy slaughtering whole Muslim towns, they fought each other.

On February 21, 1992, after much soul-searching, the United Nations called for the deployment of UN peacekeeping forces to protect relief supplies to be sent initially to Croatia and then Bosnia. The United Nations established the UN Protection Force (UNPROFOR) to guarantee the delivery of supplies, to verify cease-fires, and to disarm the combatants. The UN granted the protection force license to use armed convoys to escort relief supplies sent to beleaguered enclaves in Croatia. UNPROFOR's other missions were to demilitarize certain areas designated as UN-protected zones, to supervise the disarmament of civilians, to assist local law enforcement, to guarantee safe passages of humanitarian convoys returning resettled minorities to their homes, and to monitor the evacuation of the wounded.

Further efforts to stabilize and restore the region followed: On June 29, 1992, the United Nations Security Council passed Resolution 761, rushing humanitarian assistance to Sarajevo and its suburbs. In September, Secretary General Boutros Boutros-Ghali recommended placing the relief efforts of the UN High Commissioner for Refugees under UNPROFOR protection. In October, Resolution 781 implemented a no-fly zone over Bosnia to protect the Muslim refugees from Serb airpower, and requested its enforcement by UNPROFOR until the task was taken over by NATO six months later. In November, Resolution 787 deployed observers to the Bosnian borders "to enforce compliance of the arms embargo on Bosnia and the sanctions on Serbia." Sea and air exclusion zones were also put into place to try to stop the inflow of external aid to the warring parties. Unfortunately, these controls did little to stem the flow of the banned materials controlled by smugglers and criminals backed by the Serbian and Bosnian leaders. The embargoes merely entrenched at the head of extortion and bribery rings Serb authorities who amassed vast personal fortunes from the sanctions while their people suffered.

Tito's concept of All Yugoslav National Defense had ensured that ample arms and ammunitions were stashed throughout the hills of Yugoslavia during the long and precarious cold war. As a result there were sufficient arms for all, even without imports from abroad. Serb and Croat forces seized most of these supplies, so any embargoes hurt only the underarmed Muslim forces, who were barely scraping by on the few deliveries coming in secretly from sympathetic Muslim countries. Much of these came through Croatia, whose government exacted its own cut.

UN humanitarian assistance began to flow into the Balkans in October 1992. The UN resolution authorized member states to intervene to guarantee the arrival of relief shipments with or without invitation by the republics of Croatia and Bosnia. Initially UNPROFOR was to ensure that the relief supplies reached the needy in Croatia alone, but in October its mandate was expanded to provide convoys to escort aid to Muslim enclaves in Bosnia. A civilian international relief organization put together by the European Union coordinated with the UN armed force to deliver the relief supplies.

Unlike the combined civilian-military effort designed to help the Kurds in northern Iraq in 1991, UNPROFOR lacked muscle and the will to use force. The UN force was lightly armed and could not compete against the Serbs with their heavy weapons and armor. The UN peacekeepers were deployed to Muslim-controlled areas primarily because the Serbs simply refused to allow them in Serb-controlled areas. This soon created the appearance that the United Nations was supporting the Bosnian Muslims exclusively and contributed to the perception that the whole world was arrayed against the Serbs, a view that gradually spread until the entire Balkan population of Serbs, from Belgrade to the Albanian borders, embraced the idea of widespread anti-Serb persecution. Milosevic capitalized on this view with great skill to bolster the Serb national spirit through the very end of the conflict in Kosovo in 1999. To most involved in the Balkans it seemed that "the Serbs had all the guns, while the Muslims got all the publicity."[5] Admiral Leighton Smith, the NATO Southern Allied Forces commander from 1994 to 1996, explained that the inclination of the Balkan peoples, including children of all competing factions, to swallow the party line was uncanny. After visiting schools of all the sides—Muslim schools in Sarajevo, Serb schools in Alija, and Croat schools in Mostar—Admiral Smith observed that the youngsters in each case were totally indoctrinated by their own side. Muslim children inquired when NATO would begin pursuing Serb and Croat war criminals, whereas Serb children asked why the United Nations and whole world were against the Serbs. This united front was the unfortunate residue of years of Communist education, when the public accepted everything it was fed by the government-controlled press, and to doubt, question, or challenge official news was taboo. Each of the three disparate groups presented its own version of propaganda, which was duly swallowed by highly motivated and fanatical believers of all ages.[6]

As soon as the Serbs realized that the UN peacekeepers were reluctant to use force of any kind, they quickly began to harass and bully the aid workers until the relief effort was rendered completely ineffective. Belgian Lieutenant General Francis Briquemont, the UN military commander in Bosnia from 1992 to 1994, complained, "There is a fantastic gap between all these Security Council resolutions and the means available to execute them."[7] Admiral Leighton Smith concurred: "The UN Protection Forces were ordered to avoid using force at all costs."[8] The UN forces attempted to remain neutral during the vicious fighting and, like the U.S. Marines in Beirut in 1983, became engrossed with their own protection.

The United States had chosen not to act despite growing revulsion toward the Serbs and the feeble attempts of predominantly Canadian, French, and British UN peacekeeping forces. The Serbs undertook ethnic cleansing in besieged centers, including Banja Luka, Bihac, Gorazde, Tuzla, and Zepa, with a vengeance. By November 1992 an estimated seventeen thousand were dead and roughly half the Bosnian population of two million were refugees. Many of the Serb military formations in Bosnia by late 1992 were well armed, professionally trained, highly motivated, and capable, with heavy weapons and armor. There were clearly three warring factions: the Muslims and Croats—now in a weak federation—and the Serbs backed by Yugoslavia.

While the fighting continued, the European Union finally proffered a plan in January 1993 to all sides for an independent Bosnia. Designed by Cyrus Vance, a former U.S. secretary of state, and David Owen, a former British foreign secretary who represented the

European Union, the plan called for a seventy-two-hour cease-fire, fifteen days thereafter to withdraw forces from Sarajevo, and forty-five days to decamp major forces, as ratified by a constitutional agreement. Under the plan Bosnia would become a centralized state with ten cantons based as closely as possible on existing ethnic settlements and having significant local autonomy. But it required the Serbs to give up a large part, almost 40 percent, of the territory they had already gained. Milosevic compelled the Bosnian Serb leader Radovan Karadzic to accept the plan on May 2, 1993. However, days later, President Clinton lost confidence in the idea of enforcing the plan with American-led NATO military forces on the ground. Soon the Bosnian Serbs reversed Karadzic and rejected the Vance-Owen plan.

The Clinton administration's alternative, lifting the arms embargo and backing the UN forces with the threat of NATO air strikes, was rejected by the Europeans. America's forces would remain on the periphery of the war in Bosnia for two more years. In a compromise solution the United States agreed to a plan for a pullback of Yugoslav regular army units and the demobilization of the Yugoslav Territorial Defense Force under the conditions brokered by the Vance-Owen plan. However, the Yugoslav army, under the leadership of Defense Minister General Veljko Kadijevic, circumvented the agreement by quietly reassigning large numbers of federal Yugoslav regular troops, who were mostly Serbs, into the Bosnian Territorial Defense Force and police units and by redeploying and further arming the local Serb units already fighting in Croatia and preparing to oppose an independent Bosnia. The Yugoslav army also quickly handed over to Bosnian Serbs large amounts of arms and armored vehicles—more than 300 tanks, 100 armored personnel carriers, 250 artillery pieces, 25 combat aircraft, several dozen Soviet-designed surface-to-air missiles, and an estimated 80,000 tons of ammunition.

The Vance-Owen plan demanded that the Yugoslav army adopt the policy of "interposition and calming armed conflicts between other parties," but this was like asking the wolves to protect the sheep. The Yugoslav army units—still with red stars on their helmets and tanks—merely turned a blind eye and let Serb irregulars commit massacres of captured prisoners of war, wounded soldiers, civilians, and even children.[9] The Vance-Owen plan failed to take root, and the fighting continued.

During this time in Washington the Defense Department was busily defining what forces would need to be committed to Yugoslavia if the United States was called upon to put an end to the fighting. It was clear to military authorities that a protracted war on the ground in Bosnia was to be avoided at all costs. There was ample historical precedent to ensure that such an option was out of the question. Lieutenant General Barry McCaffrey, the head planner of the Joint Chiefs of Staff, explained to Congress that a ground force of at least four hundred thousand was required to carry out the mission.[10] Senior military leaders were vehemently opposed to going into Bosnia without sufficient force to impose a decisive result. In 1992 Secretary of Defense Richard Cheney advocated contributing only those unique American assets such as airlift, communications, and intelligence to European forces to do the job. There was sharp disagreement between advocates of intervention and the military who opposed involvement without adequate commitment. Madeleine Albright, U.S. ambassador to the United Nations, and military planners disagreed on the level of forces needed. In the early months of the Clinton administration there was little dialogue between State and Defense Department planners to seek an honest evaluation of the cost in numbers of troops, time to achieve the mission, and probable losses in a U.S. incursion. In such cases the military normally provides estimates of the best- and worst-case costs of executing the mission. The State Department suspected that General Colin Powell, chairman of the Joint Chiefs of Staff, was raising the numbers of total troops required in order to sabotage the effort.

Despite the disagreements on the levels required, the European countries led by the United States finally interceded. The United Nations began to investigate the plethora of war crimes that could no longer be ignored, and to sponsor political negotiations. Existing political and economic sanctions against the Serbs were reinforced. These late, but nonetheless more potent, UN military measures proved more effective; but even though authorized to use force, commanders on the ground were still reluctant to do so. There was little incentive for the lightly armed UN peacekeepers to start a confrontation with the heavily armed Serbs. The UN peacekeepers were not armed, equipped, or backed with enough force to compel the Serbs to do anything. There was still the growing perception that the United Nations, Europe, and the United States were supporting the Muslims alone. There was strong concern in Europe that an Iranian-backed Muslim state might emerge in the Balkans and sponsor terrorism. These fears proved to be exaggerated but seemed real to a Europe wary of that threat. Bogdan Muratovic, the head of the UN liaison to the Bosnian Muslim forces, was widely known to be dealing with Iran for arms and even buying weapons under the table from the Serbs they were fighting.[11]

The support for Bosnia shown by some Islamic countries failed to transform the struggle into a popular Muslim cause. The lack of material support from major powers for the Bosnian government encouraged some Bosnian Muslim leaders to embrace Muslim militancy; however, imposing Islamic indoctrination on young people and army units and returning women to the custom of wearing veils were not widely enforced. Prime Ministers Tansu Ciller of Turkey and Benazir Bhutto of Pakistan, neither of whom was considered an Islamic extremist, visited Sarajevo once in a futile attempt to galvanize world opinion around the belief that the conflict was a desperate struggle for survival by ill-fated Bosnian Muslims. According to James Clunan, a former political counselor in the U.S. embassies in Belgrade and Ankara, the Turks tried hard to thwart the radicalization and Islamization of the Bosnians. The presence of Muslim volunteers and mujahideen from Iran, Afghanistan, Libya, Sudan, and Saudi Arabia was confirmed but did not become a major factor in the Bosnian war.

Serbs at one time claimed there were 4,000 Muslim volunteers from abroad fighting in Bosnia. There were 160 Turkish volunteers confirmed fighting in Bosnia along with the 1,500-man Islamic legion Kata' ib el-Muminin (Phalanx of Believers) also fighting in the Bosnian hills. There were reportedly regular officers from Turkey, Pakistan, and Iran in Bosnia, hardened guerrillas who for years had fought in Lebanon and Afghanistan. The presence of a few ragtag mujahideen from failed causes in other areas reinforced the fact that the conflict in Bosnia was not a religious war but a vicious struggle among political tyrants vying for territory. Most Europeans view the Slavic Muslims in Bosnia as the unfortunate result of five hundred years of Turkish occupation. In fact, there has been little trend toward the entrenchment of Muslim fundamentalism in Bosnia or in Kosovo, where the Muslims had been secularized. Mercenaries from other lands also joined both the Croat and Serb armies in similarly small and inconsequential numbers.

The first American aircrews and logistics troops entered the former Yugoslavia in July 1992. Under the auspices of the UN relief resolutions, Operation Provide Promise was to provide an airlift for humanitarian aid. Initially two missions per day flew from Rhein-Main Air Base in Germany to Croatia. Additional daily flights of C-130 Hercules turboprop transports from U.S. Air Force Reserve and Air National Guard units delivered roughly twenty tons of humanitarian cargo each to a still-besieged Sarajevo. UNPROFOR units provided security for the supplies on the ground, while UN and volunteer relief agencies unloaded the planes. In November 1992 the United States erected a Mobile Army Surgical Hospital in Camp Pleso just outside Zagreb. American soldiers set up the sixty-bed hospital with 300 American staffers to support all UN military personnel, volunteer relief workers, and local citizens. The hospital staff was made up of members of all U.S. services who stayed for six-month assignments. The medical facility treated more than 6,000 outpatients and had a capacity for 450 inpatients, including children in a special pediatric ward. The military hospital was the first visible and permanent instance of American participation on the ground. That it was far from the ground fighting made it acceptable to most Americans still locked in debate over the acceptability of intervention of any kind.

The UN sea and air zones of exclusion came into full effect in November 1992. In reality they denied only a limited amount of external assistance to the belligerents. For the first time, the United Nations authorized the Western European Union and NATO to patrol the skies over the Adriatic Sea and Bosnia in combat aircraft not under UN command. The mission of the combined UN-NATO force was to contain the fighting on the ground in Bosnia by enforcing land cordons using sea and air forces. The air and naval forces were commanded by Admiral Jeremy M. Boorda, the American commander in chief of Allied Forces South, located in Naples, Italy. Admiral Leighton Smith succeeded him in April 1994. The military structure of the combined mission of the UN forces on the ground and the NATO aircraft and warships was unique and somewhat confusing. Supported by a strong naval and air contingent from NATO, the UN token ground forces, which consisted of small units from more than twenty countries, some of questionable effectiveness, did not constitute an army powerful enough to subdue the heavily armed Serb and Yugoslav armies well entrenched in Bosnia.

In November 1992 the naval forces began to challenge merchant ships bound for ports in the former Yugoslavia. Operation Sharp Guard placed U.S. carrier battle groups in the Adriatic—later reinforced by a French and British carrier force—with escorts from other NATO and Western European Union countries. By June 1, 1993, the blockade had challenged 11,700 ships, boarded 760, and diverted 165.[12] The sea blockade seemed initially to be working.

As the situation in Bosnia grew more and more desperate for the besieged Muslim communities, President Clinton, under increasing pressure to act, expanded the role of Operation Provide Promise to include airdrops of food and medicines to Bosnian Muslim villages isolated by Bosnian Serb and Yugoslav army forces. Relief missions flown by Americans increased to a dozen per day to Sarajevo, and another dozen missions were flown by the Germans, Canadians, British, French, Italians, and Swedes. Aircraft routinely came under fire and while on the ground were easy targets for the undiscriminating Serb gunners.

When the ground fire against the aid mission increased, President Clinton ordered supplies to be dropped by air. In March 1993, U.S. Air Force C-130 crews were flying six to twelve sorties three to four times per week from Rhein-Main in Germany. To avoid the threat of antiaircraft fire the C-130s were dropping their cargo from ten thousand feet. The inability to ensure delivery of relief supplies in earlier relief operations, specifically the year before in northern Iraq, had resulted inevitably in the deployment of ground forces. The U.S. administration was still simply not willing to deploy forces on the ground in Bosnia. Instead, coalition forces from the Fifth Allied Tactical Air Force began patrolling the no-fly zone from Del Molina Air Base near Vicenza, Italy. Predominantly manned by the U.S. Navy and Air Force, the patrols consisted of nearly seventy sorties daily. U.S. Air Force Major General James E. Chambers commanded the Yugoslav campaign of both the no-fly enforcement and the relief-supply aircraft from Vicenza. It was an unusual effort: NATO was commanding the no-fly zone while the relief effort was a U.S. command. Americans were coordinating and commanding the entire air effort, including airlift, defensive air patrol, tankers, reconnaissance, and eventually the air strikes. By early October 1993 the air effort to prevent Yugoslav air force flights over Bosnia had expanded to 130 combat aircraft flying predominantly from Aviano Air Base in northeast Italy near Venice. The multinational force at Aviano included U.S., British, Dutch, French, and Turkish aircraft. The aid operation delivered forty-six thousand tons of humanitarian assistance, more than one-quarter by parachute and packet scattering, surpassing the Berlin airlift as the longest American resupply in history.[13]

Despite the UN efforts on the ground, airdrops, and sea blockades, the Serbs continued to gain territory throughout 1993 at the expense of the Muslims. In the meantime, the lightly armed UN troops proved ineffective in attempting to pacify the area. After months of reacting to violence in one spot and meeting with obfuscation and resistance on all sides, Lieutenant General Briquemont resigned in early 1994 and was replaced by British General Sir Michael Rose.[14] Under General Rose UNPROFOR enjoyed some limited successes but spent an inordinate amount of time in fruitless bargaining with Serb, Croat, and Muslim leaders who regularly lied, prevaricated, promised, and delayed. UNPROFOR continued with a mandate that dictated minimum use of force, and General Rose resisted pressures to use more force against the Serbs. The United States pressured the United Nations to be more forceful when dealing with the Serbs, but to no avail.

On February 5, 1994, a single 120mm mortar round killed sixty-eight civilians in a Sarajevo market. Four days later a sharp reaction followed. The United States, NATO, and the United Nation gave an ultimatum to the Serbs to cease attacks on Sarajevo and pull all guns outside a twenty-kilometer radius of the city by February 20 or suffer air strikes. In this case the Serbs complied and there were no air attacks. In another exceptionally effective move, NATO and the European Union leaders obtained Russian agreement to station a battalion of Russian paratroopers alongside the UN forces around Sarajevo. This presence showed that Russia, although no longer a credible superpower, was a participant in the international move to end the hostilities. The Serbs took note.

In March 1994 the United Nations authorized NATO to fully protect the five thousand UN peacekeepers on the ground in Bosnia with airpower. The plan for this protection force had its origins in the early summer of 1992. It was created by U.S. planners in London and Stuttgart who had a mandate from General Powell to devise ways to go to the aid of allied peacekeeping forces earmarked for deployment to Bosnia. This planning, which continued quietly as the situation in Yugoslavia deteriorated, came to encompass maritime interdiction, aerial delivery of relief supplies, a no-fly zone, a bombing campaign, and the introduction of small, secret reconnaissance and communications teams on the ground in Bosnia.

With little fanfare, NATO quietly landed British Special Air Services and U.S. Tenth Special Forces teams in Bosnia in the early spring of 1993 to reconnoiter and set up communications with the various UN country commands. They were equipped with laser designators to guide precision bombs from U.S. and British Aircraft. In an attempt to replicate the successful mission of the special operations liaison detachments assigned to all coalition forces during the Gulf War, U.S. Special Forces teams were sent in to coordinate with each UN national military unit to assist with communications and air control.[15] The NATO command also established a special Rapid

Reaction Force to conduct special short-notice operations when the need arose.[16] NATO also established a special operations cell in Brindisi in Italy to be ready to conduct sensitive search-and-rescue or hostage-rescue operations should NATO aircraft go down in Bosnia.[17] The only American combat force on the ground was a battalion of paratroopers from the 502nd Infantry, which President Clinton had sent to Macedonia, where they attempted to keep the peace subordinate to a UN commander.

On February 28, 1994, six Yugoslav air force Jastreb J-1 single-seat light-attack jet aircraft took off from an airbase at Banja Luka and attempted to fly under allied radar cover to provide air support to Serb forces on the ground. They were detected, and within fifteen minutes of their takeoff four of the six were shot down by U.S. Air Force F-16 fighters. That incident ended Bosnian Serb air-to-ground attacks. Although UN and NATO rules authorized UNPROFOR to use air strikes for self-defense, the lightly armed UN forces were still reluctant to call in NATO air strikes, fearing the Serb threat to exact revenge against the UN forces following any significant air strikes.

In the summer of 1994, fearing Serb retaliation, the United Nations and NATO agreed to the plan whereby NATO forces would be used to rescue UN peacekeeping forces if the need arose.[18] This agreement with NATO was intended to encourage the UN forces to take more decisive actions on the ground. NATO was still prohibited from conducting any operations on the ground, however, even though reconnaissance was essential to plan realistically for the rescue of UN forces. To do so might demonstrate a commitment on the ground that NATO, lacking firm U.S. leadership, was still not prepared to make.

UN Resolutions 824 and 836 of 1993 had provided for "safe areas"—Bihac, Gorazde, Sarajevo, Zepa, and Srebrenica—in Bosnia that armed elements from all sides were prohibited to enter. The safe areas were meant to be eventually demilitarized. But typically, UNPROFOR under General Rose was unable to enforce the demilitarization. NATO was not permitted to assist the United Nations in reinforcing Bosnian forces in or near the safe areas. The concept was further confused by the specification that the United Nations and

NATO were permitted to defend only the people in the safe zones, not the territory itself. The primary limitation imposed on UNPRO-FOR was UN resolution 836, which stated that UN forces should deter attacks on the safe areas by all belligerents, but not in such a way as to clearly allow their firm defense by the United Nations. Still worse, the Security Council did not request a sufficient number of UN troops to seriously defend a single safe area. The UN Secretariat had requested 34,000 troops to defend the safe areas, yet the Security Council in fact provided only 7,600. And by March 1995 only 5,000 of those were in place. Like the Bangladeshi battalion at Bihac, many of these troops were so poorly equipped that they were less than models of modern and effective military forces; for example, soldiers in the battalion from Ukraine guarding the safe area of Zepa sold their shoes and weapons to the local black market, so they were unable to perform their military mission.[19]

It was hoped that NATO's threat to use airpower in support of the safe areas would make up for the lack of heavy artillery by the United Nations on the ground. Instead, the Serbs warned that they might take peacekeepers as hostages and disrupt humanitarian aid to the safe areas. Such intimidation proved to be a very effective deterrent against some of the more poorly motivated national troop formations serving as blue-helmeted UN peacekeepers. The mission of UNPROFOR on paper had grown from protecting humanitarian assistance to enforcing the sanctity of the designated safe areas. Serb forces on the ground interpreted the safe area concept as positively anti-Serb, since the Serbs posed by far the greatest threat to those designated areas. This was a change in the previous effort by the United Nations to remain impartial and to apply evenhanded pressure on each of the warring parties.

The safe areas had been declared two years earlier but had never really been free of fighting. The Bosnian Muslim forces consistently used the safe areas to improve their military position. Muslim forces attacking out of Srebrenica, before it became a safe area, had conducted raids against Serbs that killed hundreds of civilians and military personnel. General Ratko Mladic, the Bosnian Serb ground commander, later admitted that if it hadn't been for the international imposition of the safe-area restrictions on Srebrenica the Muslims would have paid dearly in 1993.

The UN High Commissioner for Refugees (UNHCR), the organization that was supposed to provide humanitarian assistance to those most in need, was caught in the middle. It could not reach those in the contested combat areas and was thwarted by the war on all sides. Even the most needy war victims, the residents of Sarajevo, interpreted the mandate of UNHCR as a weak substitute for more robust military assistance to end the protracted siege. These citizens began to block the flow of assistance to pressure the United Nations for more active military intervention. The humanitarian answer was intended to relieve political pressure in the United States and European countries, which demanded stronger measures to force an end to the conflict. Thus UNHCR had a dual mission: to get aid to the victims and to assuage public opinion in America and Europe. As a result, UNPROFOR's mission was nearly impossible, despite the twenty-eight thousand soldiers from twenty-two countries, as well as an army of relief workers, spread out in Croatia, Macedonia, and Bosnia. After two years of futile effort, the United Nation had suffered a total of 850 casualties, including 71 killed, by mid-January 1994.[20] Much like the U.S. Marines during the intervention in Lebanon in 1983, UNPROFOR tried to remain neutral in a savage fight among rival factions. When UN forces on the ground met significant Serb opposition, they would back down for fear of suffering retaliation. On several occasions, when air strikes had been called in to support the UN forces, General Rose, who was UNPROFOR commander in 1994–1995, warned the Serbs of the area and time of the strikes so they could evacuate. When his behavior was challenged by the NATO commander, General Rose responded that he did not want to endanger his forces by having the Serbs suffer serious losses.[21]

In April 1994 Dutch peacekeepers had replaced Canadians in the Srebrenica area. The Netherlands had been the sole European country to answer the UN secretary general's request for troops to enforce the safe areas. While endeavoring to keep the fragile peace in Srebrenica, Dutch forces were constantly harassed by the surrounding

Serb forces, who blocked UN fuel supplies so that the Dutch were forced to patrol by foot. On November 21, the Serbs took seventy Dutch soldiers hostage in response to a NATO bombing of a Serb air base at Ubdina. A Serb leader, General Mladic, visited them in one of their own jeeps. After intense diplomatic pressure the Serbs released the hostages a week later.

By early 1995 the Muslim military presence inside the Srebrenica safe area had swollen to more than one thousand and the Dutch efforts to disarm these Muslims in accordance with the safe-area rules were unsuccessful.[22] In the meantime special operations forces ground units joined the Dutch to coordinate air support. It was clear that the Serbs had become accustomed to threats made but not carried out by UNPROFOR. With an offensive looming and the Muslim-Croat federation pouring into the so-called safe areas, the pressure built.

Early in 1995 British General Rupert Smith replaced General Rose as commander of UNPROFOR in Bosnia. Smith had commanded the British First Armoured Division in the Gulf War and had been involved in the UNPROFOR operation for a year as the assistant chief of the defense staff for operations and plans in London. Smith believed that a peacekeeping force could achieve only four goals—ameliorate, contain, compel or deter, and destroy. When General Smith arrived in Sarajevo, a cease-fire negotiated at the end of the previous year by Jimmy Carter, the former U.S. president, and Yasushi Akashi, the head of UN forces in the Balkans, was in place. Nothing more than a convenience for the three warring sides during a period when snow and freezing weather made fighting unproductive, the cease-fire was due to end on May 1, and it was clear that the Croats and Muslims, who were now allied in a reluctant coalition as the Bosnian Federation, were preparing for a major offensive against the Serbs. Both Carter and Akashi were strongly opposed to the use of force except as a last resort, and this attitude, which was easily recognized by the Serbs, doomed the cease-fire to failure. The Bosnian Federation army was steadily growing stronger as it received more heavy weapons and training from abroad. Most of its new arms were believed to have been delivered by air in neighboring Croatia from sympathetic Muslim countries. The United States and European powers turned a blind eye to these violations of the arms embargo. At the same time, Serb forces in Bosnia were gradually being stretched thinner as they coped with many pockets of resistance throughout Bosnia. The impending spring campaign was sure to strike the UN safe areas in eastern Bosnia located adjacent to the Serb supply line, where significant numbers of Muslim forces were now concentrating.

The cease-fire expired on May 1, 1995, and hostilities erupted around all the safe areas. After one night of particularly heavy Serb shelling of noncombatants, General Smith requested NATO air strikes, but his request was denied by Secretary General Boutros-Ghali. The British foreign secretary, Douglas Hurd, protested the turndown. As a result, both the local commander, General Smith, and the overall UN commander in Zagreb recommended that the peacekeepers be withdrawn immediately from the safe areas, leaving only observers and ground spotters who could call in air strikes. This suggestion could have reduced the risk of retaliation by the Serbs after the strikes. However, Madeleine Albright, the U.S. ambassador to the United Nations, strongly opposed this action, saying it would amount to the UN's abandoning the safe areas.[23] The United States would not support the withdrawal idea. The resulting stalemate prevented the United Nations and NATO from taking more robust action to protect the safe areas. It appeared that the situation was unsolvable. Then, on May 22, the Serbs pushed aside the defending UN military protectors and forced their way into a heavy-weapons collection site near Sarajevo, where they seized several heavy artillery pieces. Once armed, the Serbs resumed shelling Sarajevo, and the Bosnian Federation forces returned artillery fire from the city. Hundreds of people were killed. The UN commanders again threatened air strikes against the Serbs if they did not stop—and this time the UN took action.

On May 25 Admiral Smith ordered NATO aircraft to attack an ammunition dump near the Bosnian Serb mountain headquarters at Pale, above Sarajevo. The next day the Serbs retaliated by shelling all the safe-area cities. In a particularly devastating attack, the Serbs killed hundreds of civilians in Tuzla. The next day NATO struck again, and General Smith complained to General Mladic, the Serb commander, that the Tuzla shelling was in violation of the safe-area restrictions. In what had become a typical type of Serb distortion, Mladic insisted to General Smith that the UN commander and NATO were guilty of killing the civilians because Smith had requested the air strikes.

General Mladic retaliated. Peacekeepers throughout Bosnia were taken hostage, including four unarmed UN observers who were handcuffed to a fence to deter further air strikes in the Serb headquarters area. Mladic's men took a total of three hundred UN soldiers hostage to prevent another NATO air strike. Again Mladic blamed General Smith personally for calling in the air strike. This pivotal moment demonstrated the futility of using peacekeepers without giving them sufficient force to defend themselves, let alone protect the victims of war. UN Secretary General Boutros-Ghali intervened and ordered the bombing stopped. He blamed the United States for not cooperating.

Also in May, the Croats and Serbs began a series of military offensives that would dramatically change the map of Croatia and Bosnia in the subsequent fifteen weeks.[24] The Croatian attack into Western Slavonia (in Croatia) in early May 1995 reclaimed land that had been controlled by the Serbs since the Vance cease-fire in January 1992. Fifteen thousand Serb refugees fled south into the Banja Luka district of Bosnia. The next Croat attack in the Krajina region of Croatia that summer drove out nearly the entire Serb population—more than 150,000 were expelled. In response the Serbs launched offensives aimed at taking possession of all of eastern Bosnia and overran Srebrenica in July. Emboldened by their overwhelming victory, Serb forces began an attack on Bihac, while they increased the shelling of Sarajevo.[25]

In July 1995 quasimilitary gangs of Serb thugs mixed with a few professionals killed more than seven thousand men trying to escape from Srebrenica in eastern Bosnia. The battle in mountainous forest terrain was over in less than forty-eight hours; there were few Serb casualties. The Serbs then managed to paralyze the command hierarchy of UNPROFOR for so long that they had time to bury the evidence, evict the Dutch defenders, and "cleanse" the town of women and children without facing a counterattack. This happened despite the availability of overwhelming NATO air and ground forces; however, the determined leadership to use those forces was lacking. During this period Washington came under increasing pressure from the newly elected French President Jacques Chirac, who began to appeal directly to the U.S. Congress. After the fall of Srebrenica, evidence emerged of a bloody massacre: Thousands of Muslim men and boys had been savagely butchered and buried (some of them alive) in mass graves. Appalled, the United States finally agreed to concrete intervention. The Serbs apparently made the decision to murder the thousands at Srebrenica only after they realized that the UN was responding hesitantly and weakly to the attacks on all the safe areas. All told, 7,414 men and boys were murdered at Srebrenica in the greatest mass killing in Europe since World War II.

The situation was confused at best. The UN commanders felt that the NATO forces were trying to start an all-out war with the Serbs. UN representative Akashi said, "We had a peacekeeping force there in the middle of a war and a war-fighting force in the middle of a peace."[26] As UN officials pondered whether or not to withdraw the peacekeepers, they realized that NATO had already been committed to supporting their withdrawal, which would be very bloody if done under fire. In anticipation of a UN pullout, and in reaction to the summer Serb offensives, General Smith created a unit of British and French troops to serve as a Rapid Reaction Force if the Serbs attacked. This cell not only was armed with heavy weapons that were superior in range, caliber, and rate of fire to the weapons of the Serb besiegers but also had excellent communications that gave it the ability to call in NATO air support directly, quickly, and without advance UN clearance.

Finally, NATO ministers met in London and made some concrete decisions. They decided that any future Serb attacks on safe areas would be met with overwhelming force, including air strikes and the heavy artillery of the British and French Rapid Reaction Force. This force was brought into place around Mount Igman, an advantageous position vis-à-vis the Bosnian Serb gun emplacements outside Sarajevo. General Bernard Janvier, the overall UN commander, and Admiral Leighton Smith, NATO's southern commander, could authorize strikes again without prior clearance from the UN secretary general.

The Croats began a successful blitzkreig in May 1995 and continued into August, which created an opportunity to impose a settlement on the three warring parties. Also that summer, NATO met and formed a list of three types of targets for the Rapid Reaction Force to strike: heavy weapons violating the safe areas, particularly Sarajevo; Serb interdict targets; and bases inside or near the safe areas. The trigger to use the revised tactic came on August 28 in the form of another horrible marketplace bombing in Sarajevo. Fortuitously UN troops had finished withdrawing from safe areas that evening, and Operation Deliberate Force, the largest NATO combat operation ever mounted, commenced on August 30. NATO aircraft struck Serb targets around Sarajevo and other Bosnian Serb positions, installations, ammunition dumps, and storage areas. The Rapid Reaction Force struck with more than six hundred rounds of heavy artillery at Serb positions around Sarajevo. The United Nations ordered General Mladic to cease all attacks against safe areas and end all hostilities in and around Bosnia. The air strikes would cease when the Serbs complied.

On September 5, after offering to cease bombing when the Serbs withdrew their heavy artillery from the safe areas, more than ninety NATO aircraft attacked the Serbs while the Rapid Reaction Force opened heavy fire. At the same time U.S. ships launched Tomahawk cruise missiles at Serb radar sites northwest of Banja Luka, an apparently severely frightening move. On September 14 the Bosnian Serbs agreed to UNPROFOR conditions and the bombing ended. The Serbs withdrew their heavy weapons from Sarajevo for the first time, and relief supplies began to flow again. The United States offered a plan for permanent peace that resulted in the Dayton accords. According to General Rupert Smith, the peace had been achieved "by the deliberate, disproportionate and extensive use of force."[27] On November 21, 1995, the leaders of all the competing powers of the former Yugoslavia signed the Dayton accords. These accords—to be enforced by IFOR, the Implementation Force of 60,000 fully armed NATO troops—were a "framework for peace" rather than a concrete peace agreement; nevertheless, they ended the fighting in Bosnia and created a single multiethnic government in an ethnically divided country. Reflecting the reality of troop dispositions on the ground, 49 percent of the country went to the Serbs and 51 percent to the Croat-Muslim Federation; Sarajevo was reunified.

The conflict in the former Yugoslavia did not end with the Dayton accords. At the end of the conflict in Bosnia, the dictator Milosevic was still in power. He soon refocused his attention on the plight of the Serb minority in Kosovo as a means of consolidating his influence. In the eyes of Serbs, Milosevic had sold them out in Bosnia, and to remain in power he had to regain their support.

CHAPTER 15

Intervention in Kosovo

1999

The war in Bosnia, which had raged until 1995, merely delayed another bloody and more disgustingly inhuman conflict in Kosovo. The Serbian dictator Slobodan Milosevic was uncomfortable splitting his attention between two main enemies, so while the Bosnian issue simmered, the Albanian ethnic majority in Kosovo festered in his mind. According to William Shawcross in *Deliver Us from Evil,* "Milosevic had begun his rise to power by promising to protect the Orthodox Kosovar Serbs from the huge and growing Muslim Albanian majority in what Serbs regarded as their traditional heartland. In 1989 he abolished the autonomy that Tito had given Kosovo within the Yugoslav federation, dismissed Albanian teachers from schools and universities, introduced a new Serbocentric curriculum, made it illegal for Albanians to buy and sell property without permission, imposed a brutal Serbian police rule and encouraged a form of apartheid in which the Albanian majority had no power."[1] During one demonstration against that decision, more than twenty Kosovars had been slain in two villages.

The following year Yugoslavia dissolved the Kosovo government and dispatched army troops to impose order, but the repression proved too much for the large Albanian majority. In 1991 Albanian separatists declared Kosovo an independent republic, which was recognized immediately by Albania. In a shadow election the public chose Ibrahim Rugova as the president of the Kosovo Republic. An advocate of nonviolence, Rugova fostered a peaceful path to independence from Yugoslavia. During this period, Serb forces and the Yugoslav army were engaged in trying to build and maintain Serb sovereignty in Bosnia. Serb police enforced the closing of Albanian schools and medical centers. Rugova avoided violence and tried to keep the more radical Albanians in check. By 1993 the Albanians in Kosovo were reestablishing their own schools and clinics in small houses to replace those shut down or destroyed by the Serb police. There was little open unrest on the streets, yet the current of resistance to Serb police measures was strong.

As soon as the Dayton accords were clinched in 1995 and the bloodletting in Bosnia ended, Milosevic's pro-Serb revival refocused on Kosovo. Now that the Serbs were no longer locked in combat in Bosnia, the leaders of the newly formed Kosovo Liberation Army (KLA), which Rugova had initially opposed, as well as Rugova himself and others, realized that any major move on their part would bring swift and bloody retribution, jeopardizing their cause of gaining full autonomy from Yugoslavia. The issue of independence had been merely set aside, not solved. During the six years since Milosevic had reduced the status of Kosovar Albanians, he had made no attempt to find a solution with the nonviolent leaders of the Kosovars who still in 1989 retained the support of most of the people and who did not pose a serious military threat to Serbs in Kosovo. However, trouble loomed. Fearing perpetual Serb domination, the small KLA advocated guerrilla violence to restore Albanian autonomy in Kosovo.

The events in Kosovo posed a series of tests for the world: When should claims of self-determination be recognized? How and when should force be used to meet challenges caused by ethnic differences? The rise of the KLA in Kosovo signaled to Milosevic that he was no longer dealing with a nonviolent group but with armed militants whose ranks were swelling with large numbers of young Kosovar men who were jobless because of Milosevic's own anti-Albanian tactics. This lightly armed but enthusiastic force began to threaten Serbs living in Kosovo. The reaction by the Serb police in Kosovo was severe as they set out to destroy the KLA.

The Serbs' own policies had abetted the formation of the KLA and its explosive growth into a significant force. Milosevic responded by seeking to rid the region of the roots of friction. He moved to eject all the Albanians, who made up nearly 90 percent of the population. He would simply kill those he could not force to resettle. This was a major undertaking, but Milosevic and the leaders of the Yugoslav army and police went about the task with little hesitation and unbelievable brutality. The Serb effort to evict all Albanians from Kosovo became the largest resettlement of a European population since World War II. To carry out the task effectively Milosevic was forced to purge his own police force and army in order to install a sufficient number of ruthless men willing to do the job.

The animosity between the Serbs and Albanians in Kosovo was much sharper than what had existed among Bosnian Muslims, Serbs, and Croats. In Bosnia intermarriage among ethnic peoples was widely accepted, while in Kosovo the rate of intermarriage was less than 20 percent. Serbs claimed that Kosovo was their historical and cultural heartland: They had resisted the Turkish occupation there, which had culminated in the Battle of Kosovo in the fourteenth century. Albanians, who were the vast majority, claimed that Kosovo was their homeland. The fighting began when KLA insurgents tried to break Kosovo away from what remained of Yugoslavia. Milosevic, who was already being investigated for war crimes in Bosnia—he was formally indicted on May 27, 1998, by the Yugoslav war crimes tribunal—threw all his efforts into resisting the Kosovars' bid for independence, causing the dislocation of hundreds of thousands of refugees.

The European attempt in February 1999 to solve these issues at a conference in a chateau in Rambouillet, outside Paris, collapsed. The effort failed because the proposed accords were based on the false assumption that the two groups could coexist in harmony while the Albanian percentage of the populace continued to skyrocket. Europeans feared that an independent Kosovo would disrupt the south Balkans. The natural aspirations of the three Albanian communities—in Albania proper, in Kosovo, and in western Macedonia—were potentially disruptive. Also destabilizing were the emotional disputes between Greece and Macedonia over Macedonian identity, and the chronic rivalry between Greece and the emerging regional giant, Turkey.[2]

In the back of some Europeans' minds, especially in Germany, Austria, and Italy, lurked the possibility, even though far-fetched, of an Iran-backed revolutionary state in Kosovo that could become the Cuba of Europe, giving succor to Islamic revolutionary causes. An underlying difficulty was that Albania had the highest birthrate in Europe. NATO and the Europeans faced a dilemma: backing independence for Kosovo could disrupt the entire Balkans; however, the atrocious human rights violations committed there were unacceptable. NATO, the Europeans, and the Americans had to do something; unfortunately, their response was late and overly cautious.

Partitioning the area was a possible solution, but given the radical views of both sides such a formula would be daunting at best. After months of threats NATO resorted to military action only after Milosevic extended his violence against the KLA to include all Albanians. From the time the violence had begun in 1995 to March 1999, more than four hundred thousand ethnic Albanians had fled from Kosovo as the Serbs burned and bombarded their villages.

As the spring of 1998 brought better weather the Serbs increased their attacks in Kosovo, forcing more and more ethnic Albanians to flee across the borders into Albania, Macedonia, and Montenegro. Evidence of large-scale massacres began to filter out of the area; Milosevic denied it. Meanwhile, Serb paramilitary security squads went from village to village separating Albanian families, selectively murdering some village leaders and abusing others, and forcing all to flee for their lives. Milosevic refused to allow any foreign troops in Kosovo. NATO argued that it already possessed the authority to act based on UN Resolution 1199 of 1998, in which the Security Council had acknowledged that the deterioration of the situation in Kosovo constituted a threat to peace and security in the region and demanded that all parties cease hostilities and maintain a cease-fire. However, NATO took no action.

As the crisis grew in Kosovo, the Clinton administration began to prepare for a showdown with Belgrade. Eyewitness accounts of Serbian atrocities in Kosovo were beginning to reach the West, and the administration warned Milosevic that he faced air strikes. However, American leaders were divided on the feasibility and effectiveness of strategic bombing alone as an instrument to force Milosevic to re-lent. Some felt that a bombing offensive alone could do the job, but others echoed the belief expressed by General Colin Powell in his memoir—the trouble with airpower alone is that it leaves the initiative to the enemy to determine when he has had enough. Many senior American military men believed that the allied bombings had forced the Serbs to the negotiating table in Bosnia and could do the same in Kosovo in short order. Unfortunately, they overlooked the impor-tance of successfully using ground forces, such as the Croatian army and the British and French Rapid Reaction Force, which had signifi-cantly reduced the Serbs' will to fight, so that a brief round of NATO bombing was all it took to make a difference. In Kosovo in 1999, however, the Serb forces were completely fresh.

On March 23, 1999, Richard Holbrooke, President Clinton's spe-cial envoy for the Kosovo crisis, held a last meeting with Milosevic, who denied that an offensive against the Albanian Kosovars was under way and blamed the reports on the KLA, which he accused of feeding propaganda to Western television. Milosevic still would not agree to the presence of foreign troops in Kosovo.

On March 24, 1999, NATO commenced air strikes against Serb forces in Kosovo and Serbia. The attacks came after the Serbs had re-jected a plan offered by the United States to restore the autonomy of Kosovo and to police the area with thousands of NATO peacekeep-ers. On the first night of the air assault the allies struck thirty targets. NATO naval and air forces launched one hundred cruise missiles during the first five nights of the offensive. During the whole cam-paign, which comprised 450 allied sorties, B-52s dropped only sixty-four bombs. The aircraft attacking in Kosovo itself were carefully limited to altitudes above ten thousand feet to minimize the risk of loss. As such these strikes could not be accurate enough to deter Serb army units that were perpetuating the expulsion of Albanian civil-ians. Nor could such bombing inside Kosovo alone force Milosevic to the bargaining table. Indeed, the strikes worsened the plight of the Albanians on the ground, for as soon as the bombing began, the Serbs' ruthless purge of the Albanians intensified. In fact, such a bombing campaign risked helping to accelerate the Serb mission of displacing all Albanians from Kosovo. NATO leaders sincerely believed that a brief but violent bombing offensive would soon bring Belgrade's surrender. This misconception was compounded when the Clinton administration continually assured the American public that the president would never embark on a ground campaign. Regardless of whether that was a clever deception, it certainly signaled to Milosevic that there was indeed no threat of allied ground forces ever entering the fray. Thus the Serbs needed only to concentrate on camouflage, hunker down, endure the high-altitude air strikes, and accelerate the killing and ethnic cleansing, a strategy that murdered hundreds and displaced thousands. It is believed that during the ensuing eleven weeks of bombing 10,000 more were deliberately murdered by the Serbs. In the year before the bombing began, about 2,500 Kosovars had been killed. By March 24 more than 260,000 Albanians had been driven out of their villages and another 200,000 had sought refuge abroad.[3] Since the Serbs could not fight back against NATO aircraft flying at ten thousand feet they merely intensified their killing of the Albanians.

As NATO focused its determined, high-tech attack on the Serbs, Milosevic unleashed an indiscriminate force of thugs and paramilitary mercenaries against the Kosovars, and although nominally striking against the terrorist KLA, they in fact accelerated their purges of the entire Albanian population of Kosovo. Unpaid Serb army "volunteers" augmented by paramilitary thugs flushed a million and a half Kosovar Albanians into the hills and across borders into sprawling refugee camps. By operating largely on foot and moving among civilians, they held key towns, roads, and borders for months; as a result, Kosovar was essentially invasion-proof and the Serbs were invulnerable.

NATO ran into problems as soon as it began to act. The NATO high command failed to foresee that Milosevic would try to stymie the alliance by expelling thousands of Albanians and creating an even greater refugee crisis. NATO was told secretly by its participating member nations that the first requirement was to avoid the loss of any aircraft. This preoccupation with avoiding NATO military casualties limited the effectiveness of the air campaign and increased the prospect of civilian casualties, because allied warplanes bombed from high altitudes. General Wesley Clark, NATO's supreme commander, defended the order to limit allied losses as necessary to maintain public support for the war.[4] France and other nations believed that air strikes should concentrate exclusively on Serbian forces in Kosovo. The Americans insisted that the strikes should be directed against command and control sites and other targets in Belgrade. In addition, well before the bombing began, a French officer compromised security by providing an early version of the air-war plan to the Serbs.

NATO inflicted significant damage only when the Serbs began to operate as conventional ground units. Columns of armor and trucks left Kosovo only when ordered, and most of the Serbs' limited numbers of fighting vehicles were unscathed. The bombing against Serbia proper, however, took a terrible toll. The destruction of bridges and power plants and the systematic, accurate strikes against military and government buildings eventually had an effect. Initially the Serbs stood united against the NATO strikes, but gradually their stoicism evaporated and Milosevic began to feel public pressure.

On June 3, after seventy-eight days of bombing, Slobodan Milosevic suddenly settled and allowed an international force of peacekeepers into Kosovo. A military agreement signed at Kumanovo Air Base in Macedonia followed on June 9. The UN Security Council passed Resolution 1244 on June 10, which officially endorsed the terms of the peace. Kosovo was divided into five zones; American, British, French, German, and Russian general officers commanded the peacekeepers in their respective zones.

The bombing in Serbia proper is believed to have led to Milosevic's capitulation; the damage to his military forces in Kosovo was a great deal less than initially claimed. Shortly after the settlement, the Kosovo Force (KFOR), the NATO peacekeeping force, drove unopposed into Kosovo and the refugees began to return home. As the NATO and Russian forces took over the security in Kosovo, it soon became clear that maintaining law and order would be a long and difficult task. It had been a NATO war and would be a UN peace, said one observer.

Conclusions

During the recurring "little wars" of the last quarter of the twentieth century, moral outrage and popular sentiment at times interfered with the creation of sound U.S. foreign policy and military strategy. After the devastating attacks in New York and Washington, D.C., in September 2001, which caused more casualties than the 1941 Japanese attack on Pearl Harbor, American resolve clearly strengthened. The emotions of the public have been brought into play more and more by the ability of the news media to broadcast real-time scenes of devastation after terror attacks and the horrible, inhuman brutality of "ethnic cleansing." That is what occurred in New York on September 11, and the years before in Lebanon, Somalia, Bosnia, and Kosovo.

America has been criticized for being morally indifferent to events abroad, for taking unilateral action, or for not responding to the appalling deeds of various despots. When the United States enforced its moral principles through the barrel of a gun or, more aptly and recently, from the bomb racks of airplanes or missile tubes of ships at sea, the result was not always what the popular will intended. Too often military responses provoked an increase in the suffering of civilians, as in Afghanistan and Kosovo, or vengeful actions against the enforcer, as in the cases of the marines in Beirut and the Rangers in Mogadishu. Moral indignation, while a laudable attribute for a powerful democracy, is no substitute for a well-thought-out foreign policy.

These failed U.S. military ventures of the past twenty-five years—the Iran hostage rescue, the Beirut intervention, and the Mogadishu incursion—foundered more because of a lack of concrete foreign policy than because of poor military execution. The successful military actions—such as the *Mayaguez* rescue, Grenada, Panama, the Gulf War, and most recently the war in Afghanistan against the Taliban—resulted from an overall national policy that either was already in force at the time of the action or had been formed just prior to it.

U.S. soldiers, sailors, and airmen fought during the last twenty-five years of the twentieth century in many more conflicts than are described in the pages of this book. Accounts of some of these actions, such as those in Colombia against drug lords and those on a global scale against terrorists, are omitted because they were covert and therefore difficult to describe in useful detail. Whether successful or not, there is nothing insignificant or dishonorable about these engagements. Peacekeeping interventions by U.S. military forces in Haiti and in African nations where Americans participated in noncombat operations were also appropriate.

As the world's foremost military power since World War II, the United States is not accustomed to wrenching defeats or lost campaigns. The price of world military leadership has proved difficult to bear; modest achievements in battle and major victories were interspersed with bitterness, disappointment, and loss. Today the United States also controls the majority of military technology and airpower. This exceptional position in history promises neither a future of untroubled peace nor open-ended interventionism. Because most Western populations seem unwilling to tolerate military casualties, the United States and its allies may not often commit ground forces in future conflicts. However, the exceptional technological advantage enjoyed by the United States does ensure that those who threaten American interests risk their own destruction by a broad spectrum of long-range "standoff" missiles, severe air attacks, and assaults on the ground by highly trained and superbly equipped special operations warriors. In short, there is not a tidy military solution to every problem.

Notes

Chapter 1. Recovering SS *Mayaguez* and the Fight on Koh Tang

1. Journalist Ralph Wetterhahn visited the island several times in search of evidence of the lost marines and wrote in January 2000 that he had uncovered evidence that the three were no doubt killed later by the Khmer Rouge. The bodies of nine marines killed in the downed CH-53 helicopter have been returned and identified, but the remains of the three missing have still not been repatriated. For more information, see Ric Hunter, "Marine MIAs, Fate Unknown," *Veterans of Foreign Wars Magazine*, May 2000, 22–24.

2. USS *Pueblo*, an unarmed signal intelligence reconnaissance ship, was seized by the North Koreans in 1968. The eighty-two crewmen were held for eleven months and suffered terrible treatment. The United States did not respond with force to that act.

Chapter 3. The Hostage Rescue Attempt

1. Roosevelt described the events in a short book, *Countercoup: The Struggle for the Control of Iran* (New York: McGraw-Hill, 1979). Release of the book was delayed for a time in 1979 for fear that its publication could aid the revolution against the monarch whom the operation had helped to save.

2. Author's interview with retired Foreign Service Officer James Clunan in Hiram, Maine, on June 30, 2001.

3. Gary Sick, *All Fall Down: America's Tragic Encounter with Iran* (New York: Random House, 1985), 11.

4. Ibid., 40.

5. Zbigniew Brzezinski, *Power and Principle: Memoirs of the National Security Advisor, 1977–1981* (New York: Farrar, Straus & Giroux, 1983), 489.

6. Ibid.

7. Author's interview with Sikorsky helicopter test engineer Andrew Lapati, on Frye Island, Maine, on September 22, 2000.

8. The pilots of the two helicopters that aborted were following the precise rules in their Naval Air Training and Operating Procedures Standardization Program (NATOPS) manual, which governed the mechanical failure procedures for that type of helicopter. Both pilots chose not to risk the lives of their troop passengers by continuing onward. Author's interview with Sikorsky helicopter test engineer Andrew Lapati on September 22, 2000.

9. Admiral James L. Holloway III, *Rescue Mission Report*, August 1980.

10. Gary Sick gives an account of the hostage crisis in his book *All Fall Down*, 356.

11. Author's interview with Brigadier General David Grange, March 11, 2001.

12. Moorhead Kennedy, *The Ayatollah in the Cathedral–Reflections of a Hostage* (New York: Hill and Wang, 1986), 131.

13. Charlie A. Beckwith and Donald Knox, *Delta Force: The U.S. Counter Terrorist Unit and the Iran Rescue Mission* (New York: Harcourt Brace Jovanovich, 1983), 196.

14. Byron Farwell, *Queen Victoria's Little Wars* (New York: W. W. Norton and Co., 1972), 166–73.

Chapter 4. Intervention in Lebanon

1. Ze'ev Schiff and Ehud Ya'ari, *Israel's Lebanon War* (New York: Simon and Schuster, 1984), 32–34.

2. Initially the PLO complied with the cease-fire, which frustrated Israeli Defense Minister Ariel Sharon. See Caspar Weinberger, *Fighting for Peace: Seven Critical Years in the Pentagon* (New York: Warner Books, 1990), 140–41.

3. Some believed that the Reagan administration may have agreed in principle to allow Israel to deal a mortal blow to the PLO by invading Lebanon. See Alexander M. Haig Jr., *Caveat* (New York: Macmillan, 1984), 317–18.

4. Mission as stated in the 32nd MAU After Action Report, Sept.–Nov. 1982. USMC Historical Center, Washington, D.C.

5. U.S. Department of Defense, *Report of the Department of Defense Commis-*

sion on Beirut International Airport Terrorist Act, October 23, 1983 (Washington, D.C.: U.S. Government Printing Office, December 20, 1983), 35.

6. Russell F. Weigley, *The American Way of War: A History of United States Military Strategy and Policy* (Bloomington, Ind.: Indiana University Press, 1973), 467: "The ultimate objective of all military operations is the destruction of the enemy's armed forces and his will to fight."

7. Daniel P. Bolger, *Savage Peace: Americans at War in the 1990s* (Novato, Calif.: Presidio, 1995), 198–99.

8. Benis M. Frank, *U.S. Marines in Lebanon 1982–1984* (Washington, D.C.: U.S. Government Printing Office, 1987), 152.

9. UPI, "House Subcommittee Report," *Washington Post*, December 21, 1983, 23.

10. U.S. Department of Defense, *Report on Beirut International Airport Terrorist Act*, 43; House Armed Services Committee, *Full Committee Consideration of Investigation Subcommittee Report on Terrorist Bombing at Beirut International Airport*, 98th Cong., 2d sess., January 31, 1984, 358.

11. Author's interview with Admiral Robert Long in Annapolis, Maryland, on April, 22, 2000.

Chapter 5. Intervention in Grenada

1. In 1983 members of the Organization of Eastern Caribbean States (OECS) included Antigua and Barbuda, Dominica, Grenada, Monserrat, St. Kitts and Nevis, St. Lucia, and St. Vincent and the Grenadines. The Caribbean Community (CARICOM) had fourteen members, including the seven members of OECS plus seven additional states, as well as two associate members and nine observer states. Both organizations required a consensus on all important matters.

2. According to material and documents uncovered during the U.S. intervention, weapons arriving in 1979 included more than three thousand rifles, such as Soviet AK-47 assault rifles, American M-16s, and British .303s; two hundred machine guns; one hundred grenade launchers; twelve 82mm mortars; and twelve 12.7mm antiaircraft machine guns and the accompanying ammunition. See Major Mark Adkin, *Urgent Fury: The Battle for Grenada* (Lexington, Mass.: Lexington Books, 1989), 22.

3. Ibid., 21.

4. Caspar Weinberger, *Fighting for Peace: Seven Critical Years in the Pentagon* (New York: Warner Books, 1990), 102.

5. Lehman, John F., Jr. *Command of the Seas: Building the 600 Ship Navy* (New York: Charles Scribner's Sons, 1988), 293.

6. Adkin, *Urgent Fury*, 98.
7. Weinberger, *Fighting for Peace*, 99.
8. Author's interview with Vice Admiral Joseph Metcalf III in Washington, D.C., on November 17, 2000.
9. Ibid.
10. Author's interview with Brigadier General David Grange on March 11, 2001.
11. According to Admiral Metcalf the order originated in the office of Secretary of Defense Caspar Weinberger. In his memoir *Fighting for Peace*, Weinberger writes that the request to ban the press had originated with Metcalf and Weinberger's office approved it and issued the order.
12. Weinberger, *Fighting for Peace*, 124.
13. Dov S. Zakheim, "The Grenada Operation and Superpower Relations: A Perspective from the Pentagon," in *Grenada and Soviet/Cuban Policy*, ed. Jiri Valenta and Herbert J. Ellison (Boulder, Colo.: Westview Press, 1986), 180.

Chapter 6. Retaliatory Attacks on Libya

1. John F. Lehman, Jr. *Command of the Seas: Building the 600 Ship Navy*. (New York: Charles Scribner's Sons, 1988), 357.
2. Freedom of Navigation Operations also challenged policies such as the failure to observe the right of "innocent passage" by ships sailing through territorial waters, a custom recognized for centuries in international law. The U.S. Navy's Black Sea operation in February 1988, for example, was designed to assert the right to transit Soviet territorial seas in innocent passage. According to maritime law, while doing so the transiting ships would be required "to conduct a continuous and expeditious transit in a manner that is not prejudicial to the coastal state's peace, good order, or security." At issue was recent Soviet legislation that allowed innocent passage in only five specific locations around the USSR and excluded the right in other areas.
3. Lehmann, *Command of the Seas*, 372.

Chapter 7. Escort and Retaliation in the Persian Gulf

1. Admiral James L. Holloway III, COMIDEASTFOR Report, July 29, 1960.
2. Admiral William J. Crowe, Jr., *In the Line of Fire: From Washington to the Gulf, the Politics and Battles of the New Military* (New York: Simon and Schuster, 1993), 181.

3. Congressman Les Aspin's press conference prior to the first convoy may have helped cause the *Bridgeton* mining. It most certainly cost the southern overflight rights for AWACS that the United States had delicately obtained from Gulf Emirates and agreed to keep confidential–Aspin's press conference hit all the newspapers the next day and forced a renegotiation of the AWACS agreements. See Caspar Weinberger, *Fighting for Peace: Seven Critical Years in the Pentagon* (New York: Warner Books, 1990), 410–11.

Chapter 8. Storming Panama

1. This view was provided by Ambassador Paul D. Taylor, a State Department Latin American specialist who served in Panama and many other diplomatic posts in Latin America.
2. Colin Powell with Joseph E. Persico, *A Soldier's Way: An Autobiography* (London: Hutchinson, 1995), 434.

Chapter 9. The Gulf War: Desert Shield

1. *Newsweek Commemorative Edition,* "America at War," Spring–Summer 1991, p. 35.
2. Central Command had been formed out of the Rapid Deployment Joint Task Force that had been created during the Carter administration in the late 1970s to face the threat of the Soviet Union attacking our then-ally Iran.

Chapter 10. The Gulf War: Desert Storm

1. On the initial day of air action 668 allied aircraft attacked Iraq: 530 U.S. Air Force (79 percent), 90 U.S. Navy and Marine Corps (13 percent), 24 British (4 percent), 12 French (2 percent), and 12 Arabian (2 percent). See Richard P. Hallion, *Storm over Iraq: Air Power and the Gulf War* (Washington, D.C.: Smithsonian Institution Press, 1992), 165–66.
2. Although the eight suspected nuclear targets were struck, the U.S. Air Force concluded that it had failed to eliminate the entire Iraqi nuclear weapons program. See U.S. Department of the Air Force, *Gulf War Air Power Survey: Operations and Effects,* vol. 2 (Washington, D.C.: U.S. Government Printing Office, 1993), 225–27.
3. *Newsweek Commemorative Edition,* vol. 117, Summer 1991, 101.
4. Lawrence Freedman, *The Gulf Conflict, 1990–1991: Diplomacy and the New World Order* (Princeton, N.J.: Princeton University Press, 1993), 328–29.

5. When the warhead reached the end of its powered trajectory it apparently tumbled and broke up into parts, which prevented it from being tracked by a defending Patriot antimissile system. It struck a warehouse that had been converted to a barracks for Americans, starting a massive fire that killed twenty-eight soldiers.

6. See Lawrence Freedman and Efraim Karsh, *The Gulf Conflict 1991: Diplomacy and War in the New World Order* (Princeton, N.J.: Princeton University Press, 1993), 436.

7. U.S. Department of Defense, *Conduct of the Gulf War, Final Report to Congress* (Washington, D.C.: U.S. Government Printing Office, 1992), 609.

Chapter 11. The Rescue of the Kurds in Northern Iraq

1. The journalist Seymour Hersh charged that Division Commander General Barry McCaffrey and his Twenty-fourth troops killed Iraqi prisoners while they were surrendering. In a *New Yorker* article entitled "Annals of War: Overwhelming Force" (May 22, 2000, 48), Hersh accused McCaffrey and his men of pounding elite Republican Guard units as they fled north in panic. His account, which accuses the Twenty-fourth of the systematic destruction of Iraqis who were generally fulfilling the requirement of the cease-fire, ignores the fact that the Hammurabi Armored Division was attempting to break out of the allied encirclement and to proceed north to stop the revolt of the Kurds. See Lawrence Freedman and Efraim Karsh, *The Gulf Conflict 1990–1991: Diplomacy and War in the New World Order* (Princeton, N.J.: Princeton University Press, 1993), 407.

2. Michael M. Gunter, *The Kurds of Iraq: Tragedy and Hope* (New York: St. Martin's Press, 1992), 57.

3. The task force included U.S. Special Forces in Silopi, Turkey; a U.S. Marine Expeditionary Unit and French, British, Dutch, Australian, and Italian units in Zakho, Iraq; and combined air forces and the headquarters in Incirlik, Turkey.

Chapter 13. President Clinton Crosses the Mogadishu Line

1. Walter S. Clarke, "Testing the World's Resolve in Somalia," *Parameters* (Winter 1993–94): 47; Major General Waldo D. Freeman, Captain Robert B. Lambert, and Lieutenant Colonel Jason D. Mims, "Operation

RESTORE HOPE: A USCENTCOM Perspective," *Military Review* (September 1993): 68.

2. Secretary of Defense Les Aspin said he did not wish to create the appearance that the United States was increasing forces in Somalia, when in fact the Americans were trying to reduce their presence. He later conceded, "Had I known at the time what I knew after the events of Sunday [October 3] I would have made a very different decision." He resigned in December 1993. Quote from John L. Hirsch and Robert B. Oakley, *Somalia and Operation Restore Hope* (Washington, D.C.: U.S. Institute of Peace Press, 1995), 132.

3. Muhammad Hassan Awale's interview with William Cran of InVision Productions in Mogadishu on February 15, 1999.

4. Frederick Sleigh Roberts, an officer of the Indian army who won the Victoria Cross in the Umbeyla Expedition during the 1863 Indian Mutiny, wrote about fighting during a withdrawal from Kabul, Afghanistan, with masses of Afghans closing in on his troops from three directions, forcing them to retire to Sherpur: "It is comparatively easy for a small body of well-trained soldiers, such as those of which the army in India is composed, to act on the offensive against Asiatics, however powerful they may be in point of numbers. There is something in the determined advance of a compact, disciplined body of troops which they can seldom resist. But a retirement is a different matter. They become full of confidence and valour the moment they see any signs of their opponents being unable to resist them, and if there is the smallest symptom of unsteadiness, wavering, or confusion, a disaster is certain to occur." From Byron Farwall, *Queen Victoria's Little Wars* (New York: W. W. Norton, 1972), 212.

5. William Shawcross, *Deliver Us from Evil: Peacekeepers, Warlords and a World of Endless Conflict* (New York: Simon and Schuster, 2000), 122.

Chapter 14. Intervention in Bosnia

1. Warren Zimmerman, *Origins of a Catastrophe* (New York: Random House, 1999), 133.

2. Ibid., 135.

3. Foreign military attachés who watched the Slovenian secession closely reported that journalists from many western European nations—in particular Germany, France, and Austria—had gathered at fourteen of the country's forty-two border-control stations with Serbia, at each of which

shooting incidents erupted. Obviously, Slovenian officials had tipped off the media in advance. From Brigadier General Jacques de Laigue, French military attaché in Belgrade at the time.

4. Anton A. Beber, "The Yugoslav People's Army and the Fragmentation of a Nation," *Military Review* (August 1993): 41.

5. Author's interview with NATO's Balkan commander, Admiral Leighton Smith, in Bowie, Maryland, on November 28, 2000.

6. Ibid.

7. Carol J. Williams, "Belgian Quitting Post as Commander of UN Peace-keepers in Bosnia," *Washington Post,* January 5, 1994.

8. Interview with Admiral Leighton Smith.

9. *Amnesty International Newsletter,* vol. 21, no. 11 (November 1991), 1.

10. Interview with Admiral Leighton Smith.

11. Ibid.

12. Christopher Wode, "USACOM Mixes New Recipe," *Defense News,* March 28–April 3, 1994, 32.

13. Rick Atkinson, "Bosnia Airlift Delivers the Goods: More Support for Bosnian Effort," *Air Force Times,* vol. 10 (January 1994), 32.

14. Carol J. Williams, "Frustrated U.N. Troops Humiliated in Bosnia," *Los Angeles Times,* January 16, 1994; "Belgian Quitting Post."

15. Edward Gorman and Michael Evans, "SAS Active Behind the Front Lines in Bosnia," *London Times,* March 17, 1994.

16. NATO used this force to neutralize an Iranian terrorist faction that began storing arms and equipment in support of Bosnian Muslim forces in a town called Kuznica.

17. Interview with Admiral Leighton Smith.

18. Author's interview with James Clunan in Hiram, Maine, July 1, 2001.

19. Interview with Admiral Leighton Smith.

20. Daniel P. Bolger, *Savage Peace: Americans at War in the 1990s* (Novato, Calif.: Presidio, 1995), 346.

21. Ibid.

22. Dutch officers in Srebrenica saw the leader of the Muslim forces there, Naser Oric, as a gangster who was profiting from the refugee situation and from pilfered Western aid. The aid agencies insisted that the local Muslims elect their own leader; they did so, and their elected official was immediately murdered by Oric's men. Oric left the enclave in April 1995 and disappeared.

23. Interview with Admiral Leighton Smith.

24. David Owen, *Balkan Odyssey* (New York: Harcourt Brace, 1995), 386.

25. In early August a force of Croatians attacked Krajina, the Serb strong-
    hold near coastal Croatia, and evicted 250,000 Serbs who were then
    forced to march to Serbia. Hundreds of Serbs were murdered by the
    Croats—an act that appeared to the world to have been sanctioned by
    the United States.
26. Interview with Admiral Leighton Smith.
27. William Shawcross, *Deliver Us from Evil: Peacekeeping, Warlords and a
    World of Endless Conflict* (New York: Simon and Schuster, 2000), 186.

Chapter 15. Intervention in Kosovo

1. William Shawcross, *Deliver Us from Evil: Peacekeeping, Warlords and a
   World of Endless Conflict* (New York: Simon and Schuster, 2000), 360.
2. Misha Glenny, *The Fall of Yugoslavia: The Third Balkan War* (New York:
   Penguin, 1993), 238.
3. Shawcross, *Deliver Us from Evil*, 368.
4. Michael R. Gordon, "General in Balkans Says Pentagon Hampered
   NATO," *New York Times*, May 21, 2001, 6.

Bibliography

Chapter 1. Recovering SS *Mayaguez* and the Fight on Koh Tang

Cable, James. *Gunboat Diplomacy 1919–1979*. New York: St. Martin's Press, 1981.

———. *Navies in Violent Peace*. London: Macmillan, 1989.

Ford, Gerald R. *A Time to Heal*. New York: Berkley Books, 1979.

Guilmartin, John F., Jr. *A Very Short War: The* Mayaguez *and the Battle of Koh Tang*. College Station, Tex.: Texas A&M University Press, 1995.

Hunter, Ric. "Marine MIAs, Fate Unknown." *Veterans of Foreign Wars Magazine*, May 2000, 22–24.

Kennedy, Paul M. *The Rise and Fall of British Naval Mastery*. London: The Ashfild Press, 1983.

———. *The Rise and Fall of Great Powers: Economic Change and Military Conflict from 1500 to 2000*. New York: Random House, 1987.

Lamb, Christopher. *Belief Systems and Decision Making in the* Mayaguez *Crisis*. Gainesville, Fla.: University of Florida Press, 1989.

Rodgers, Captain John Michael, U.S. Navy (Ret.). Interview with author, Hiram, Maine, April 15–16, May 28, 2000.

Rowan, Roy. *The Four Days of* Mayaguez. New York: W. W. Norton and Co., 1975.

Thucydides. *History of the Peloponnesian War*. New York: Penguin, 1954.

Wetterhahn, Ralph. *The Last Battle: The* Mayaguez *Incident and the End of the Vietnam War*. New York: Carroll and Graf, 2001.

Chapter 3. The Hostage Rescue Attempt

Arostegui, Martin C. *Twilight Warriors: Inside the World's Special Forces.* New York: St. Martin's Press, 1995.

Beckwith, Charlie A., and Donald Knox. *Delta Force: The U.S. Counter-Terrorist Unit and the Iran Hostage Rescue Mission.* New York: Harcourt Brace Jovanovich, 1983.

Brzezinski, Zbigniew. *Power and Principle: Memoirs of the National Security Advisor, 1977–1981.* New York: Farrar, Straus, Giroux, 1983.

Clunan, James C., Foreign Service Officer (Ret.). Interview with author, Hiram, Maine, June 30, 2001.

Farwell, Byron. *Queen Victoria's Little Wars.* New York: W. W. Norton, 1972.

Fredericks, Pierce G. *The Sepoy and the Cossack.* New York: The World Publishing Company, 1971.

Grange, Brigadier General David L., U.S. Army (Ret.). "Making Peacetime Engagement Work." *U.S. Naval Institute Proceedings* 127, no. 7 (July 2001): 30–33.

——. E-mail interviews with author, March 9 and 11, 2001.

Holloway, Admiral James L., III, U.S. Navy (Ret.). *Rescue Mission Report,* August 1980.

Jordan, Hamilton. *Crisis: The Last Year of the Carter Presidency.* New York: Putnam, 1982.

Kennedy, Moorehead. *The Ayatollah in the Cathedral—Reflections of a Hostage.* New York: Hill and Wang, 1986.

Lapati, Andrew. Interview with author, September 22, 2000, Frye Island, Maine.

McFadden, Robert D., Joseph B. Treaster, and Maurice Carroll. *No Hiding Place.* New York: Times Books, 1981.

Nixon, Richard M. *The Memoirs of Richard M. Nixon.* New York: Grosset and Dunlap, 1978.

Powell, Colin, with Joseph E. Persico. *My American Journey.* New York: Random House, 1995; London: Hutchinson, 1995.

Powell, Jody. *The Other Side of the Story.* New York: William Morrow, 1984.

Rubinstein, Alvin Z., ed. *The Great Game: Rivalry in the Persian Gulf and South Asia.* New York: Praeger, 1983.

Scott, Charles W. *Pieces of the Game: The Human Drama of Americans Held Hostage in Iran.* Atlanta: Peachtree Publishers, 1984.

Sick, Gary. *All Fall Down: America's Tragic Encounter with Iran.* New York: Random House, 1985.

Waller, Douglas C. *The Commandos: The Inside Story of America's Secret Soldiers*. New York: Dell, 1994.

Weigley, Russell F. *The American Way of War: A History of United States Military Strategy and Policy*. Bloomington, Ind.: Indiana University Press, 1973.

Weinberger, Caspar. *Fighting for Peace: Seven Critical Years in the Pentagon*. New York: Warner Books, 1990.

Woodward, Bob. *Veil: The Secret Wars of the CIA 1981–1987*. New York: Simon and Schuster, 1987.

Chapter 4. Intervention in Lebanon

Benis, Frank M. *U.S. Marines in Lebanon 1982–1984*. Washington, D.C.: U.S. Government Printing Office, 1987.

Bolger, Daniel P. *Savage Peace: Americans at War in the 1990s*. Novato, Calif.: Presidio, 1995.

Friedman, Thomas L. "America's Failure in Lebanon." *New York Times Magazine*, April, 8, 1984, 33.

Gutman, Robert. "Battle over Lebanon." *Foreign Service Journal* (June 1984): 32.

Haig, Alexander M., Jr. *Caveat*. New York: Macmillan, 1984.

Lehman, John F., Jr. *Command of the Seas: Building the 600 Ship Navy*. New York: Charles Scribner's Sons, 1988.

Long, Admiral Robert, U.S. Navy (Ret.). Interview with author, Annapolis, Maryland, April 22, 2000.

Moskin, J. Robert. *The U.S. Marine Corps Story*. 3d rev. ed. Boston: Little Brown and Company, 1992.

Paret, Peter. *Makers of Modern Strategy from Machiavelli to the Nuclear Age*. Princeton, N.J.: Princeton University Press, 1986.

Schiff, Ze'ev, and Ehud Ya'ari. *Israel's Lebanon War*. New York: Simon and Schuster, 1984.

32nd MAU After Action Report, Sept.–Nov. 1982. USMC Historical Center, Washington, D.C.

UPI, "House Subcommittee Report," *Washington Post*, December 21, 1983, 23.

U.S. Department of Defense. *Report of the Department of Defense Commission on Beirut International Airport Terrorist Act, October 23, 1983*. Washington, D.C.: U.S. Government Printing Office, December 20, 1983.

U.S. House Armed Services Committee. *Full Committee Consideration of Investigation Subcommittee Report on Terrorist Bombing at Beirut International Airport*. 98th Cong., 2d sess., January 31, 1984.

Weigley, Russell F. *The American Way of War: A History of United States Military Strategy and Policy*. Bloomington, Ind.: Indiana University Press, 1973.

Weinberger, Caspar. *Fighting for Peace: Seven Critical Years in the Pentagon*. New York: Warner Books, 1990.

Chapter 5. Intervention in Grenada

Adkin, Major Mark. *Urgent Fury: The Battle for Grenada*. Lexington, Mass.: Lexington Books, 1989.

Arostegui, Martin C. *Twilight Warriors: Inside the World's Special Forces*. New York: St. Martin's Press, 1995.

——. E-mail interviews with author, March 9 and 11, 2001.

Headquarters U.S. Special Operations Command. *History: U.S. Special Operations Command*. Tampa, Fla.: November 2000.

Lehman, John F., Jr. *Command of the Seas: Building the 600 Ship Navy*. New York: Charles Scribner's Sons, 1988.

Metcalf, Vice Admiral Joseph III, U.S. Navy (Ret.). Interview with author, Washington, D.C., November 17, 2000.

Moskin, J. Robert. *The U.S. Marine Corps Story*. 3d rev. ed. Boston: Little Brown and Company, 1992.

Schwarzkopf, Norman H. *It Doesn't Take a Hero*. New York: Bantam, 1992.

Waller, Douglas C. *The Commandos: The Inside Story of America's Secret Soldiers*. New York: Dell, 1994.

Weinberger, Caspar. *Fighting for Peace: Seven Critical Years in the Pentagon*. New York: Warner Books, 1990.

Zakheim, Dov S. "The Grenada Operation and Superpower Relations: A Perspective from the Pentagon." In *Grenada and Soviet/Cuban Policy*, edited by Jiri Valenta and Herbert J. Ellison. Boulder, Col.: Westview Press, 1986.

Chapter 6. Retaliatory Attacks on Libya

Arostegui, Martin C. *Twilight Warriors: Inside the World's Special Forces*. New York: St. Martin's Press, 1995.

Crowe, Admiral William J., Jr. *In the Line of Fire: From Washington to the Gulf, the Politics and Battles of the New Military*. New York: Simon and Schuster, 1993.

Headquarters U.S. Special Operations Command. *History: U.S. Special Operations Command*. Tampa, Fla., November 2000.

Lehman, John F., Jr. *Command of the Seas: Building the 600 Ship Navy.* New York: Charles Scribner's Sons, 1988.

O'Connell, D. P. *The International Law of the Sea.* Vol. 2. Oxford: Clarendon Press, 1984.

Schachte, William C. "The Black Sea Incident." *U.S. Naval Institute Proceedings* 114/6/1024 (June 1988): 62.

Weinberger, Caspar. *Fighting for Peace: Seven Critical Years in the Pentagon.* New York: Warner Books, 1990.

Chapter 7. Escort and Retaliation in the Persian Gulf

Arostegui, Martin C. *Twilight Warriors: Inside the World's Special Forces.* New York: St. Martin's Press, 1995.

Crowe, Admiral William J., Jr. *In the Line of Fire: From Washington to the Gulf, the Politics and Battles of the New Military.* New York: Simon and Schuster, 1993.

Headquarters U.S. Special Operations Command. *History: U.S. Special Operations Command.* Tampa, Fla., November 2000.

Hiro, Dilip. *The Longest War: The Iran-Iraq Military Conflict.* London: Paladin, 1989.

Lehman, John F., Jr. *Command of the Seas: Building the 600 Ship Navy.* New York: Charles Scribner's Sons, 1988.

Naff, Thomas. *Gulf Security and the Iran-Iraq War.* Washington, D.C.: National Defense University Press, 1985.

O'Connell, D. P. *The International Law of the Sea.* Vol. 2. Oxford: Clarendon Press, 1984.

Waller, Douglas C. *Commandos: The Inside Story of America's Secret Soldiers.* New York: Dell, 1994.

Weinberger, Caspar. *Fighting for Peace: Seven Critical Years in the Pentagon.* New York: Warner Books, 1990.

Chapter 8. Storming Panama

Arostegui, Martin C. *Twilight Warriors: Inside the World's Special Forces.* New York: St. Martin's Press, 1995.

Donnelly, Thomas, Margaret Roth, and Caleb Baker. *Operation Just Cause: The Storming of Panama.* New York: Lexington Books, 1991.

Moskin, J. Robert. *The U.S. Marine Corps Story.* 3d rev. ed. Boston: Little Brown and Company, 1992.

Powell, Colin, with Joseph E. Persico. *My American Journey.* New York: Random House, 1995; London: Hutchinson, 1995.

Waller, Douglas C. *Commandos: The Inside Secret Story of America's Secret Soldiers.* New York: Dell, 1994.

Chapter 9. The Gulf War: Desert Shield

See Chapter 11 below.

Chapter 10. The Gulf War: Desert Storm

See Chapter 11 below.

Chapter 11. The Rescue of the Kurds in Northern Iraq

Bolger, Daniel P. *Savage Peace: Americans at War in the 1990s.* Novato, Calif.: Presidio, 1995.

Chandler, Robert W. *Tomorrow's War, Today's Decisions.* McLean, Va.: AMCODA Press, 1996.

Frazar, Brigadier General Joe, U.S. Army (Ret.). Interview with author, March 22, 2001.

Freedman, Lawrence, and Efraim Karsh. *The Gulf Conflict 1990–1991: Diplomacy and War in the New World Order.* Princeton, N.J.: Princeton University Press, 1993.

Grange, Brigadier General David L., U.S. Army (Ret.). "Making Peacetime Engagement Work." *U.S. Naval Institute Proceedings* 127, no. 7 (July 2001): 30–33.

Gunter, Michael M. *The Kurds of Iraq: Tragedy and Hope.* New York: St. Martin's Press, 1992.

Hallion, Richard P. *Storm over Iraq: Air Power and the Gulf War.* Washington, D.C.: Smithsonian Institution Press, 1992.

Headquarters U.S. Special Operations Command. *History: U.S. Special Operations Command.* Tampa, Fla., November 2000.

Hersh, Seymour M. "Annals of War: Overwhelming Force." *The New Yorker,* May 22, 2000, 48–82.

Howe, Jonathan T. "NATO and the Gulf Crisis." *Survival* 23, no. 3 (May/June 1991): 246–59.

Mueller, Lieutenant Colonel Peter, U.S. Army. Interview with author on Frye Island, Maine, July 5, 2000.

Powell, Colin, with Joseph E. Persico. *My American Journey.* New York: Random House, 1995; London: Hutchinson, 1995.

U.S. Department of Defense. *Conduct of the Gulf War: Final Report to Congress.* Washington, D.C.: U.S. Government Printing Office, 1992.

U.S. Department of the Air Force. *Gulf War Air Power Survey,* vol. 1: *Planning and Command and Control.* Washington, D.C.: U.S. Government Printing Office, 1993, 159–60.

U.S. Department of the Air Force. *Gulf War Air Power Survey: Summary Report.* Washington, D.C.: Government Printing Office, 1993, 32.

Weiss, Lieutenantt Colonel Benjamin, U.S. Army (Ret.) Interviews with author in Cornish, Maine November 21 and February 8 2000.

Chapter 12. President Bush Responds to Starvation

See Chapter 13 below.

Chapter 13. President Clinton Crosses the Mogadishu Line

Arostegui, Martin C. *Twilight Warriors: Inside the World's Special Forces.* New York: St. Martin's Press, 1995.

Awale, Muhammad Hassan. Interview with William Cran in Mogadishu on February 15, 1999.

Bolger, Daniel P. *Savage Peace: Americans at War in the 1990s.* Novato, Calif.: Presidio, 1995.

Bowden, Mark. *Black Hawk Down: A Story of Modern War.* New York: St. Martin's Press, 1999.

Church, George J. "Anatomy of a Disaster." *Time,* October 8, 1993.

Churchill, Winston S. *The River War: An Account of the Reconquest of the Sudan.* New York: Carroll & Graf Publishers, 2000.

Clarke, Walter S. "Testing the World's Resolve in Somalia." *Parameters* (Winter 1993–94).

Clunan, James L. Interviews with author in Somesville and Hiram, Maine, in October 2000 and June 2001.

Cran, William. *Ambush in Mogadishu.* Public Broadcasting System television documentary, WGBH Boston. London: In Vision Productions, 1999.

Drew, Elizabeth. *On the Edge: The Clinton Presidency.* New York: Simon and Schuster, 1994.

Headquarters U.S. Special Operations Command. *History: U.S. Special Operations Command.* Tampa, Fla., November 2000.

Hirsch, John L., and Robert B. Oakley. *Somalia and Operation Restore Hope.* Washington, D.C.: U.S. Institute of Peace Press, 1995.

Oakley, Robert B. "An Envoy's Perspective." *Joint Forces Quarterly* (autumn 1993): 45.

Shawcross, William. *Deliver Us from Evil: Peacekeepers, Warlords and a World of Endless Conflict.* New York: Simon and Schuster, 2000.

Steele, Dennis. "Army Units Deploy to Assist Starving, War-torn Somalia." *Army* (February 1993): 25.

Chapter 14. Intervention in Bosnia

Amnesty International Newsletter, vol. 21, no. 11 (November 1991).

Atkinson, Rick. "Bosnia Airlift Delivers the Goods: Move Support for Bosnian Effort." *Air Force Times,* vol. 10 (January 1994).

Beber, Anton A. "The Yugoslav People's Army and the Fragmentation of a Nation." *Military Review* (August 1993).

Bennett, Christopher. *Yugoslavia's Bloody Collapse.* London: Hurst, 1995.

Bolger, Daniel P. *Savage Peace: Americans at War in the 1990s.* Novato, Calif.: Presidio, 1995.

Clodfelter, Mark. *The Limits of Airpower: The American Bombing of North Vietnam.* New York: Free Press, 1989.

Clunan, James. Interviews with author, July 1, 2001.

Cohen, Roger. "Bowing to NATO, Serbs Pull Back from Muslim City." *New York Times,* April 25, 1994.

Draganich, Alex N. *Serbs and Croats: The Struggle in Yugoslavia.* New York: Harcourt Brace & Company, 1992.

Drew, Elizabeth. *On the Edge: The Clinton Presidency.* New York: Simon and Schuster, 1994.

Gorman, Edward, and Michael Evans. "SAS Active Behind the Front Lines in Bosnia." *London Times,* March 17, 1994.

Honig, Jan Willen, and Norbert Both. *Srebrenica: Record of a War Crime.* New York: Penguin, 1997.

Malcolm, Noel. *Bosnia: A Short History.* New York: New York University Press, 1994.

Owen, David. *Balkan Odyssey.* New York: Harcourt Brace, 1995.

Reid, Robert H. "Serbs Move Most Guns, Avert Attacks." *Washington Times,* February 21, 1994.

Rieff, David. *Slaughterhouse: Bosnia and the Failure of the West.* New York: Simon and Schuster, 1995.

Rose, Sir Michael. *Fighting for Peace.* London: Harvill, 1998.

Shawcross, William. *Deliver Us from Evil: Peacekeepers, Warlords and a World of Endless Conflict.* New York: Simon and Schuster, 2000.

Silber, Laura, and Allan Little. *The Death of Yugoslavia.* London: Penguin, 1995.

Smith, Admiral Leighton, U.S. Navy (Ret.). Interview with author, November 28, 2000.

Williams, Carol J. "Belgian Quitting Post as Commander of UN Peacekeepers in Bosnia." *Washington Post,* January 5, 1994.

——. "Frustrated U.N. Troops Humiliated in Bosnia." *Los Angeles Times,* January 16, 1994.

Wode, Christopher. "USACOM Mixes New Recipe." *Defense News,* March 28–April 3, 1994.

Zimmerman, Warren. *Origins of a Catastrophe.* New York: Random House, 1999.

Chapter 15. Intervention in Kosovo

Clodfelter, Mark. *The Limits of Airpower: The American Bombing of North Vietnam.* New York: Free Press, 1989.

Drew, Elizabeth. *On the Edge: The Clinton Presidency.* New York: Simon and Schuster, 1994.

Gordon, Michael R. "General in Balkans Says Pentagon Hampered NATO." *New York Times,* May 21, 2001.

Judah, Tim. *Kosovo: War and Revenge.* New Haven, Conn.: Yale University Press, 2000.

Myers, Lieutenant Colonel Gene, U.S. Air Force (Ret.). "Do Smoking Hulks Measure Success?" *U.S. Naval Institute Proceedings,* 127, no. 6 (June 2001): 75–76.

Shawcross, William. *Deliver Us from Evil: Peacekeepers, Warlords and a World of Endless Conflict.* New York: Simon and Schuster, 2000.

Silber, Laura, and Allan Little. *The Death of Yugoslavia.* London: Penguin, 1995.

Conclusions

Griffith, Samuel B. *Sun Tzu: The Art of War.* London: Oxford University Press, 1963.

Index